T0227863

Virtual Character Design

for Games and Interactive Media

Robin J.S. Sloan

ABERTAY UNIVERSITY, DUNDEE, UK

CRC Press
Taylor & Francis Group
Boca Raton London New York

CRC Press is an imprint of the
Taylor & Francis Group, an **informa** business

AN A K PETERS BOOK

CRC Press
Taylor & Francis Group
6000 Broken Sound Parkway NW, Suite 300
Boca Raton, FL 33487-2742

First issued in hardback 2017

© 2015 by Taylor & Francis Group, LLC
CRC Press is an imprint of Taylor & Francis Group, an Informa business

No claim to original U.S. Government works

Version Date: 20150407

ISBN-13: 978-1-4665-9819-5 (pbk)
ISBN-13: 978-1-138-42771-6 (hbk)

Visit the Taylor & Francis Web site at
http://www.taylorandfrancis.com

and the CRC Press Web site at
http://www.crcpress.com

Contents

Acknowledgments

I'm grateful to both my colleagues in academia and my friends in the games industry for the many conversations about virtual characters we've had over the last few years. I am also thankful to my undergraduate and postgraduate students, both past and present. Arguably one of the most rewarding aspects of university life is getting to work with students who are so enthusiastic and knowledgeable about their subject. And with so many of them now in top games jobs around the world, I'm grateful that they continue to keep me informed about developments in game making.

It is clear to me that this book would never have been written if my parents hadn't purchased a ZX Spectrum when I was six years old. My fascination with playing, writing, and building games can be traced to the day that I loaded *Manic Miner* for the first time. More recently, if it wasn't for my patient wife, I would never have found the time to assemble these chapters into a more coherent whole. All the while, my daughter has insisted that I come outside and play. With the book now complete, I guess it is time to venture outside—at least until she gets the hang of *Mario Kart*.

About the Author

Dr. Robin J.S. Sloan is a lecturer at Abertay University in Dundee, Scotland. Robin attained a first degree in computer arts and worked in the Scottish games industry before researching for a PhD in character animation. His doctoral research focused on the development of emotional animation for interactive characters, with emphasis on both the psychological principles of facial expressions and the creative principles of animated performance. Robin currently teaches Game Art and Game Design to students studying for degrees within the School of Arts, Media and Computer Games, which houses the UK's first Centre for Excellence in Computer Games Education. Besides character design, his research interests include game-design processes, games nostalgia and culture, and games education.

Introduction

THROUGHOUT THE DEVELOPED WORLD, most people have now grown up with video games and interactive media. It wasn't that long ago that video games were regarded as an emerging entertainment medium, junior to more established forms of artistic expression such as cinema and popular music. Many people considered games to be trivial. Even among those who appreciated and played games, the capacity for games to communicate complex themes and intricate narratives was not universally accepted. In the late twentieth and early twenty-first centuries, it would be safe to say that many critics, politicians, and commentators saw games as a medium of low social, cultural, intellectual, and educational value. At best, games were for children, and even then parents would argue that games were preventing kids from doing more worthwhile activities. At worst, games were accused of containing excessively violent or explicit content that had adverse effects on the behavior of young people, particularly teenage boys.

And yet, despite the troubled development of the medium, it is clear today that video games are of enormous interest to academics, artists, designers, critics, and the general public. Children still play games, but they are no longer the presumed demographic. After all, the children of today are being raised by parents (and grandparents) who have played games for decades. Similarly, the traditional assumption that gamers tend to be young men has also faded. The rapid development of a variety of game platforms, genres, stories, and play styles has transformed the video game into a mass-market medium. Violent games are still in the mix, but they are regulated in the same way that violent films and television programs are. Games are played by men and women, by children and parents, by artists and critics, and by teachers and politicians. What's more, it would be exceptionally difficult to deny that games are now of immense social, cultural, and historical value. Mobile devices, online connections, and cloud services have helped to embed games into the fabric of our daily lives. Gamer achievements and experiences are recorded and shared with friends and family through social media. Games technology has been appropriated, developed, and deployed in areas as diverse as education, health, social care, finance, commerce, transport, and defense. The cultural impact of games has been showcased at exhibitions such as The Art of Video Games at the Smithsonian American Art Museum (March–September 2012), and the growing field of game studies has generated a wealth of scholarly papers concerning the design, aesthetics, and art history of games.

We can confidently argue that video games play a significant role within contemporary culture. Video games are no less capable of generating meaningful and emotional experiences than film, television, music, literature, or even the fine arts. We could take this sentiment even further by arguing that the video game might become one of the highest forms of art and most pervasive forms of digital design in the twenty-first century. The flexibility of game technologies has opened the doors for contemporary artists to develop concepts and ideas that simply cannot be communicated through the more established art forms. The same technological potential has enabled engineers and designers within the field of Human–Computer Interaction (HCI) to develop digital interfaces that augment and improve our lives. Games can still be trivial; they can still be simplistic; and they can still be violent and action-oriented. But they can also be used to tell deep emotional stories, to explore complex themes and ideologies, to analyze history, and to critique society. Essentially, they can be used to examine, show, and discuss what it means to be human. And they can present us with interesting and dynamic characters that not only embody all of the above concepts, but that also challenge us to reflect on who we are.

With this in mind, this book specifically looks to discuss the design of virtual characters. The term *virtual characters* is used purposefully for two reasons: first because characters within computer media need not be limited to just video games (and so video game characters might seem a restrictive term), and second to draw attention to the fact that these are characters that have the *potential* to exist. They are characters that exist within simulations, that only come to life when a user runs the software, and whose lives (and deaths) are ultimately determined by the interactions that a player performs. This virtuality is arguably the defining property of characters in media such as video games, and it is this quality that sets them apart from characters in other media such as film and television.

A BRIEF HISTORY OF VIRTUAL CHARACTERS

In order to provide a general context for the ideas and examples discussed in the following chapters, it would be appropriate to spend some time considering the history of virtual character development. Clearly this is an extended and deeply complex history, with characters appearing not only across an eclectic range of gaming platforms, but also within a variety of styles and genres. Additionally, virtual characters have achieved varying degrees of success in different regions of the world. Rather than attempt to exhaustively document and discuss this detailed history, we instead seek to establish a basic timeline of the key artistic, conceptual, technological, cultural, and aesthetic developments in the design of virtual characters.

First, we need to acknowledge the earliest digital games. (Note that the Ludography—literally from the Latin *ludus* [game] and -graphy [a descriptive study in a specific field]—at the end of this book documents the sources of the various computer games cited in this book. These citations appear in braces to distinguish them from the citations to the references in each chapter, which appear in parentheses.) Some of the titles typically identified as being among the first computer games include *Tennis for Two* {Higinbotham 1958}, an experimental game that served as the predecessor to *Pong* {Atari 1972}; *Mouse in the Maze* {MIT 1959}, which featured a "mouse" (represented by a dot) working its way through a maze under the player's guidance; *Spacewar!* {Russell 1962}, which required two players to take control of spaceships and compete against each other; and *Computer Space* {Nutting Associates 1971}, the first coin-operated game to be sold commercially. In all of these early games, we would probably fail to recognize a clear example of a virtual character as we would define one by today's standards. In a modern game, not every game object that we directly manipulate is necessarily a character. Some games allow for control over vehicles, and we would be hard-pushed to call a car in a racing game a "character." Some games allow for direct control over inanimate objects or even the world itself. These, too, are not really what we tend to call virtual characters. However, it would be a mistake to skip over these early, noncharacter-based games when trying to establish a historical timeline for virtual characters. While they might not be characters as we know them today, the early novelty of having direct control over a digital object is vital to our understanding of player interaction within digital worlds. The forming of a link between player input and visual feedback on a digital display—seeing an object move left or right, up or down, forward or backward when explicitly commanded to do so—is really our starting point for virtual representation of player intent in a digital space. Furthermore, interaction with computer-controlled objects could be considered the genesis of digital nonplayable characters, or NPCs. Again, these might not have looked or sounded like the characters we see in games today. But players interacting with these limited graphical objects could project human personalities onto the blocky graphics, accusing them of malice or of cheating, of being sly, or of being ruthless. In other words, although it was only a dot-shaped "mouse" or a visual blip that looked something like a spaceship, we could argue that these objects were effectively early examples of NPCs.

The first games may have grappled more with the core technological underpinnings of computer interaction and visual displays than they did with characterization, but it wasn't long before more complex concepts were developed and clearer examples of virtual characters started to emerge. Based on a premise put forward by Alan Turing (discussed in more detail in Chapter 9), computer scientists started to experiment with artificial intelligence (AI) and the creation of interactive characters that could potentially pass for real humans. Obviously, these characters were not presented visually or sonically, given the limitations of the technology. Instead, these characters were represented through text generated by a rudimentary AI that could respond to human questions and statements. The most famous of these characters was ELIZA: a program written by Joseph Weizenbaum in 1966 that aimed to simulate a psychotherapist. By selecting therapy as the context for ELIZA, Weizenbaum was able to program the software to respond to questions in a vague manner, often answering human questions with further, fairly generic questions. Following ELIZA, other conversational character programs (such as PARRY) were created. Where ELIZA was designed to simulate a therapist, PARRY—created by Kenneth Colby in 1972—was designed to simulate the features of a paranoid schizophrenic. ELIZA and PARRY were even introduced to each other so that the two programs could interact. While these early simulations of character intelligence were basic programs that simply generated statements and questions, their impact on the development of more complex character interactions in video games was clear to see (in early text adventure games, for example). Ultimately, we could point to programs such as ELIZA and PARRY as the starting point for the conversational NPCs that are commonplace in today's video games.

Following the early development of games and character simulations in universities and research facilities, the commercialization of computer games via the arcades in the 1970s led to rapid improvements in virtual character visuals. Graphics that could be recognized as characters, however loosely, helped to grab consumer attention and provide video games with basic narrative contexts. One of the first games to clearly depict representations of humanlike characters was *Gun Fight* {Taito 1975}. Played as either a single- or two-player game, *Gun Fight* featured simplistic animated character graphics, with gameplay based on a Western-style duel. In 1976, Sega developed *Fonz* {Sega 1976}, a racing game based on the hit US television series *Happy Days*. Although it was a racing game, the Fonz character was shown in the game world. This milestone arcade game also demonstrated that characters from existing media franchises and storyworlds could make the leap into cyberspace, foreshadowing the potential for video games to take influence from narrative media such as television and film.

Among the most noteworthy examples of early arcade games featuring virtual characters were *Space Invaders* {Taito 1978}, *Pac-Man* {Namco 1980}, *Donkey Kong* {Nintendo 1981}, and *Frogger* {Konami 1981}. These classic games set new benchmarks not only for gameplay quality, but also for virtual character presentation. In particular, *Pac-Man* was one of the first games to establish a cast of characters—Pac-Man as the player character (or PC) and a set of four distinctive NPCs (Blinky, Pinky, Inky, and Clyde), each of which had its own color and personality (represented through subtle variation in their gameplay actions). By the end of this period, it had become clear that virtual characters were vital to the branding and success of many games. Limitations in computer power still meant that characters had very basic graphics and sound effects, but this was rectified through the use of detailed art on the physical arcade cabinets, encouraging players to imagine that the pixelated forms shown on the screen were actually much more complex characters. Games that featured distinctive characters were also able to make the leap from game products to cross-media franchises. Virtual characters were becoming stars in their own right, driving sales of plush toys, figurines, board games, television series, books, clothes, alarm clocks, and even cereals.

The arcades established video games as a commercially viable entertainment medium; however, it was the emergence of affordable home computers that really brought gaming and virtual characters to the masses. A multitude of game systems made their way into living rooms and bedrooms in the late 1970s and early 1980s. Not all of these devices achieved great success, but platforms such as the Atari VCS (or Atari 2600), Commodore 64, ZX Spectrum, and the hugely influential Nintendo Entertainment System (NES) changed the nature of home entertainment forever. Virtual characters became more graphically advanced, showcased more detailed animation, were empowered with a wider set of gameplay actions, and found their voice through dialogue and narrative exposition.

Pitfall Harry from the iconic Atari 2600 game *Pitfall!* {Activision 1982} was one of the first video game action heroes, ushering in the era of platform games. This important game genre was best defined on the NES when Mario—originally featured as Jumpman in *Donkey Kong*—debuted in his own game. Widely regarded as a pioneering and genre-defining game, *Super Mario Bros.* {Nintendo 1985} can also be identified as the launchpad for arguably the most important game character of all time. The *Super Mario Bros.* storyworld would soon expand to encompass a cast of influential characters, which we consider in more detail in Chapter 8. Other notable Nintendo characters still in active service today made their debuts in the 1980s, including Samus Aran in *Metroid* {Nintendo 1987} and Link in *The Legend of Zelda* {Nintendo 1986}. Across the games platforms and into the early 1990s, a range of action and role-playing game (RPG) characters were debuted that left lasting impressions on gamers. Games that spawned memorable characters included: *Dizzy—the Ultimate Cartoon Adventure* {Oliver Twins 1987}, a peculiarly British reply to *Super Mario Bros.*; *Final Fantasy* {Square 1990}, a Japanese RPG that cultivated a large and devoted fan base; and *Sonic the Hedgehog* {Sonic Team 1991}. The introduction of Sonic set up one of the first and most divisive virtual character rivalries, with Sonic and Mario coming to represent the corporate rivalry between Sega and Nintendo.

While many designers were presenting players with skill-based and strategic challenges, others were looking to create games that more closely resembled a form of interactive fiction. Early text adventures operated much like ELIZA, in that players interacted with the world through typed or selected statements and were presented with text-based responses. However, text adventures soon gave way to graphical adventures. Don Bluth's *Dragon's Lair* {Advanced Microcomputer Systems 1983} was a very early example of what might be considered an interactive movie. Using traditional animation to create prerendered scenes, *Dragon's Lair* was limited in terms of the capacity for interaction but showcased graphics similar to those seen in animated films. Subsequent graphical adventure games demonstrated how interactive narrative and animated characters could be combined to create games that would find mass appeal. Although the genre ultimately declined in the mid 1990s, it gave rise to some of the most important and influential virtual characters of all time. Arguably, it was LucasFilm Games (later LucasArts) that became the master of the graphical adventure. Games such as *Maniac Mansion* {LucasFilm Games 1987} introduced characters that had a greater quality and depth of personality than many of the other virtual characters of the day. These games also featured cutscenes that allowed for more advanced narrative exposition.

Perhaps the most memorable adventure-game characters of this period were the characters that were first featured in *The Secret of Monkey Island* {LucasFilm Games 1990}. Guybrush Threepwood, the PC in *The Secret of Monkey Island*, was a groundbreaking virtual character. Guybrush demonstrated a range of subtle yet easily recognizable personality traits, delivered memorable lines of dialogue, and frequently engaged with the player directly by breaking the fourth wall. The player had the ability to treat Guybrush like a puppet, instructing him to talk to NPCs, to make particular dialogue choices, and to interact with objects in the world. The *Monkey Island* series delivered some of the most engaging, credible, and humorous virtual character performances. Not only was Guybrush a fairly useless hero, but the supposed damsel character of the series, Elaine Marley, was also much more courageous, competent, and capable than Guybrush. Given the criticism of damsel characters in contemporary games (as we discuss in Chapter 3), *The Secret of Monkey Island* was fairly ahead of its time in terms of characterization.

The graphical adventure game went into decline in the mid '90s as three-dimensional (3D) graphics were on the rise. Although 3D games had existed on earlier computers and platforms, it was the arrival of the PlayStation and Sega Saturn in 1994 (and later the N64 in 1996) that marked the widespread use of 3D characters in games. Characters such as Lara Croft in *Tomb Raider* {Core Design 1996} and Crash in *Crash Bandicoot* {Naughty Dog 1996} opened up new possibilities for the performance of virtual characters. Full movement in the *X*, *Y*, and *Z* axes of 3D space helped to bridge the gap between reality and virtual reality, and in consequence what followed was a gradual enhancement in the realism of virtual characters. The first problem to be solved was one of 3D navigation. Many of the early 3D characters were immensely difficult to control. Not only did game and hardware developers have to figure out how to design control schemes that involved 3D camera manipulation, but players (who were attuned to the traditional two-dimensionality of virtual space) also had to learn new skills in 3D control. Once again, it was Nintendo that set the standard for intuitive and engaging 3D character manipulation, first with the landmark *Super Mario 64* {Nintendo 1996} and later with *The Legend of Zelda: The Ocarina of Time* {Nintendo 1998}.

Once controls improved, 3D games benefited from iterative enhancements in graphical power. Virtual characters received higher-resolution meshes and textures, leading to increasingly realistic humanlike appearances. At the same time, first-person perspective games—games viewed through the eyes of the PC—were emerging as a new game genre. In particular, the first-person shooter (FPS) would soon become one of the most popular game genres. The game most frequently cited as the landmark FPS is *Doom* {Id Software 1993}. *Doom* was neither the first game to use this type of camera nor the first to integrate it with shooting gameplay, but it was *Doom* that essentially defined the genre of the FPS. Although the PCs in FPS games are rarely (or never) seen, some of the most memorable virtual characters of the 1990s were presented in games such as *GoldenEye 007* {Rare 1997} and *Half-Life* {Valve 1998}. FPS games like *Doom* also contributed to much of the early media controversies regarding violence in video games, along with other games that depicted violence against increasingly realistic characters, such as *Mortal Kombat* {Midway Games 1992}.

The switch away from cartridges and toward optical discs was another key factor in the development of virtual characters in the 1990s. Discs had been used by previous computer and console manufacturers, but it was the PlayStation (and to a lesser extent the Saturn) that popularized disc-based games on mainstream consoles. Perhaps the most significant impact of optical discs was the opportunity to include a large amount of audio and video data in a video game, meaning that characters could finally speak at length. Games such as *Resident Evil* {Capcom 1996} were notable for characters that spoke throughout gameplay, and games such as *The X-Files Game* {HyperBole Studios 1998} made use of full-motion video (FMV), representing filmed or animated characters within an interactive media product. FMV was also used within 3D games to depict higher-resolution characters in cutscenes, but ultimately this mode of visual presentation faded as the technology behind real-time 3D graphics advanced.

In the mid to late 1990s, another technological evolution impacted on virtual character design: the widespread availability and increasing speed of Internet connections. Online gaming became more accessible, and RPG developers were among the first to capitalize on this new aspect of game design. MMORPGs (massively multiplayer online role-playing games) such as *Ultima Online* {Origin Systems 1997}, *EverQuest* {Sony Online Entertainment 1999}, *Asheron's Call* {Turbine Entertainment Software 1999}, and *Star Wars Galaxies* {Sony Online Entertainment 2003} opened up new opportunities for virtual character customization and social interaction in virtual worlds. The term *avatar* entered the mainstream gaming vocabulary, and players became increasingly attached and devoted to their virtual identities. While online play had existed for many years, the arrival of MMORPGs toward the end of the twentieth century changed the way gamers engaged with characters, with some players spending years controlling and developing just one avatar. Virtual worlds that contained little or no traditional gaming elements—such as the online life simulation *Second Life* {Linden Research 2003}—became a popular new form of digital interaction. As Internet capability spread from computers to consoles at the start of the twenty-first century, virtual characters in all manner of game genres made the leap into the online world. Today, many of the biggest video game releases, such as Bungie's landmark title *Destiny* {Bungie 2014}, have an explicit focus on online multiplayer interactions.

The combination of advanced graphics, complex audio, and online capability underpinned the design of Triple A (AAA) games in the late 1990s and the first decade of the twenty-first century. On the mainstream consoles and on Windows PCs, it was the big-budget video games that dominated. Some of the most memorable virtual characters appeared in games such as *Final Fantasy VII* {Square 1997}, *Silent Hill* 2 {Konami Computer Entertainment Tokyo 2001}, *Grand Theft Auto III* {DMA Design 2001}, *Halo: Combat Evolved* {Bungie 2001}, and *Call of Duty* {Infinity Ward 2003}. In more recent years, we have seen a rise in the independent (or indie) game development scene. Once constrained to making browser-based games or free downloads for Windows PCs, many indie game developers now achieve high levels of critical, commercial, and financial success. Much of this has to do with the evolution of the Steam video games platform, which revolutionized digital download games for PC, Mac, and Linux platforms. Steam made it much easier for indies to find a large, paying audience. Following the success of Steam, indie games were subsequently given a strong presence on mainstream consoles such as the

Xbox 360 and PS3, and the provision of indie games has become one of the most important selling points for the eighth generation of game consoles. Indie games contain what could be considered the most diverse range of virtual characters ever seen in video games. Many indie game characters purposefully reference 8-bit or 16-bit aesthetics as a means of establishing a connection with gaming history and nostalgia, such as *Fez* {Polytron 2012} and *Superbrothers: Sword & Sworcery EP* {Capybara Games 2012}. Others marry gameplay mechanics with narrative themes to generate characters that facilitate meaningful play, such as *Braid* {Number None 2008} and *Thomas Was Alone* {Bithell 2012}. Indie games have become the site of some of the most innovative and creative virtual characters of the last few years, with many of the larger studios taking note.

Today, video games and virtual characters are ubiquitous. There is no single, dominant interactive media platform. Neither is there a dominant game genre. Games are played on consoles and home computers, on phones and handheld devices, online, using virtual-reality headsets, and, of course, in the arcades. The technological limitations of computer hardware will continue to be pushed, but achieving the most advanced feats of technical wizardry is no longer the universal ambition of virtual character creators. Games are developed in a wide range of visual styles, from the photorealistic down to the purposefully low-fi (low fidelity). Video game genres have merged to the point that many games can't be so easily categorized. And, as we noted earlier, gamer demographics are more diverse than they have ever been. It is an exciting time to be making and studying games and, by extension, an excellent time to be discussing virtual character design.

AN OVERVIEW OF THE BOOK

Given the importance of video games within our modern world, it is reasonable that we would want to examine them and try to understand their qualities, techniques, and sociocultural impacts. This is largely what the field of game studies is concerned with, and there are wide ranges of books and journals within this field that offer insights into game design and culture.

In this book, the virtual characters that can be developed using games technologies are specifically targeted for study. When it comes to character design—both in general and for games—there are many excellent books that identify key steps in the design process and that demonstrate best practices in the production of game characters. However, this book is not concerned with the actual building of characters for games. There are no technical step-by-step guides or tutorials that direct readers to draw, model, or implement characters in specific game engines. Instead, the focus of this book is on establishing critical frameworks that can be used to both design and analyze virtual characters. In other words, this book is about the overarching conceptual underpinnings of virtual character design, irrespective of the particular technologies or pipelines that might be used.

Most of us will have encountered a virtual character that has made us smile, laugh, cry, or frown. Maybe this was due to the visual presentation of the character or the way it acted. Alternatively, maybe we were engrossed in the character's story or challenged by the gameplay actions it performed. By extension, it is highly likely that you will have played a game in which a virtual character has completely frustrated you or broken your suspension of disbelief. And, occasionally, our encounters with virtual characters can be truly emotional and moving. By developing critical frameworks, the intention of this book is to provide a means of identifying the qualities and inadequacies of virtual characters and, in turn, to understand how these elements can contribute toward our overall aesthetic experience of a game.

This book is aimed at a wide audience, including students of game studies and game design, academics with interests in video games, and games industry professionals. The book has been written to be as accessible as possible to all readers, but in particular to undergraduate students who might be studying character design for games for the first time. For these readers, it would be a good idea to read the whole book to get a feel for the range of theories that impact upon the design and aesthetics of game characters. Academics and industry professionals may want to skip straight to the chapters that interest them most. It's likely that these readers will already be familiar with some of the core concepts covered in the following chapters.

The book has been structured in three sections. Section I (Chapters 1–3) focuses on the presentation of virtual characters. The emphasis of Chapter 1 is on the biological factors that influence the visual design of characters. This covers the fundamentals of human anatomy as well as factors that influence our perception of character age, health, and attractiveness. Chapter 2 lays out the basic visual and audio theories that underpin effective character design, including issues such as visual composition, visual style, and sound implementation. Chapter 3 then looks at how the appearance of a virtual character can reflect issues of identity. This encompasses systems that permit customization of virtual characters (allowing players to express themselves) as well as issues of representation within games.

In Section II (Chapters 4–6), the discussion shifts to the performance of virtual characters. The core psychological principles of emotion, personality, and nonverbal communication are covered in Chapter 4. Chapter 5 then considers external factors that affect character performance, including archetypes and backstories, the design of interactive narratives, and the design of gameplay. The final chapter of Section II encompasses theories of acting, movement, and animation as well as methods for creating and displaying animation. This chapter identifies both technical and conceptual issues that arise when attempting to strike a balance between high-quality acted performance and the responsive animation of virtual characters.

Having covered a range of theories across Sections I and II, Section III (Chapters 7–9) presents a series of applied virtual character design examples, broken down into three categories. Chapter 7 first considers the control of characters and, in particular, how players take on virtual roles. Chapter 8 then looks more widely at the cast of characters within video games, including how casts are designed to appeal to consumers and how virtual characters interact with each other. Finally, Chapter 9 looks to some of the most complex issues facing virtual character design, from the difficulty in establishing credible human appearances and performances through to the simulation of authentic virtual intelligence.

TERMINOLOGY

Throughout the book, the terms *games* and *video games* are used interchangeably. The view is taken that the terms do not solely apply to interactive entertainment products that have both explicit rules and competitive play. Instead, when the terms *games* and *video games* are used, it is implied that this encompasses not only the entertainment games that we consume on consoles, computers, and mobile devices, but also the wide array of art games that are being produced by innovative designers, the experimental games that emerge as an output of game jams, "games for change" that are developed in order to achieve social impact, educational games for children and adults alike, so-called serious games that are used in training and in visualization, and also collective intelligence games such as *Foldit* {University of Washington 2008}. Put simply, this book takes the stance that all of these varied types of audiovisual interactive products are best described holistically as games or video games, regardless of their target audiences or their intentions. Nevertheless, the title of the book identifies the place of virtual characters not only in games, but also in interactive media more generally. Interactive media can be taken to include apps, websites, digital television, kiosks, self-service technologies, and digital signage, among many other new and exciting technologies. The book frequently turns to video games that readers might be familiar with for applied examples, but hopefully it will be willingly accepted that the principles that underpin virtual character design for mainstream entertainment video games are transferable to other forms of interactive media.

There are some specialist terms that are used repeatedly in the book, and in order to aid the flow of the text, it is necessary to present these in an abbreviated form. As such, a Glossary has been provided at the end of the book. Whenever you see an abbreviation used, you will be able to refer to the Glossary to check its meaning.

I

Presentation

IN SECTION I, we look at some of the theories that can be applied to the design and analysis of virtual character appearance. We start with biological principles that inform character design, including anatomical cues that are affected by body type, sex, age, and health. From there, we progress to the core artistic principles that are commonly applied to character design, before finishing with a discussion of the sociological factors that can impact on character presentation and audience reception. By the end of Section I we should be better prepared to evaluate and discuss the audiovisual design of virtual characters.

CHAPTER 1

Anatomy and Physical Cues

THE VISUAL STYLE OF VIRTUAL CHARACTERS varies enormously from game to game. Appearance can be influenced by game genre, target-audience preferences, cultural differences, the brand of the development studio, or even the gaming platform. In any analysis of a character's appearance, the visual style is typically the most obvious element to consider first. For instance, the photorealism of a character is frequently highlighted in criticism of video game graphics, and for many game developers photorealism is a stylistic ideal. When working with more distinctive styles, the aesthetic choices of a developer might have an even greater impact on the presentation of a character. Regardless of whether a developer opts to create a bespoke style or conform to an established style, the application of style can have a dramatic effect on character appearance and, subsequently, on player perception and interpretation. As such, it would seem logical to begin our discussion of virtual character appearance by first considering artistic and visual design principles.

However, as any artist will be well aware, the development of good character art is not possible without a solid understanding of nature. When it comes to the visual design of characters—irrespective of whether they are photorealistic, stylized, or abstract—understanding the structure and movement of humans is essential. The literature on character design often covers this topic in some detail, drawing particular attention to the need to use references when producing character concepts. From observation of life to the study of photography, detailed analysis and imitation of anatomy is considered an essential skill for practicing character artists. Most practical books on character design will specifically identify the need to take part in life drawing classes in addition to spending thousands of hours practicing drawing using reference images. The premise is simple: Original character design and distinctive styles can only be achieved once the artist thoroughly understands how humans look and move in nature.

The importance of natural forms and phenomena is so fundamental to character design that we address this topic first before moving on to discussion of artistic principles and visual style in Chapter 2. We start with a discussion of anatomy, identifying the core principles that inform good artistic practice. Here, we consider how we might deconstruct virtual characters by using concepts such as proportions, body types, and sex differences. Moving on from anatomy we consider nature more broadly, taking into account some of the most important physical attributes that affect how humans perceive each other, including cues to attractiveness, age, and health. This chapter aims to develop our first critical framework for the analysis of virtual character presentation, with specific emphasis on natural reality and perception.

ANATOMY

As we have acknowledged, because anatomy is the cornerstone of character art production, it is logical for us to examine human anatomy early on in the book. The degree to which a design conforms to, exaggerates, or confounds the principles of anatomy can have a significant effect on how we observe and interpret a character. So let us begin by going over the anatomical criteria that artists need to take into account when designing a character. As this book is intended for anyone who is studying virtual character design, and not just for artists, our discussion of anatomy is not exhaustive. Our focus is on the core principles that inform the production of anatomically accurate character designs, and does not include detailed illustrations of the human form. However, it is highly recommended that further study of anatomy be carried out in order to enhance your ability to deconstruct the design of virtual characters. While drawing classes are by far the best way of developing a working knowledge and understanding of anatomy, it is not always possible or practical to attend classes locally. As such, acquiring and reading books that focus on anatomy would be useful. There are many classic texts that are recognized by artists as core reading that you might want to consider (e.g., Bridgman 2009; Peck 1982; Simblet 2001).

Body Proportions

First, a holistic evaluation of character anatomy ought to take into account the body proportions. In nature, this varies tremendously based on a number of factors. Even two very similar people are unlikely to have exactly the same anatomical measurements. But there are general rules of thumb that underpin the proportions of human anatomy and, thus, character design. The principle most commonly applied by character artists involves the use of head height (from the top of the head to the chin) as a comparative unit of measurement. Although in many ways this is an artistic principle, it is reflective of detailed observation of life. It is also one of the simplest ways of making sense of what might be a highly complex character image, because the key unit of measurement is contained within the image.

The overall height of an ideal character is considered to be roughly eight head heights. This is of course a simplification in order to make analysis more straightforward. In reality, the proportion for a typical adult may well be closer to seven and a half head heights, but as this is a general principle rather than a hard rule, there is some room for maneuver. It is also clear that the overall height of the character is not relevant here. On average, a typical adult woman is likely to be shorter than a typical adult man, but the basic eight-head-heights principle still applies. The main factor that will manipulate the head-to-height ratio is the age of the character. Broadly speaking, we can consider younger teenagers to be roughly seven head heights, older children roughly six head heights, younger children roughly five head heights, and infants roughly four head heights (see Figure 1.1). Furthermore, the head unit can be used to analyze the length of the torso, arms, and legs. By using the principle of head measurements to determine overall height as well as internal proportions, it is therefore possible to determine whether a virtual character's anatomy is in line with what is typically observed in nature, or whether it has been exaggerated for effect.

A cartoon character such as Sackboy from *LittleBigPlanet* {Media Molecule 2008} can make use of highly exaggerated proportions to manipulate our perception. At roughly two heads high, Sackboy has a head-to-height ratio which exceeds that of a typical baby, greatly exaggerating his childlikeness and cuteness. The titular character from *Bayonetta* {Platinum Games 2009}, on the other hand, is an example of a character whose overall height and leg-to-torso ratio are massively exaggerated to enhance our perception of her athleticism and dominance. However, many virtual characters are designed to map on to realistic anatomical proportions. The physical

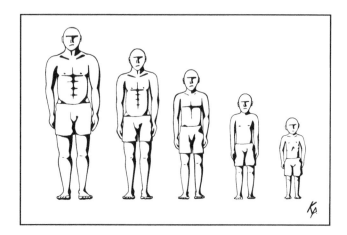

FIGURE 1.1 Approximate body proportions for a range of age groups. From left to right: adults (8 heads tall), teenagers (7 heads tall), older children (6 heads tall), younger children (5 heads tall), and toddlers (4 heads tall).

appearance of the characters Joel and Ellie from *The Last of Us* {Naughty Dog 2013} were carefully designed to ensure that a believable relationship could be implied (with Ellie acting as a teenage daughter substitute for the bereaved father Joel). The head-to-height ratios of these characters roughly map on to expected ratios for a typical teenager and a typical adult.

Body Type

Moving on from the principles of proportion, we can next consider body types. As before, we can look at these as general rules of thumb without having to drill down too deeply into the minutiae of human anatomy. In the case of body type, one of the most common systems of categorization concerns the extent to which the body builds muscle and stores fat. Known as somatotypes, the three categories used to describe body type based on these factors are the ectomorph, the mesomorph, and the endomorph (see Figures 1.2 and 1.3). You will see these terms used not only in the character design literature (particularly for fantasy design), but also in literature that discusses human anatomy. In the mid twentieth century, these categories were controversially associated with intelligence and personality, leading to a general sense of skepticism regarding their usage in psychology today. However, the underlying concept of categorizing body appearance based on predisposed tendencies to store fat and build muscle remains useful, particularly within studies of health, sport, and

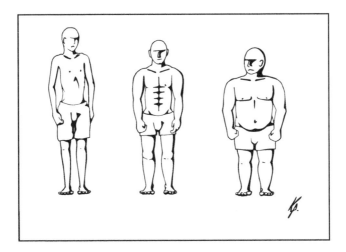

FIGURE 1.2 Male ectomorph, mesomorph, and endomorph body types.

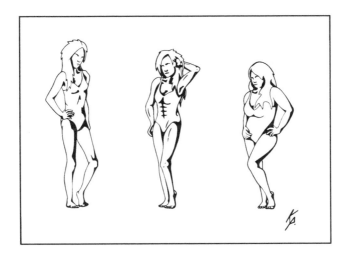

FIGURE 1.3 Female ectomorph, mesomorph, and endomorph body types.

exercise. Furthermore, although a direct connection between body type and individual personality is unfounded, it is common for audiences to project traits onto characters based at least partially on their observation of body type. Let's discuss what the physical traits associated with these body types are, before going on to consider what possible connotations these forms might have.

- *Ectomorphs*: The ectomorph body type can be assigned to people who are typically considered to be of a light build, with small bones and lean muscle tone. They are likely to have narrow shoulders and little body fat due to a high metabolism, and may also have long limbs or be taller than average.

- *Mesomorphs*: People who are more solidly built with bigger bones can be categorized as mesomorphs. They are likely to have a naturally athletic build and, while they may have some limited body fat, their muscles will be larger and more clearly defined.

- *Endomorphs*: The endomorph types will have a higher proportion of body fat to muscle. They will find it harder to lose fat than people who are more closely aligned with ectomorph or mesomorph types. They are typically shorter, rounder, and stockier, and may have strong arms and legs.

These categories are used to describe general body types, so it is important to bear in mind that not all humans (and therefore not all virtual characters) can be so neatly pigeonholed. It is likely that a character will fit a combination of two categories, particularly a combination of ectomorph and mesomorph or of endomorph and mesomorph. However, it is worth considering what these broad categories might communicate to a player, particularly as they are often chosen by designers to appeal to our common preconceptions and prejudices about body type. For example, ectomorphs could be regarded as being fast and relatively fit due to their low weight. In combination with other design factors, though, the ectomorph body type can suggest traits such as thoughtfulness, introversion, emotional control, shiftiness, intensity, or creativity. On the other hand, the mesomorph body type clearly suggests strength and physical ability, but it can also suggest courage, adventurousness, dominance, assertiveness, competitiveness, and a tendency to take risks. Finally, endomorph body types might typically suggest a preference for food over exercise, even though this is not necessarily the case in nature. Dependent on the exact depiction of an endomorph, this body type can insinuate that a character is good-humored, fun-loving, sociable, tolerant, lovable, or strong.

The somatotype categories can be useful for describing a character's physique, but it is important to consider the potential impact of certain body shapes—particularly idealized body shapes—in visual media such as video games. Market preferences are a common consideration in game development, particularly for big-budget games. This can lead to a prevalence of body types such as mesomorphs for heroes, with the heavier or scrawnier characters being relegated to minor (and often comedic) roles. The problem can become even more pronounced with regard to the exaggeration of sexual characteristics in body shape.

Sex Differences

Although somatotypes can be used to generalize the effect of muscle density and fat storage on the appearance of the body, it is important to bear in mind that biological sex has a clear impact on human anatomy, including the shape of both the body and face (see Hyde and DeLamater [2013] for extensive information). There are discernible differences in male and female human anatomy that go without saying. However, when we consider that the body and face shapes of men and women are largely dictated by the balance of sex hormones (particularly during puberty), it becomes obvious why we should note sex differences in our analysis of virtual characters. Figure 1.4, for example, shows how sex differences might impact on face shape.

The sex hormones that influence body and face shape are testosterone and estrogens. Men typically have a much higher proportion of testosterone than estrogens, while women typically have a higher proportion of estrogens than testosterone. Note the use of *typically* here: Hormones can be naturally produced in different quantities and ratios, and so treating men and women as two distinct categories is problematic, even when we

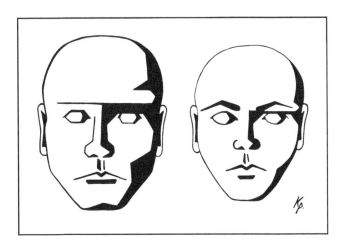

FIGURE 1.4 Generalized differences in face shape determined by sex.

are considering biological factors rather than psychological factors such as gender identity. The biological interactions are complex, and there are many other variables that determine the precise shape of any individual (including genes, exercise, and eating habits). Nevertheless, certain body characteristics of typical men and women can be associated with sex hormone levels, and understanding these characteristics can help us to analyze and discuss critically the presentation of virtual characters. To do this, let's examine what the effects of the sex hormones are on the body and the face and see how these effects can, in turn, describe biological masculinity (more testosterone than estrogens) and femininity (more estrogens than testosterone).

- *Masculine body shape*: Testosterone, a steroid hormone, has the effect of enhancing body mass—building muscle and bones—leading to larger and heavier bodies. It broadens the shoulders and expands the rib cage in puberty. Because male bodies have a higher proportion of testosterone than female bodies, men tend to build larger muscles more quickly, have larger hands and feet, and be both taller and stronger than women. If we correlate masculinity with testosterone levels, a highly masculine body would be tall and broad across the chest, with well-defined muscles and low levels of body fat, similar to the mesomorph body type. When men gain fat, their low levels of estrogens (which interact with fat deposits) means that weight is typically added around the waist and belly.

- *Masculine face shape*: As with the body, testosterone enhances the growth of facial features. Both the jawbones and the ridge of the eyebrows tend to become more pronounced, and throughout puberty the face will shift from being rounded to being squarer. In particular, a notable characteristic is that the relative proportions of the face will change, so that the face appears wider. All of these characteristics can be considered descriptive of a highly masculine face.

- *Feminine body shape*: As noted previously, while testosterone impacts on bone and muscle development, estrogens interact more with the storage and distribution of fat. Estrogens typically distribute fat around the buttocks, hips, thighs, and breasts. They also widen the hips, leading to more marked differences in body shape between men and women during puberty. The biological function of these effects is to enhance fertility and maternity. Consequently, if we correlate femininity with estrogen levels, a highly feminine body would be shorter and more lightly built than the masculine body. Additionally, a highly feminine body might have an hourglass shape (a proportionately narrower waist when compared with the chest and hips). As women's estrogen levels reduce later in life, fat distribution in women can shift to the waist and belly.

- *Feminine face shape*: Because it is primarily testosterone that dramatically impacts on the shape of the face, the lower levels of testosterone in women means that faces do not change as much in adulthood. Indeed, many of the characteristics of a highly feminine face (a face representative of a woman with low levels of testosterone) are, in effect, a continuation of childlike features. Highly feminine faces are smaller and rounder than masculine faces, have less pronounced jaws and brows, contain proportionately larger lips and eyes, and have smaller noses.

Before we go any further, it is important to note that the above descriptions are biological in nature and, therefore, are not sensitive to the sociological and cultural impact of male and female representations in media. There are clearly issues of representation in video games, particularly of exaggerated, idealized, or even fantastical feminine bodies. It is also important that we note that biological sex is not the same thing as gender identity, although the two concepts obviously overlap. We come back to issues of representation in Chapter 3. For now, we look to focus strictly on anatomical differences determined by sex hormones, and what potential impact this has on our perception of human characters.

When looking at a character's anatomy, the physical effects of both testosterone and estrogens can tell us something about the implied nature of a character, regardless of whether the character is male, female, or of an unspecified sex. It's likely that most audience members will be able to detect varying levels of masculinity and femininity in a character through recognition of sexual characteristics. And, in turn, identification of masculine or feminine characteristics in the physical appearance of a character can impact on how an audience interprets the character.

The physical effects of testosterone can suggest masculine traits such as strength, power, and dominance, whereas the physical effects of estrogen can suggest feminine traits such as care and compassion. When the physical characteristics of testosterone and estrogens are pronounced or caricatured, the effect can be to imply a high level of masculinity or femininity in a character. Conversely, the reduction of these physical characteristics could in turn adjust our perception of the manliness or womanliness of a character. In both instances, the sex of the character impacts on our interpretation because we have preconceived notions of masculine and feminine body shapes. In other words, we have the tacit ability to discriminate between the effects of testosterone and estrogens on body shape, and are naturally capable of associating the former with masculinity and the latter with femininity.

Consider how varying levels of testosterone and estrogens in male and female characters can affect their physical body shape and, in turn, how a player might perceive and interpret them. The difference in appearance is quite pronounced and, as such, this is clearly an important visual element to consider in an analysis of a virtual character.

There are many virtual characters that make explicit use of sex differences in body type to accentuate ideas of masculinity and femininity. Given the historical gaming audience of young males and continued issues with representation in both games worlds and games development, it is particularly easy to find stereotypical examples of masculine and feminine body shapes in games. Many male characters fulfill commanding and/or violent roles, and subsequently are designed with highly masculine forms. On the other hand, for much of the history of games, female characters have had a less inclusive role and have commonly been deployed to act as damsels in distress or simply to provide sex appeal. As such, there are lots of examples of virtual women with highly feminine body shapes. However, there are still interesting examples of character designs that play with commonly held notions of body shape. A good example is Samus Aran from the *Metroid* series of games, who was famously revealed as a woman at the end of *Metroid* {Nintendo 1987}, the first game in the series. Although her reveal also involved being scantily clad, this was a major twist at the time. To the gamers of the day, it would have been naturally assumed that any main player character (PC) in an action game would be male, and her sex was deliberately disguised until the final screen. Furthermore, her visual design intentionally embeds and exaggerates masculine body characteristics to maintain an air of ambiguity over her sex. While her Power Suit is effectively her equipment and not subject to her biological development, its shape still triggers our ability to recognize sex differences in the human form. When in her Power Suit, Samus arguably appears more masculine than feminine, with characteristically broad shoulders and chest as well as armor that suggests dense muscle. There are feminine characteristics in the Power Suit design as well, notably the chest-waist-hips proportions. Overall, the suit acts to muddy the apparent sex of the character by blending masculine and feminine characteristics. Out of her suit, Samus becomes highly feminine, with accentuated curves. There is clearly an element of female sexuality and sex appeal within this aspect of her visual design, but the unambiguously feminine body shape of Samus also provides a stark contrast with the Power Suit design, ensuring that the femininity of this archetypically masculine sci-fi action hero is communicated effectively. Today, as a well-known character, the continued use of exaggerated masculine characteristics in the Power Suit is of particular relevance, as the role of women characters in games is a hot topic of debate, and the desire to see leading women is as strong as ever.

PHYSICAL CUES

So far, we have considered human anatomy and the factors that define the proportions, shape, and size of the human form. When discussing these physical attributes, we alluded to the impact that physical appearance could potentially have on observer interpretation. For the remainder of the chapter, we turn our attention to specific physical properties and discuss how manipulation of these might influence our opinion of the attractiveness, age, and health of a character. By considering these factors, you can build on your observations of a virtual character's anatomy by discussing the likely effect its appearance could have on player perception. While we touch on some of the common cues that impact on our perception, Perret (2010) offers a much more extensive and detailed discussion of this topic in his book *In Your Face: The New Science of Human Attraction*.

Attraction

As the adage goes, beauty is in the eye of the beholder. There are certainly elements of the human form that individuals will find more or less attractive, and there is cultural variation in terms of how people modify their bodies in order to accentuate or disguise anatomical features. However, there is a body of scientific evidence showing that there are certain qualities which are widely regarded as being physically attractive. In this section, we focus on the qualities that interact with the perception of attractiveness and that could subsequently inform the presentation of characters.

One of the most widely discussed factors for physical attraction is symmetry (see Figure 1.5). Studies have shown that symmetry is a fairly strong

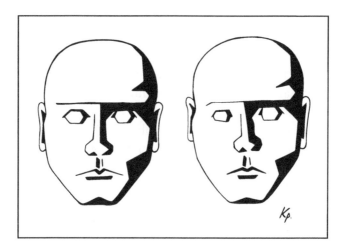

FIGURE 1.5   Observer judgment of attractiveness can be affected by asymmetry.

indicator for general attractiveness, with the most symmetrical forms being regarded as more attractive than asymmetrical forms. Given that humans (like most animals) are fundamentally symmetrical anyway, it is somewhat understandable that the differences must be quite subtle. And they are: Even very slight alterations in the symmetry or asymmetry of the human form (particularly within the face) can be picked up by observers and, in turn, these observations subconsciously affect the perception of an individual. Clearly this is a very basic way of considering physical attractiveness, and of course people with evidently asymmetrical features can be widely regarded as attractive. Nevertheless, symmetry is a useful consideration in virtual character design, as it can help to heighten appeal, generate a sense of apathy, or even create a feeling of revulsion toward a character.

As a significant element of heterosexual attraction concerns sexual reproduction, it would be a fair bet that the perceived genetic and biological qualities of the opposite sex are a factor for attractiveness. And this appears to be largely true. Physical traits associated with highly feminine and masculine forms can be correlated with ratings for attractiveness. The effects of estrogens on the female body, as we discussed earlier, make the female form more attractive to heterosexual men, a consequence of perceived fertility and capacity for child rearing. However, feminine features seem to be regarded as broadly attractive by observers of either sex and with different sexual preferences. Highly feminine faces and body shapes can therefore be seen as a standard concept for feminine beauty, but it is possible to exaggerate these traits to the point of caricature (which many games are guilty of). When pushed too far, these traits actually create less attractive face and body shapes—shapes that we find odd. The presence of masculine traits within men, interestingly, is more complex. The way heterosexual women rate male faces for attractiveness is dependent on the context. Highly masculine features, as a result of higher levels of testosterone, indicate improved immunity and physical ability. These features are perceived as positive qualities when it comes to reproduction, and so highly masculine forms do create sex appeal. However, the same features also trigger preconceptions such as aggression, dominance, and the potential for infidelity. As such, men with less masculine and more feminine features are typically regarded as more attractive as long-term partners. All of this is of course subject to individual preference, and it does not account for same-sex attraction. But the fact remains that the biological factors that impact on body and face shape have a subsequent impact on a general perception of physical attractiveness.

As well as visual cues to attraction, we are also naturally inclined to pick up on audio cues. The properties of the voice can be connected to the appearance of a character, with a subsequent effect on attraction. Within men, the deepness of a voice can be directly associated with body shape. Deeper voices have been shown to correlate with larger bodies, particularly taking into account shoulder and chest size and upper-body musculature (Evans, Neave, and Wakelin 2006). This aligns with a mesomorph body type and more highly masculine body shape. Heterosexual women perceive these deep voices as being more attractive. When the roles are reversed, heterosexual men are likely to align voice with visual appearance, detecting cues to attractiveness in both the voice and face, with higher pitched voices being most attractive (Collins and Missing 2003). In character design, then, there is a need to consider the pitch of voice in relation to physical appearance.

Health

Being able to detect the health of another individual is vital to survival. As such, there are certain cues to health and illness that we as a species are particularly adept at picking up on. This ensures not only that we can avoid potential infection, but also that we can pick a suitable mate. As this would suggest, there are some problems separating perceived attractiveness from perceived health, as the two factors are clearly related in terms of our natural ability to conduct a physical assessment of another individual. The three aspects of a character's appearance that have the strongest impact on our perceptions of healthiness are:

- Amount of body fat
- Skin texture
- Skin color

Perhaps the easiest aspect of physical appearance to align with perception of healthiness is weight. Studies have shown that weight clearly impacts on how healthy we perceive someone to be. There is no universal ideal weight: it varies slightly from culture to culture, dependent on the environment in which a culture exists. But a healthy individual is typically perceived to be someone with low to moderate levels of body fat—what we might consider to be a typical body weight. Obviously, as levels of body fat increase, we perceive individuals to be increasingly unhealthy. But it also works the other way around. Despite a Western fascination with beauty in underweight individuals, people with very low levels of body fat are also perceived to be unhealthy. This makes a lot of sense when considered in biological terms, as extreme thinness can indicate starvation or disease, while extreme obesity can suggest risk of heart disease and a lack of physical fitness. As individuals move away from normal body weights toward these two extremes, our interpretation is prone to be that these individuals are unhealthy.

In most video games, characters typically fit within low to normal body weight ranges, particularly for PCs and allies. We could read from this that part of the appeal of a character relates to how healthy it appears to be. A character that looks unhealthy automatically loses some of its appeal, and thus most characters will appear to have fairly healthy weight levels. On the other hand, manipulation of character weight can be used effectively with characters that we are meant to regard negatively. This may seem somewhat politically incorrect, but from a purely evolutionary perspective, our species has every reason to avoid individuals that are overly thin or obese. An extremely thin game character can trigger our natural ability to detect potential signs of ill health. This is a character that we want to avoid, as there is a potential threat of disease. Similarly, an extremely obese character can suggest potential genetic flaws and, as such, we might find this type of character both unhealthy and also unattractive.

The texture and color of the skin might seem a much more subtle consideration than body shape. This is particularly clear if you consider the importance that is placed on character shape and silhouette in character art production (discussed in Chapter 2). Nevertheless, the skin of a virtual character can be an extremely powerful means of communicating not only the character's health, but also its lifestyle.

If we examine texture first, one of the most important considerations is the evenness of the skin (see Figure 1.6). A lack of consistency of skin pigmentation can be a signal for poor immunity and, therefore, susceptibility to disease. As the appearance of spots, blotches, and variation in skin pigment increases, we perceive a reduced capacity to fight off disease, whereas smoother skin with little variation in pigment indicates strong genes. This can of course be taken to extreme levels, with inclusion of warts and scarring where the skin has been damaged by some ailment. As noted in the previous section on attraction, physical symmetry can be a cue to attractiveness, with asymmetry being perceived as less attractive. We could extend that to the perceived healthiness of the skin. Prevalence of asymmetric artifacts within skin texture could accentuate the lack of healthiness, as healthy skin would be not only smooth and consistent, but also fairly symmetrical in its texture.

In the case of skin color, studies have shown that an individual is perceived as more healthy if the level of redness in the skin is increased

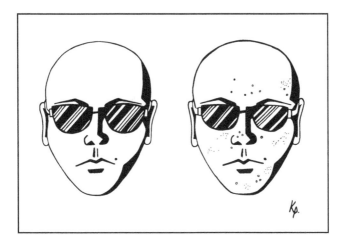

FIGURE 1.6   Skin texture can affect the perceived healthiness of a character.

slightly. This, as you may imagine, has a lot to do with the type and amount of blood under the skin. When blood is oxygenated it turns a brighter red. This can occur after the body has undergone some form of exertion, such as physical exercise. If the body has not been subject to exertion, the proportion of deoxygenated blood increases. This type of blood is more of a blue-purple color and is perceived as less healthy than oxygenated blood. Furthermore, a lack of blood in the skin can also be a sign of poor health. If the amount of blood drops, the skin becomes paler, which makes the person appear unhealthy. As such, shifting skin color toward red can improve the player's perception of a character's health, whereas skin that is closer to blue-purple or pale tones will make a character look unhealthy. This is true regardless of the ethnicity of the character. But there is, of course, a limit. If the skin becomes too red, this can be perceived as unhealthy. All that is required to adjust our perception is a subtle shift in color.

One final property of skin color that is an indicator of healthiness concerns the amount of yellow in the skin. This has been linked to a healthy diet rich in fruit and vegetables. Consumption of vitamin A has the effect of making a person's skin more yellow, which in turn is picked up by observers and identified as a sign of good health. It is believed that it is this connection that makes people associate a tan with healthiness. It is not that the tan in itself is seen as healthy, but that the increase in yellowness that comes with a tan imitates the yellowing effect of a healthy diet rich in vitamin A. As with the addition of red to the skin, this applies to all people, regardless of ethnicity. Again, only a subtle application is required: if there is too much yellow, a character will appear jaundiced.

The various cues to healthiness are readily applied in virtual character design. Generally, you will observe that characters are provided with cues to good health through use of low to medium fat levels and healthy skin. When cues to poor health are present, this is often more interesting. Even when ill-health cues are used subtly, they can be highly effective at making a character appear unsettling, unnerving, or generally disturbing. A good example of subtlety in the application of health cues is the G-Man character from *Half-Life* {Valve Corporation 1998} and *Half-Life 2* {Valve Corporation 2004}. This mysterious character is presented as menacing and threatening. The G-Man appears particularly thin, has uneven skin texture, and has a lack of redness in his skin color. These cues combine to present a person that we naturally find unhealthy and, thus, a character that we want to avoid.

Age

While our natural ability to detect subtle cues to health might seem surprising, most of us will be fairly confident that we can estimate the age of an individual based on appearance alone. There are visual cues to age that are more noticeable than the slight variations in skin tone that are indicators of health. We've already covered proportions earlier in the chapter, for instance, and we saw that proportions are a fairly good indicator of a character's age. On top of this, the striking visual changes that occur in skin texture and hair color are fairly recognizable signals. Nevertheless, the aspects of our appearance that can be associated with age are worth dwelling on, as they can be appropriated and implemented in virtual characters to create powerful aesthetic effects.

One of the cues to age that is discussed frequently in relation to character design is the appearance of babylike faces (see Figure 1.7). The facial proportions of babies have been shown to be effective at grabbing our attention, with the normal response being one of affection and warmth. In other words, we find babies to be much cuter than older children and adults. This feature is well understood by character designers, and you will notice that characters in games aimed at younger audiences take full advantage of this natural reaction by including more baby-faced characters. However, there are specific details that we ought to be aware of. The first is that cuteness diminishes with age, from approximately age 1 onwards. So toddlers are less cute than babies; younger children are less

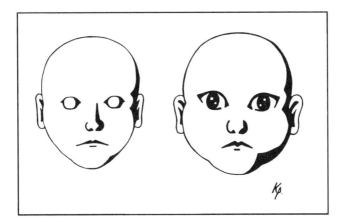

FIGURE 1.7 The facial features of toddlers can be adopted and exaggerated to enhance the cuteness of a character.

cute than toddlers, and so on. Perhaps more surprising is that cuteness doesn't diminish from birth. Instead, babies approaching their first birthday are cuter than younger babies. It is believed that cuteness actually peaks around the ages 9–11 months. This is because these babies are making the transition to toddlers. They are starting to move around and, as a result, are likely to get themselves into bother. Consequently, we have adapted to find these babies the cutest, as this means that adults will give them the most attention and protection.

With an approximate age for maximum cuteness identified, the facial proportions that we are inclined to find the cutest can be examined more closely. The notable features that trigger a feeling of cuteness (and that can therefore be associated with cute character design) are:

- Large forehead
- Large eyes
- Small nose
- Small mouth
- Small chin
- Narrower face below the eyes

It should be noted that these features, while generally observed most often in babies approaching their first birthday, are not explicitly a sign of age. Instead, they are better identified as the features we find most cute. They can be observed in very young babies and older children. Indeed, the features can somewhat persist into adulthood. As we discussed earlier, a highly feminine face maintains childlike features, because testosterone is one of the most important factors to impact on face shape in puberty. The fact that we find highly feminine faces more appealing and worthy of our attention than masculine faces can be related to this extension of cuteness into adulthood.

At the other end of the scale, the most prominent aspect of appearance that provides an indication of advancing age is the texture of the skin. What makes this more complex is the fact that the appearance of the skin isn't dictated by biological age alone. The texture of our skin changes over time due to both genetic and environmental factors. From a biological perspective, skin elasticity is a major contributor to skin texture appearance and indicative of approximate age. With a high level of skin elasticity in youth, skin appears smooth and tight with little or no wrinkles. The appearance of incredibly smooth skin can therefore enhance the youthfulness of a character, as can be seen in many examples of characters aimed at younger audiences. As elasticity reduces with age, skin becomes looser and wrinkles become more pronounced. It therefore seems fairly straightforward to align skin elasticity with the intended age of a character in order to produce a believable design.

However, our overall perception of the age of an individual based on his or her skin texture has more to do with the life that the individual has lived. The presence of wrinkles and liver spots on the skin will vary from individual to individual based primarily on exposure to the environment. A lot of time spent outside can lead to sun-damaged skin, which will make people appear older than they actually are. Using sun protection or staying out of the sunlight when possible will significantly impact on the appearance of the skin, prolonging a youthful appearance. On the face in particular, permanent creases can form that mimic the types of expressions the person has most frequently produced. Heavy creases in the forehead could reflect a life spent frowning, whereas wrinkles in the corners of the eyes (known as crow's feet) could suggest that the person smiles a lot. Additionally, there are obviously links between age and health. In older age, people are more likely to suffer from health-related problems. They've also had more time to contract diseases or develop illnesses over the course of their life that might have had a lasting impact on appearance. As such, skin texture as a cue to actual age is not so useful. Instead, when looking at a virtual character's skin appearance, consider what the texture of the skin might infer in relation to the wider context of the character's story.

SUMMARY AND ACTIVITY

In this chapter, we have started our discussion of the presentation of virtual characters by considering the underlying biological factors that impact on the appearance and observer's perception of the human body. We looked first at human anatomy, identifying what the typical body proportions are in relation to age. By caricaturing these proportions, we saw that this can manipulate how players perceive and interpret a character, accentuating properties such as cuteness, dominance, and athleticism. From there we looked at body types, in particular the three somatotypes: endomorph, ectomorph, and mesomorph. Our discussion showed that the application of these body types in character design can trigger preconceived characteristics such as strength, intensity, and tolerance. Sex differences were shown to be of particular importance to virtual character design, and the physical effects of sex hormones during development were discussed. The effects of sex hormones were again examined in relation to our perception of attractiveness, which is of particular relevance to studies of beauty and aesthetic ideals in virtual character design. Finally, factors that impact on the perceived health and age of a character were considered.

To build on these concepts, two exercises are proposed. Both exercises challenge you to consider virtual character design from a biological perspective, incorporating evaluation of the use of anatomy and visual cues to attraction, health, and age. As the visual presentation of characters amalgamates these factors, it is anticipated that you'll want to account for most if not all of them when analyzing and designing characters. In any case, it is good practice to conduct further reading in order to enhance your critical understanding of human anatomy and perception. The reference list identifies the sources that have been cited in this chapter, and this would be a good starting point for further reading. In particular, it is worth noting that there is a wealth of information on human appearance and perception of appearance in academic journals, and so it is a good idea to become accustomed to developing keywords and searching appropriate journals to access the most up-to-date information. Perret's (2010) book includes scores of references to academic journals related to expression and the face, and so demonstrates the value of the information contained within these more scholarly publications.

Exercises

CHARACTER ANALYSIS

Identify and discuss examples of virtual characters that make effective use of anatomical and biological factors in their design.

1. Identify a range of characters that illustrate strong application of the scientific fundamentals that have been covered in this chapter (including both accurate and exaggerated applications).

2. From this list, try to group your examples under each of the following headings:

    a. Presentation of sex, sexuality, and attractiveness

    b. Presentation of age, fitness, and health

3. For each category, analyze the characters in order to establish how anatomy and other physical cues are used to enhance the designs.

4. Take into account the wider context of the characters within the games, that is, their role in the narrative, their role in the game design, and so on.

5. Write an evaluation of the characters drawing on examples from your notes and screenshots to illustrate key points.

6. Aim to discuss the examples critically, making connections between your observations and the related literature, other media, and so on. Identify strengths and weaknesses in the character(s) you studied.

CHARACTER DESIGN

How can observations of human anatomy be used to enhance the design of video game characters and improve communication of character attributes?

1. Take an existing character design or a character concept that you have developed yourself.

2. Using this character as the basis, imagine how the character can be visually redesigned to reflect a change in:

   a. Sex (increasing the perceived masculinity or femininity of the character)

   b. Age, fitness, and health (turning the character into an infant, teenager, elder, etc., and making the character appear more or less healthy)

   c. Attractiveness and demeanor (making the character more or less attractive, making the character appear more or less friendly)

3. In all instances, consider how you can manipulate the anatomy and other physical cues to enhance your redesign.

REFERENCES

Bridgman, G. 2009. *Bridgman's complete guide to drawing from life.* New York: Sterling.

Collins, S. A., and C. Missing. 2003. Vocal and visual attractiveness are related in women. *Animal Behaviour* 65 (5): 997–1004.

Evans, S., N. Neave, and D. Wakelin. 2006. Relationships between vocal characteristics and body size and shape in human males: An evolutionary explanation for a deep male voice. *Biological Psychology* 72 (2): 16–163.

Hyde, J., and J. DeLamater. 2013. *Understanding human sexuality.* 12th ed. Boston: McGraw-Hill.

Peck, S. R. 1982. *Atlas of human anatomy for the artist.* Oxford, UK: Oxford University Press.

Perret, D. 2010. *In your face: The new science of human attraction.* Basingstoke, UK: Palgrave Macmillan.

Simblet, S. 2001. *Anatomy for the artist.* London: DK.

CHAPTER 2

Visual and Audio Design Principles

V ISUAL PRESENTATION IS EASILY one of the most discussed topics in the character design literature. In the games industry, artists are typically charged with imagining, developing, and constructing the visual appearance of a character from concept through to finished, animated assets. This work can vary, depending on the nature of the role. For instance an art generalist might be responsible for the complete pipeline, whereas a concept artist is likely to focus on the visual design but not the production of the in-game assets. Regardless of the specific art role, all video game artists require a strong understanding of line, shape, silhouette, color, and composition. The direct connection between visual design theory and professional practice in video game art validates the prominence that character design books place on discussion of character appearance.

By extension, understanding the theories behind character audio—while not discussed to the same extent in the character design literature—can be directly related to a game development role. Audio engineers are responsible for developing concepts and final assets for the vocals, sound effects, and even the music that will be associated with a game character. But it is not just the professional artists and audio engineers who need a foundation in visual and audio theories for character design. Writers and game designers are also tasked with developing ideas for the characteristics, personality, aesthetics, and functionality of a character, all of which inform a character's audiovisual design.

In this chapter, we look in detail at the visual principles that can be used to describe a virtual character, and then we go on to examine the components and aesthetics of character sound design. Throughout the chapter, the focus is on artistic principles, rather than hard and fast rules. While there can be connotations associated with particular visual and audio elements, these are always subject to interpretation, and conventions can be broken, downplayed, or modulated by context. As such, it is crucial that audiovisual principles be considered critically. For instance, there are no definitive meanings behind the color red or the use of triangles. But an understanding of common visual associations and an appreciation of the subtlety of human perception can inform our critical interpretation of a character. By the end of this chapter, we will have devised a critical framework that can be applied to a virtual character in order to analyze and understand its visual and audio qualities.

LINE AND SHAPE

When it comes to character design principles, line and shape are two of the most common concepts discussed in the literature. One of the main reasons for this is that, as a species, we are naturally skilled at recognizing patterns and identifying outliers. Babies, for example, are capable of discriminating between face and nonface shapes from birth. This tacit ability to perceive shape and pattern has been exploited by artists for centuries. The silhouettes of figures in both historic artworks and contemporary media have been used as a compositional tool that not only guides the eye of the spectator, but that also visually communicates or reflects the themes of an artwork.

To begin our formal analysis of the spatial elements of a character, it is sensible that we first consider the most basic element of all: the line. Although this is less well discussed in the character design literature, it is fundamental to formalist analysis. The line is not only responsible for outlining shapes within a character, but also for leading the eye, making connections between and intersections with shapes, and communicating movement and direction. The first application is perhaps best recognized in characters that are produced in a cartoon style that makes specific use of outlines. In more realistic character design, line for shape definition is often an abstract consideration, as lines are alluded to rather than explicitly shown. Nevertheless, the thickness, orientation, position, and type of line should be taken into account when conducting a visual analysis of a character, irrespective of the art style.

Consider how the following attributes can define the visual appearance of a character:

- *Line thickness*: Technically, lines are one-dimensional and are therefore infinitely thin. In order to perceive them, however, some thickness must be shown. How we perceive thickness is based on the ratio between width and length. This thickness of a line can have an effect on the impression it creates. For instance, a thin line has less impact than a bold line. A line can be uniform—maintaining consistent thickness—or loose and rough. The former can convey precision, clarity, honesty, and seriousness, whereas the latter might create an impression of triviality, ambiguity, and playfulness. Furthermore, lines do not need to be continuous. Broken lines made up of repeated elements can be used to create more texture in an image, and they potentially can even embed depth of meaning if shapes or symbols are used as the repeated elements.

- *Line orientation*: The next attribute to consider is the orientation of a line. The angle at which a line is oriented in relation to the rest of the design can affect the perception of a character's appearance. Lines that are horizontal suggest restfulness and steadiness: conceptually, they are parallel to the ground. They can also be used to emphasize or exaggerate the width of a character. In contrast, vertical lines are best used to convey height, balance, and significance, as they are conceptually perpendicular to the ground. Lines that are diagonal or oblique can create an impression of dynamism, movement, and instability, as they suggest either a line that is falling from or rising to a vertical orientation.

- *Line position*: As well as considering orientation, it is important to think about how lines are positioned. Lines can be positioned to create outlines, as has been previously discussed. This might be an explicit line that outlines a shape, implied lines that highlight shapes or elements of a character, or lines that are positioned to surround (and therefore group) several elements together. These are powerful techniques when it comes to guiding the viewer's eye and drawing attention to key features. Another use of line position is to make visual connections between elements, which can in turn infer metaphorical connections. For instance, lines may be used to link two or more elements together, to intersect and divide elements, or to support elements. Line combinations can also be of value. Combining vertical and horizontal lines, for example, can produce rigid shapes that create an impression of stability, permanence, and strength.

- *Line type*: Finally, it is important to consider that lines are not always straight. While straight lines can complement uniform thickness and horizontal/vertical orientation to reinforce notions of strength and consistency, curved lines can instead connote dynamism, energy, and nature. Deep curves can be used to emphasize playfulness and joy, whereas shallower curves can give an impression of softness, gentleness, sensuality, and femininity.

In analysis of line within the visual appearance of a character, it is important to be sensitive to both the explicit and implicit use of line. Visual analysis can scrutinize the use of explicit line in the outlining of character elements, but it can also consider the implied lines that are apparent within a character. In both instances, the criteria discussed here can aid interpretation of how line is used to communicate the nature or personality of a character. The characters of *Super Meat Boy* {Team Meat 2010} are outlined in bold, ragged lines that vary in thickness and that lack precision. The use of line emphasizes the connection to alternative cartoons and a 1980s gaming aesthetic, reflects the wacky humor of the game, and also makes a connection to the independent development of the game itself. In contrast, the use of line in the design of GLaDOS in *Portal 2* {Valve 2011} is less explicit. Here, a combination of straight diagonal lines and subtle curves is used throughout, flowing from top to bottom but in an erratic and unstructured manner. The implied lines serve a functional purpose, leading the eye to the character's "face," which could easily be lost in the scene, given that it contains few familiar features. More than this, though, the lines within the GLaDOS design reflect her part-feminine/part-machine nature, and the erratic line placement reflects her madness, menace, and despotism.

Progressing from line, the next visual element that can be examined within character design is shape. The application and connotations of shape usage are widely discussed not only in the character design literature, but also in other visual design fields, such as graphic design and architecture. As with line, shape may be explicitly used to define the internal elements of a character (as is common in cartoon design for younger audiences) or implied within the overall design of a character.

The most common shapes discussed in the literature are the circle, triangle, and square: the primary shapes. These are the simplest shapes that observers can reduce an image down to. Making sense of complex scenes through simplification to base elements is an important aspect of perception and cognition. These basic shapes do not need to conform to a geometric ideal—for example, the perfect circle, equilateral triangle, or square—but instead can be loosely interpreted by their definitions.

- *Circles*: Any rounded shape defined by a continuous introverted curve may be considered a circle and associated with common connotations. These connotations have a tendency to focus in two broad categories: youth and goodness. In the former category, it can be inferred that circular shapes communicate ideas such as playfulness, childlikeness, energy, and innocence. The latter category can be broken down into ideas such as positivity, grace, unity, balance, nature, and protection. In consequence, circular shapes are more frequently observed within characters aimed at younger audiences or within more conventional, uncomplicated heroes.

- *Triangles*: Triangular shapes can offer quite different interpretations, depending on their usage. Triangles that are oriented to point toward the sky can communicate stability, rest, and strength, while triangles that point toward the ground suggest precarious balance, instability, and tension. Overall connotations of triangular shapes may be grouped into two categories: energy and temperament. Energy can include concepts such as dynamism, movement, and speed. Temperament simply means the implied human characteristics that can be projected onto triangular shapes, which are typically ideas such as aggression, hostility, deviousness, passion, and sexuality.

- *Squares*: Finally, squares and rectangles are typically considered to be the strongest and most stable shapes. This breaks down with quadrilaterals that contain more acute angles and therefore look more triangular in shape. As well as connoting ideas such as strength and stability, square shapes can be associated with masculinity, security, orthodoxy, rationality, and purity. In general, these ideas are strongly emphasized with perfect squares and can be gradually weakened as the square becomes more rectangular or rhomboid.

FIGURE 2.1 Shapes such as squares, circles, and triangles can be implied within a character's design in order to trigger common shape connotations. (Image courtesy of Rory Jobson.)

In considering shape within character design, it is imperative to be open to both the explicit use of shape as well as implied shapes. Normally, primary shapes are not used wholesale in character design. Characters such as *Pac-Man* {Namco 1980} and *Dizzy* {Oliver Twins 1987} are effectively circular in nature, but this was an outcome of technical limitations in the 1980s rather than intentional visual design. Visual analysis should account for identification and critique of both the clear use of primary shapes in a character design as well as the less obvious use of shapes. Consider the characters in Figure 2.1, for example. These character designs make use of implied squares, circles, and triangles to generate not only distinctive character appearances, but also connotations of character type and personality.

SILHOUETTE

The overall spatial appearance of a character can be analyzed by considering its silhouette. This is a key technique used by character designers and an important stage of the design process. By removing all (or most) internal details and discounting color, silhouettes are used to ensure that the complete outline of a character can be clearly recognized from a range of angles and in different poses. Examining characters through silhouette can enhance analysis of both line and shape. Thus, as well as being a vital design tool in the production of a virtual character, it can also be used to aid visual deconstruction. In addition to line and shape criteria, however, there are other factors that can be considered when analyzing a character silhouette:

- *Recognizability*: Arguably the most important aspect of the silhouette is whether or not it makes the character distinctive. This works on two levels that can be considered in the visual analysis of a character. The first level is the purely aesthetic response. Is the character sufficiently distinctive, interesting, and pleasing to look at? In an ideal situation, all virtual characters will generate this response. But typically you'd expect the prominent characters (PCs and leading NPCs) to receive the most iteration and refinement. The use of line and shape within the character can be examined to determine what exactly makes the character satisfying or unsatisfying. These can be expanded upon to account for other visual factors that impact upon our value judgments, such as use of weight and proportion (as discussed in Chapter 1). The second level of recognizability is more practical. Does the silhouette work to successfully make the character stand out from the background? This doesn't mean that more complex silhouettes are more recognizable; simple designs can be easy to spot when they are juxtaposed with the wider visual design of a game. When characters are insufficiently distinctive, the player's ability to identify and track them within a game world can have negative impacts on both the gameplay experience and navigation.

- *Hierarchy*: Visual hierarchy extends the notion of the recognizability of a character by paying particular attention to how visual elements are used to infer the importance of particular characters in relation to other characters, or to reflect the relationships between characters. In graphic design, visual hierarchy is primarily about making information easier to understand by providing visual cues, for instance through use of size and shape. When we take this theory forward into virtual character design, we can consider how a cast of characters can be made easier to understand through explicit use of visual design elements evident in the silhouettes. Within hierarchy, there are three key concepts we can look for: contrast (e.g., size contrast to reinforce the dominance of one character over another), repetition (e.g., the repeated use of a particular shape to suggest association between characters and to create a visual theme), and alignment (e.g., the uniform configuration of visual elements across characters to create a strong sense of order and a lack of individual differences).

- *Functionality*: Beyond the practical implications of the silhouette, analysis should also consider the intrinsic functionality of the design in terms of whether the character silhouette appears logical or illogical within the game world. The clothing, armor, and equipment that a character wears can suggest a lack of maneuverability or even an inability to stand or move appropriately. The size and placement of equipment, including weapons, can even place the character in peril should they move in such a way that they become impaled. The functionality of the visual design can be formally analyzed at first, but, as noted previously, the context of the game interacts with the plausibility of design. For instance, comedic, fantasy, and science-fiction genres can play down (or indeed subvert) the logic that dictates character functionality. As such, sensitivity to context is important in consideration of functionality inherent in silhouette.

- *Metaphor*: Building on an interpretation of the use of line and primary shapes within a character, the overall silhouette can be analyzed to determine whether it acts as a metaphor. In its broadest sense, we can look at the complete outline of the character and determine whether it makes a connection with a recognizable form from nature, a work of art, or a cultural icon. A character that has been purposefully designed to suggest the shape of a flower, for instance, could convey connotations of nature, growth, fertility, fragility, or beauty, which may reinforce (or perhaps even subvert) our understanding of the character's personality and place in the world. Or a character silhouette may provide a parody or pastiche of an existing design from art and media, which in turn alters our perception and interpretation of a character.

- *Dynamism*: Finally, and of particular importance to virtual characters, is the notion of dynamism. By definition, virtual characters are interactive and have the potential to be modulated by player action. As a consequence of this, there is a strong likelihood that a virtual character—particularly a playable character observed from a third-person camera—will have a silhouette that changes based on player action. Consider how the silhouette of a character shifts—using all of the criteria we have discussed here—within the context of player interaction and the game narrative. A character may go through a story arc that suggests a change in its worldview or belief system: how does the visual design adapt to reflect this change? Similarly, a character might experience physical changes—both short and long term—that can be reflected in the silhouette. For example, consider how a character silhouette can be modified to mirror a severe depletion in health, or how a buildup of physical strength or skill over the course of a game can be reinforced with complementary changes in silhouette design. Additionally, there is the possibility that a player may have the power to manipulate cameras or character positioning to such a degree that a range of silhouettes can emerge. The Batman character from the *Batman: Arkham* series {Rocksteady Studios 2009, 2011; Warner Bros. Games Montreal 2013} is an excellent example of a virtual character with a dynamic silhouette. He can appear square-like and solid when standing, emphasizing his strength and dominance, but break into more angled and triangular shapes (aided by his cape) when gliding, fighting, or moving with speed.

Overall, the silhouette is arguably the foundation of a virtual character's appearance, and careful analysis of a silhouette using the criteria discussed here (in combination with specific application of line and shape) can help to reveal what effects the appearance can have on an audience. Silhouettes can be used to reflect personality, to create contrast or continuity, and to convey potentially complex ideas.

COLOR

Up until now, we have focused on the spatial elements of a character's visual design. We have seen that the silhouette and the use of line and shape within a design can greatly manipulate how a player might perceive a character. When we introduce color into the mix, the potential for visually communicating ideas through character appearance increases exponentially. The wealth of publications on color theory is a treasure trove for character designers and researchers alike. This chapter cannot go into the same level of detail as these specialist books, particularly with regard to the physical and psychological components of color and light. For more in-depth reading, it is recommended that readers look to books such as *Colour and Light* by Gurney (2010). Nevertheless, because color is such a crucial factor, we need to identify the core concepts that are of relevance to the successful study of character design.

First, it should be noted that there are several systems for understanding color that have been used across artistic and scientific disciplines. From the perspective of visual design, the artist's color wheel is arguably the best-known system for organizing color. Breaking down the spectrum into twelve general colors and into three categories, the artist's color wheel identifies: red, yellow, and blue as the primary colors; green, orange, and purple as the secondary colors; and blue-purple, blue-green, yellow-green, yellow-orange, red-orange, and red-purple as the tertiary colors. On the face of it, this is a relatively solid system for analysis of color with respect to perception, as it reflects how humans see color rather than how color actually exists in nature. In reality, the spectrum from yellow to orange on the artist's color wheel is exaggerated, as there are more subtle variations of purples, blues, and greens than there are of yellows and oranges. This can make the artist's color wheel quite problematic. Many artists have turned to other systems (such as the Munsell color system) that provide a more accurate representation of color in nature. Furthermore, digital artists are far more likely to work with color using systems that operate with a different set of primaries: red, green, and blue (RGB) for screen images, and cyan, magenta, and yellow (CMY) for print. As such, a universal color wheel that combines these primaries is the one that most designers will use daily, placing six primaries around the wheel in the following order: red, yellow, green, cyan, blue, magenta.

Although there is a degree of flexibility in the use of color systems, for the purposes of analysis in this book we stick with the artist's or traditional color wheel, which is based around the conceptual primaries of red, blue, and yellow. This color wheel is shown in Figure 2.2. While inaccurate when it comes to reflecting the real color spectrum, this wheel does provide a closer representation of how we tend to see and understand color, in particular when it comes to considerations such as color opposites. With this wheel in mind, let's now consider the basic color components before looking at color relationships:

- *Hue*: When we say *color*, what many of us actually mean is *hue*. Hues are the general ranges of color as seen on any color wheel. All color can be considered in terms of just eight hues: red, orange, yellow, green, cyan, blue, purple, and magenta. This list contains the six hues of the combined RGB and CMY color systems, plus orange and purple. This categorization might seem quite simplistic, but it aligns with our natural ability to perceive and discriminate between colors. Furthermore, hues are often associated with connotations that we can utilize in our analysis of a character's appearance. At the most basic level, we can split hues into warm (magenta to yellow) and cool (green to purple) colors. Cool colors can be associated with calmness,

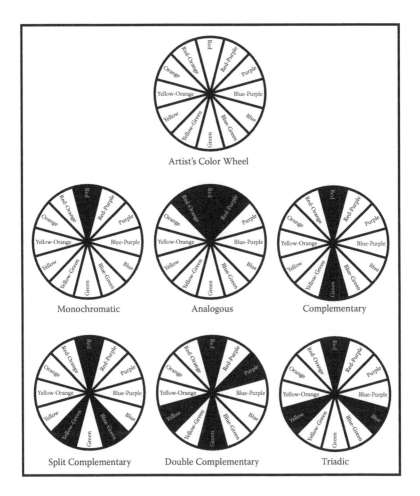

FIGURE 2.2 The traditional artist's color wheel along with some of the commonly applied color schemes.

objectivity, comfort, and nurture, while warm colors can be associated with passion, optimism, and excitement. Potential meanings for each of the hues are identified in Table 2.1.

- *Value*: The value of a color relates to its brightness or how much light it reflects. Essentially, value can be considered on a scale of black to white, with the brightest colors (those with the highest value) at the white end of the scale. Hues combined with high values and lower saturation create pastel colors, which can be associated with delicate, playful, and innocent characters, and in particular are suitable to designs that are intended for very young audiences. Conversely, use of low values can

TABLE 2.1   Hues and Potential Meanings

Hue	Type	Potential Connotations
Magenta	Warm	Sweetness, romance, playfulness, uplifting, freedom
Red	Warm	Power, love, passion, sex, energy, danger, anger
Orange	Warm	Enthusiasm, joy, creativity, fun, warmth
Yellow	Warm	Cheerfulness, joy, sunshine, remembrance, intellect
Green	Cool	Nature, growth, healing, health, fertility, harmony, envy
Cyan	Cool	Relaxation, fresh, peace, tranquility, imagination, femininity
Blue	Cool	Depth, stability, peace, trust, ocean, strength, masculinity
Purple	Cool	Royalty, wealth, power, influence, ambition, dignity

create darker, murkier, earthier colors that are more naturalistic (reds become maroons, oranges become browns). One of the most effective uses of value is to create value contrast, also known as *chiaroscuro*. Mixing high- and low-value colors can create one of the most effective contrasts achieved with color. Consider the conceptual extreme: the contrast of black and white. This most extreme of value contrasts can be used to accentuate the differences between two characters.

- *Saturation*: Color saturation is a hue's degree of purity: in effect, how colorful it appears to be. Highly saturated colors are bold, striking, fairly unnatural, and can be used to exaggerate or enhance the connotations of a hue. Due to their relative simplicity and strength, saturated colors can be appropriate for characters aimed at a younger audience or, conversely, can be effective when used sparingly to create saturation contrast within a character or between characters. Low saturation mixes hues with grays to create more realistic, mature colors that can make a character appear more subtle, distant, thoughtful, and complex. Tints are hues that are mixed with white, while shades are hues that are mixed with black.

Beyond looking at specific color components, we can consider the presence and potential effect of color relationships. When colors within a character (or within a group of characters) are combined in particular configurations, further meanings can be implied. The following color schemes are shown in Figure 2.2:

- *Monochromatic*: A color scheme used within a character or group of characters that is centered on one hue—with variation largely limited to adjustments in value and saturation—can be considered a monochromatic color scheme. These schemes often appear quite stylized and unnatural, drawing clear attention to the chosen hue. As a result, a monochromatic scheme can act to exaggerate common interpretations of a hue. Within character design, monochromatic schemes might be regarded as a means of simplifying a character and directly associating it with a color, to the point where it is in effect an embodiment of the hue. The Nintendo character Kirby, for instance, is effectively a monochromatic character centered on variations of magenta, accentuating his playfulness, energy, and sweetness.

- *Analogous*: Analogous colors are colors that are adjacent to each other on a color wheel (for instance blue, cyan, and green), providing a sense of continuity and progression. These color schemes can produce the most naturalistic results, as the colors are aligned with each other, creating a very pleasing appearance. The color at the center of the range of colors is typically the dominant color (e.g., cyan from the example given here). Within a character design, an analogous color scheme will convey a sense of harmony, serenity, and comfort, with no glaring contrast. You should consider how a character's analogous color design might amalgamate the potential meanings of the applied colors, allowing for a more complex reading of the color connotations we commonly hold. Analogous schemes can also allow for a broader application of warm or cool colors within a character.

- *Complementary*: Colors that are complementary are those that, when mixed, achieve a neutral color. One of the easiest ways to identify complementary colors is to identify the hues that are opposite each other on the color wheel you are working with. In our case, as we are sticking with the traditional artist's color wheel, the complementary colors are red and green, blue and orange, and yellow and purple. In character design, the application of complementary color is a key aesthetic consideration, as it can create a pleasing contrast and convey a sense of balance. From a practical point of view, complementary colors also provide a high degree of visibility and dynamism. For instance, many characters that are inspired by comic books make use of complementary colors in their design to emphasize their energy, vitality, and fantastical nature.

- *Split complementary*: The split complementary scheme can be considered a less jarring variation of the standard complementary scheme, whereby two colors are provided as a contrast to the dominant color. The two alternative colors would be placed on either side of the typical complementary color on a color wheel. Thus, where the dominant hue was green, the complementary hues would be red-orange and red-purple rather than red. This can create the same feeling of contrast and visibility while reducing the tension and simplicity that a straight complementary might otherwise create. As such, this can introduce more subtlety and complexity to a character and also draw on a wider range of connotations.

- *Double complementary*: A combination of four colors in a character design may fall within a double complementary scheme, where two sets of standard complementary colors are used. Typically, these are not used equally, as the design can become overpowering and garish unless one of the pairs is selected as the dominant complementary. Given the range of colors used, there is plenty of scope here for playing with color application. In virtual character design, a common application of the double complementary is not within a single character, but between two characters who sit in opposition to each other. The use of two complementary schemes serves to draw further attention to the differences between, say, a protagonist and his primary antagonist.

- *Triadic*: Finally, triadic color schemes make use of three colors that are typically evenly spaced around the color wheel (for instance red, blue, and yellow). This creates a vibrant appearance, can produce highly stylized results, and is often difficult to implement. The three colors are normally in equal balance, as the dominance of one color over the others can create very unpleasing results.

When it comes to character design and analysis, the basic color components and color relationships provide us with a means of deconstructing and making sense of color use. As with all visual principles, though, the interpretation of a color based on hue, value, and saturation is fundamentally subject to cultural connotations, and there are no universal rules that link color and meaning.

VISUAL STYLE

In the previous sections, we looked closely at the component parts of a character's visual design, interrogating the potential applications and connotations of elements such as line, shape, and color. This deconstruction of visual presentation offers us a means to analyze, interpret, and discuss a character at an intricate level. However, it is unlikely that audiences or designers will really dwell on these elements when contemplating and responding to a character's appearance. When we look at a character, we tend to consider its appearance more holistically: as a combination of lines, shapes, and colors that are arranged to create a more complete and distinctive image. It is this total image that tends to (a) communicate the nature and personality of a character most effectively and (b) have the most profound impact on the audience in terms of aesthetic quality and narrative appeal. What we are really concerned with, then, is the visual style that a character is presented in.

And yet, visual style can be a very complex concept to tackle. While we previously sought to break visual presentation down to elemental parts that we could then examine and discuss, the potential for variety in visual style makes it much more difficult to categorize. We know different visual styles when we see them—that a character might be presented in the style of classical Disney animation or in the manga-informed style of Studio Ghibli—but these points of reference are very specific and don't necessarily provide insight into how visual style works. References can be useful when developing a concept, of course. When attempting to describe what a character should look like, it can be pragmatic to suggest that it will be presented in a style reminiscent of 1960s Marvel comics, of the films of Tim Burton, or of the animations of Seth MacFarlane. Nevertheless, it would be valuable if we could discuss visual style more broadly in order to understand how style might affect audience interpretation.

At the most general level, we can seek to define the visual style of a character using scalar measures. One of the simplest yet most effective means of achieving this is provided by Scott McCloud (1994) in his book *Understanding Comics*. In the first instance, McCloud asks us to consider how cartoony a character is. In McCloud's example, he argues that, as a character representation moves from photorealism toward cartoony, there is a greater likelihood that the character will be seen to represent a wider range of people. In other words, a photographic image provides a specific representation of an individual, but a plain cartoon face with no detail could represent millions of individuals. The significance of this proposition is that a very cartoony character could be seen to represent the audience as a whole, whereas a photographic representation is more difficult to identify with. McCloud hammers home this point by suggesting that when we see a photographic representation, we see another person, but when we see a highly simple cartoon character, we can more easily see ourselves.

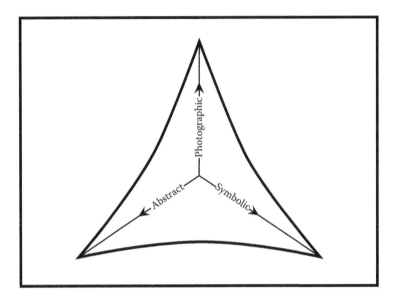

FIGURE 2.3 Visual style can be defined in relation to how abstract, photographic, or symbolic the images are.

Taking this a step further, McCloud (1994) provides a framework for the visual style of a character. McCloud's framework uses three types of representation that can be considered extremes of character presentation. McCloud suggests that these extremes can be considered the picture plane, reality, and language. These terms can essentially be equated to the abstract, the photographic, and the symbolic. I find that the latter terms more clearly communicate the building blocks of visual style, and so I have used these terms in an adapted framework (shown in Figure 2.3). When planning or analyzing a visual style, this framework can be used to identify where the style sits in relation to each of the three extremes. The extremes can be defined as:

- *Abstract*: The image consists entirely of the visual elements discussed earlier in the chapter: lines, shapes, and colors. At the extreme, these elements are neither arranged to produce a higher-level depiction of reality nor combined to communicate any clear or coherent meaning.

- *Photographic*: An image that provides a photographic representation of reality. At the extreme, a photographic image is indistinguishable from the reality that it represents: the character looks like an exact copy of a real person.

- *Symbolic*: An image focused entirely on the communication of meaning through visual symbols. At an extreme level, letters and numbers can be considered symbols that infer clear meanings. Within character design, the use of a circular shape with an internal curved line in its lower half and two dots in its upper half can be considered a symbol to connote the human face.

Others have looked to identify a means of breaking down and discussing visual style. In animation, for instance, Maureen Furniss (1998) has discussed how representation in film can be considered on a scale from live-action to animation, which can broadly be associated with concepts of mimesis (imitation of reality) and abstraction, as described in the previous discussion. Much like McCloud's (1994) framework, this concept allows for identification of a given character's visual style along a trajectory from the photographic to the purely abstract. Also like McCloud, this covers a comprehensive range of styles, as both end points are fairly extreme.

These concepts offer us a theoretical framework for identifying and positioning a particular style according to extreme points. In most instances, the visual style a character is depicted in is unlikely to exist at an extreme, as the extremes can create undesirable issues for audiences. Clearly, a character depicted in a purely abstract form will be very difficult to read and interpret. Bear in mind that a truly abstract image should not be recognizable as a character form. A purely abstract image contains no representational or symbolic images. Characters depicted at the symbolic end of the scale will essentially be reduced to visual objects that communicate specific ideas. As we have identified, letters and numbers (as well as other symbols) exist at this extreme. This style offers lots of scope for clear and effective communication through visual language, but it can be limiting in terms of the nuance of representation or aesthetic qualities that can be achieved by moving more toward photographic and abstract extremes.

The photographic extreme seems to be less troublesome: How can an exact replica of reality be as problematic as extremely abstract or symbolic styles? But two key problems exist for this extreme: one that is technical in nature and the other conceptual. First, perfect imitation of reality in any character design is highly prone to create feelings of uneasiness in the audience, popularly referred to as the *uncanny valley* effect. This theory (based initially on a proposition about the potential ill effects of a human-like form for robots) states that the closer a representation gets to that of a real human, the more likely it is to be perceived as imperfect, unusual, or unfamiliar. There isn't scope to delve deeply into this theory in this chapter, but we return to the uncanny aesthetic in relation to applied examples in Chapter 9. In terms of further reading for now, Angela Tinwell (2014) provides an exhaustive and deeply insightful discussion of the theory in relation to character design. The conceptual problem of photographic realism is perhaps more straightforward. An exact copy or imitation of a real human form offers no freedom of imagination. Character design would be fairly dry if there were no scope for creative license to imagine and visualize humans that are augmented, exaggerated, or stylized.

All of which brings us back to where we started: Visual style is most neatly defined through comparison to existing styles. These styles can exist on the scales that we have looked at, so we are better equipped to discuss a style in relation to how abstract, photographic, or symbolic it is. But really, what we need to do is categorize a character's visual style using existing conventions and style types.

Categorization is an easy enough concept to understand, but it nevertheless is dependent on a number of factors. When it comes to visual style categorization for video games and other interactive media forms, we need to be conscious of the fact that we are building upon millennia of arts practice. The category of a virtual character's visual style is not only based upon visual concepts associated with video games and games culture, but also upon categorization within film theory, animation theory, comic studies, and indeed the entire history of the visual arts. To approach a categorization of a given visual style, we should therefore be prepared to consider the relevance and value of a number of factors from across the range of visual art forms. The following list identifies some of the key factors that are likely to influence visual style:

- *Period*: This is commonly used within the field of art history to define a particular phase of artistic development, both in terms of the general movement of the time as well as a period in a particular artist or auteur's development (e.g., Picasso's Blue and Rose Periods). More generally, consideration of period should serve to identify a particular point in time that can be aligned with a particular visual style in painting, sculpture, film, gaming, and so on.

- *Location*: Alongside period, it will typically be important to identify a location in order to provide context. In other words, identification of the early sixteenth century as a period is not sufficient to define a particular visual style in image making: it would also be important to identify whether the period is in relation to work being created in Italy, the Netherlands, Russia, China, and so on.

- *Art movement*: Both periods and locations can also interact with a finer description of visual style, which is the associated art movement. For example, period and location might be narrowed to look at Western European styles of the early twentieth century, but we can also identify a plethora of art movements (Cubism, Dadaism, German Expressionism, etc.) within this time and setting that more concisely communicate visual style.

- *Individual or studio style*: Looking at particular artists, auteurs, and studios, it may be possible to identify a consistent style that can be used to help define the appearance of a character. We alluded to this earlier in this section when we suggested that a style might be defined through reference to the style of an individual creative such as Tim Burton in film, the early Disney Studio in feature animation, or Seth MacFarlane in television animation. But of course we can look more broadly at the visual arts to define and interpret a visual style, for instance the individual styles of Vincent van Gogh or Henri Matisse.

- *Genre*: Genre is a useful factor to consider in all visual art forms, but it is clearly of importance when looking to draw influence from the style conventions seen in film, animation, comics, and video games. Overarching genres such as science fiction can be broken down into subgenres that more succinctly inform visual style, for example, space opera, steampunk, dieselpunk, and the like. Additionally, we can also see that the period and location interact with genre to more clearly communicate a style, for example, the visual style of 1950s American alien-invasion B movies.

- *Culture and subcultures*: In a more contemporary sense, a visual style might be best defined along cultural or subcultural lines rather than national ones. For instance, modes of cultural activity and engagement can inform a particular visual style (e.g., punk, hip-hop, pro wrestling, extreme sports, *Dungeons & Dragons*, etc.). There are also very clear examples where a cultural aesthetic has emerged that could be used to greatly support a visual style, for example, the modern Japanese aesthetic of *kawaii* that is now widely recognized and consumed globally. The kawaii aesthetic emphasizes cuteness and is associated with a range of characters and brandings.

- *Audience*: With all of these considerations, it would seem that we have a fairly exhaustive range of criteria with which to identify, research, and shape a character's visual style in order to achieve a particular aesthetic effect. But of course, we must also be mindful of the target audience and pay heed to how the tastes of different age groups and different cultures might inform and alter a visual style.

By using the factors presented here, we can home in on particular visual styles that are appropriate for our character design based on the requirements of our projects. For example, some projects may place greater emphasis on the need to address a particular audience using a given genre, while other projects may stress the need to explore an aesthetic associated with an art movement or the style of a particular studio. Similarly, when researching virtual characters, we can use these factors to more rigorously and systematically analyze visual style, identifying potential links to existing art movements, periods, genres, and cultures and, therefore, discuss the design in a wider visual arts context.

SOUND DESIGN FOR VIRTUAL CHARACTERS

So far in this chapter, we have focused on the visual design of characters. This would seem reasonable, given that character presentation is the opening theme of the book. It would be easy to correlate character sound design with narrative and gameplay design (which we come to in Section II of this book), given that the most obvious application of audio is for scripted dialogue, sound effects (SFX) to accompany character actions, and music to complement game scenes. However, it is important that we demonstrate a critical awareness of the properties of sound if we are to thoughtfully and creatively design audio that enhances the presentation of a character. Therefore, just as we have covered the fundamental elements of visual imagery and style, we also look at the components of sound and consider how sound design can be used to generate particular effects.

The book does not have the scope to go into great detail, and further reading into sound aesthetics and sound design for games is recommended. In particular, it is suggested that readers look to books by Chion (1990) and Collins (2008) in order to develop a more thorough appreciation of sound design that is applicable to games and other interactive media. First, the three main types of sound asset that will likely be associated with a virtual character are voice, SFX, and music. These three elements are rarely going to exist in complete isolation. Typically they will be balanced so that they work together to create a consistent and pleasing sound track. For media such as film and television, this involves mixing the sound so that one fixed soundtrack is produced. This can then be aligned with the visuals. For games, however, the sound track is likely to be interactive to some degree. This can involve triggered dialogue, dynamic modulated sound effects, or a score that adapts to map onto player action. The addition of complex interaction can make sound balancing for virtual characters quite challenging, and it is not uncommon to encounter imperfections in a game soundtrack, particularly outside of cutscenes. While this is largely an issue for the wider game design (Collins 2008), virtual character design and analysis ought to be sensitive to the role and impact of player agency on the presentation of all types of associated audio. We come back to the interactivity of characters in Chapters 4, 5, and 6. For now, we focus on sound design and audio qualities in general, concentrating on the key principles and concepts that are useful to character design and analysis.

In order to describe the sonic qualities of any of the identified audio elements, it is important to be at least aware of the technical vocabulary used in sound production, editing, and analysis. Table 2.2 lists some of the key components of sound, as discussed by Mott (2009).

These elements provide us with a fundamental language with which to describe the sound design of a virtual character. As with the visual elements discussed earlier in the chapter, it is unlikely that any one of these component parts of sound will provide exceptional insight into a character or, on its own, communicate the personality or nature of a character. Ultimately, what we are really concerned with is how these elements of sound design and application can be combined and utilized aesthetically, creating an overall audio style for a given character. As before, the concepts that we cover are primarily artistic in nature. In other words, they are general principles that can be used to guide the design of audio to achieve a particular aesthetic. In this sense, there are no right or wrong answers. Instead, these concepts will help you to break down, interpret, and discuss the qualities of a character's sound design.

Diegetic, Synchronous, and Empathetic Sound

We earlier identified a book by Michael Chion (1990), and the following concepts are drawn from this text, which lays out a wider theoretical

TABLE 2.2   Nine Components of Sound Discussed by Mott

Type	Component	Description
Musical	Pitch	Sound frequency. Low or bass frequencies can create warm and powerful sounds, while high or treble frequencies can create a sense of closeness.
	Harmonics	Component frequency waves that are associated with a fundamental (or base) frequency. The combination of fundamental frequency and harmonics determines how pleasant or unpleasant a sound is (e.g., minor and major chords in music).
	Timbre	The tonal quality of a sound based on its pitch and harmonics that helps to describe the texture or aesthetic of a sound (e.g., the differences between instruments or differences in the sound of people's voices).
	Loudness	The perceived loudness of a sound, which is determined by both the source and other environmental factors. The latter can include spatial variation (e.g., small room or open field) and the presence of other sounds (e.g., an explosion is perceived as very loud in a quiet room but less so in a busy street with heavy traffic).
	Rhythm	The recurrence of a sound with variation in strength. In music this is comprised of beat, tempo, and accent. But voice can also have rhythm (distinctive patterns in speech that can infer character personality) as can SFX (e.g., breathing, footsteps, etc.).
Sound envelope	Attack	A sound envelope defines the complete life of a given sound. The attack is the initiation of the sound, from the initial event that caused the sound to the peak of the sound. Fast attacks are very short, such as handclaps or slamming doors, and can create a sense of impact and passion. Slow attacks are used in sounds that build up gradually—such as the slow raising of a voice as anger builds—and can create a sense of anticipation.
	Sustain	Sustain is the length of time a sound is held at the peak. Extending the sustain could create a feeling of suspense or monotony.
	Decay	Decay is the fading of a sound from peak to no sound, and is typically manipulated by the environment. Environments that are absorbent of sound will lead to shorter decays, whereas exterior environments or environments with reverberant surfaces will create echoes and thus longer decays.
Record/ playback	Speed	Manipulation of the overall speed of a sound will affect our perception of its meaning (e.g., speeding up or slowing vocal sounds to create more feminine or masculine voices).

framework for sound design and analysis within visual media. Rather than going into Chion's framework in detail, we instead isolate three key concepts that are of particular interest to virtual character designers and researchers: diegetic and nondiegetic sound, synchronous and asynchronous sound, and empathetic and anempathetic sound. As this list would suggest, these are effectively binary concepts, where a given sound can be considered to belong to one or the other category from each pair. These pairs can be succinctly defined as follows:

- *Diegetic and nondiegetic sound*: Diegetic sound has a clear source from within the scene, for example, present characters' voices, music played from instruments present in the scene, SFX created by objects in the scene, and so on. Conversely, nondiegetic sound seems to emanate from a source outside of the scene, for example, a narrator's voice, music with no source within the story or scene, sounds added to create dramatic effect, and so on.

- *Synchronous and asynchronous sound*: Synchresis concerns the timing of visuals and associated sounds. Synchronous sounds are vocals, SFX, and music that are presented perfectly in time with related visuals, so that the visual focus in a scene is also the audio focus. This can help to support the realism of a character. Asynchronous sound is not matched to the visuals and may serve as a counterpoint. For example, the visual focus might be a character speaking, while the audio focus might be the exaggerated sound of their increasing heartbeat. In this case, it is the asynchronous sound of the heartbeat that grabs our attention.

- *Empathetic and anempathetic sound*: These terms relate to the emotional agreement between story, visuals, and sounds. Empathetic sounds are SFX and music that support the mood of the narrative and of the visual imagery, whereas anempathetic sounds are SFX and music that appear indifferent or emotionally detached from the context.

Careful consideration of character sound design using these criteria can greatly support the overall presentation and audience interpretation of a character's emotions and personality. A good example is the Big Daddy characters in *BioShock* {2K Games 2007}. These adversaries are genetically altered humans who have been conditioned to protect Little Sister characters. Slow moving and without free will, the sadness and the protective nature of Big Daddies is greatly enhanced through the empathetic use of whale cries instead of human vocalizations.

Sound Motifs

Finally, in considering the sounds associated with a virtual character, you should try to establish whether the character has been provided with a sound motif. Sound motifs are audio elements—typically sound effects or music—that are correlated with not only characters, but also environments or ideas within the story. They can be particularly useful for audiences, as they can help them to distinguish between characters, prepare them for the entrance of a character, allude to a character, reinforce a character's presence, or reflect a character's mood or state of mind through shifts in tempo or pitch. Overall, they can be considered an effective narrative device that is used in support of the story. But they can also be extremely effective at enhancing the aesthetic and emotional impact of a character.

When studying sound motifs for virtual characters, a good approach is to consider them in terms of both form and function. In the previous sections on sound design, we have discussed sound design techniques that can be used to create particular effects. If a sound motif is identified, you can attempt to break it down aided by these criteria.

SUMMARY AND ACTIVITY

In this chapter, we focused on the principles of visual and audio design that most often inform the presentation of successful virtual characters. As stressed at the outset, creative practice in the visual and sonic arts is primarily guided by rules of thumb rather than hard-and-fast rules. From the fundamental elements of visual images such as use of line, shape, and color, to discussion of the creation and application of visual style, to the artistic use of sound in relation to visuals, all of the ideas we addressed in this chapter are best used to frame rather than dictate the design and analysis of virtual characters. As always, there is only so much we can cover in this book, and so further reading into graphic design, visual arts, art history, sonic art, sound engineering, or music composition may be necessary to enhance your design practice or aid your development of critical frameworks for the study of virtual characters. The list of references provided at the end of the chapter may prove to be a useful start point for this further reading. For now, two exercises are proposed that challenge you to take the fundamental concepts discussed in this chapter and put them to use.

Exercises

CHARACTER ANALYSIS

How are the principles of visual and sound design used to enhance the presentation of virtual characters in games aimed at a range of different audiences?

1. Identify at least three major nonplayable characters in games designed for the following broad audience types: one for children aged between 7 and 12, one for teenagers aged between 13 and 17, and one for adults aged 18 and over.

2. Ensure that you pick three characters that are well featured in the game (or game series) so that you have sufficient visual and audio data to use in your analysis.

3. Play through the games and/or watch videos of gameplay that heavily feature the characters, with a view to capturing data and writing notes on the following:

   a. Use of line and shape in the visual design of the character

   b. Use of silhouette

   c. Use of color

   d. Identification of overall visual style

   e. Use of sound design and presence of sound motifs

4. Comparing the three characters, write a case study that considers the visual-audio design of each character in reference to the discussion points in this chapter, to additional books relevant to the topic, and to the demands of different audience age groups.

CHARACTER DESIGN

How can subtle changes in visual and audio design manipulate the presentation of a character to an audience?

1. Take an existing character design or a character concept that you have developed yourself.

2. Identify the following elements of the original design and describe how these might interact with an audience's interpretation of the character:

   a. Use of line and shape in the visual design of the character

   b. Use of silhouette

   c. Use of color

   d. Visual style

   e. Use of sound design and presence of sound motifs

3. Through a series of iterative redesigns, look to destabilize or subvert each of these categories, making a range of alternative character descriptions, visualizations, and sonifications.

4. How might these redesigns undermine, enhance, exaggerate, or otherwise manipulate the potential interpretation of the character?

REFERENCES

Chion, M. 1990. *Audio-vision: Sound on screen.* New York: Columbia University Press.

Collins, K. 2008. *Game sound: An introduction to the history, theory, and practice of video game music and sound design.* Cambridge, MA: MIT Press.

Furniss, M. 1998. *Art in motion: Animation, aesthetics.* Sydney, Australia: John Libbey.

Gurney, J. 2010. *Colour and light: A guide for the realist painter.* Kansas City, KA: Andrews McMeel.

McCloud, S. 1994. *Understanding comics: The invisible art.* New York: Harper Collins.

Mott, R. L. 2009. *The audio theater guide: Voice acting, writing, sound effects and directing for a listening audience.* Jefferson, NC: McFarland & Co.

Tinwell, A. 2014. *The uncanny valley in games and animation.* Boca Raton, FL: CRC Press.

CHAPTER 3

Representation, Customization, and Transformation

O NE OF THE MOST COMMONLY DISCUSSED ISSUES concerning virtual characters relates to audience identity. Given the once widely held view that gamers are typically young males, it is not surprising that the identity of game players has emerged as a key topic for game studies. And when we look at games today, it is clear that there are issues of identity representation. It doesn't take a thorough analysis to establish that white male characters are by far the most common lead characters in games, that female characters are more typically presented in supporting roles or as characters to be saved, and that nonwhite characters are underrepresented and rarely placed in player control. But this anecdotal evaluation of identity in games offers little in the way of insight, and it overlooks much of the complexity of identity and of representation. As we show, identity is a multifaceted, dynamic, and personal construct: ethnicity is not easily summed up by one overarching category, and gender is not simply about biological sex. Furthermore, issues of nationality, religion, age, and social class all interact with identity. We therefore need a more thorough understanding of identity and the intricate nature of human society before we can begin to analyze virtual character design via a sociological lens.

In this final chapter on the presentation of virtual characters, three concepts are discussed: representation (the use of media to construct meaning), customization (the ability of the player to alter how a character appears), and transformation (the appropriation and use of existing characters by individuals or groups, for instance by fan subcultures and amateur artists). Throughout the chapter, we look to discuss virtual characters in relation to identity. Essentially, this chapter aims to lay out a sociological framework for character analysis to complement the biological and artistic frameworks defined in Chapters 1 and 2.

IDENTITY

First, it is important to note that identity is not necessarily something that is easily quantifiable, for instance by choosing categories from a list. In the modern world, our identity is often closely associated with a set of documents, including ID cards, passports, birth certificates, and driver's licenses. The existence of the phrase *identity theft* implies that this information can be acquired and permanently removed from an individual. But identity is not about statistics and, in a sociological sense, cannot be stolen. Additionally, the sociological concept of *identity* is not as simple as using a label to describe someone. Identity is a process by which individuals understand who they are in relation to other individuals and is not assigned at birth. Indeed, our sense of identity can and will change over time. It is a complex and multidimensional construct that we build for ourselves based on a number of biological, social, political, cultural, and environmental factors. As Hall (1966) discusses, identity is assembled by the individual through a process of self-identification, not through the application of external definitions imposed by other groups or by society as a whole. Nevertheless, there is a range of commonly used identity factors that can be helpful when it comes to understanding how individuals and groups of people formulate a sense of self-identity. Some of these factors include gender, sexuality, race, nationality, faith, age, and class. We look at each of these shortly, using examples of existing virtual characters that may represent (or misrepresent) these aspects of identity.

While identity is a personal construct, its counter may be considered the *other*. Otherness is one of the most important topics within studies of representation, as it concerns how groups other than the typical or target group are depicted. As Spencer (2006, 8) states, the other can be simply understood as "not self," that is, "an alien subjectivity, a being who exhibits characteristics notably different from our own, whether gender, race, class, custom or behavior." In this sense, the other (the nonself) is interlinked with identity (the self). We can articulate who we are sociologically and culturally by contrasting this with what we are not. From one point of view, self-identity and otherness are positive concepts, where an understanding of the self and an appreciation of the diversity of human society and culture can make for a richer and more meaningful existence. But, as we discuss shortly, media can seek to stereotype and control depictions of otherness in order to retain power, authority, or wealth for one particular group—commonly the group that happens to control the media and major institutions of society. As a result, critique of identity and otherness in virtual character design needs to be sensitive to how groups are represented: to understand which groups may be given privileged status (e.g., young, middle class, white, Western males) and which groups may be underrepresented or misrepresented (basically, everyone else).

It has been noted that both literature and history provide us with examples of identities with which we can associate (Lawler 2008, 21). These are presented to us in the form of characters embedded in larger narratives. By listening to, reading about, or otherwise engaging with the stories of these characters, we can come to better understand ourselves, who we are, and how we fit into the social world. Narratives, regardless of whether they are fictional or based on historical fact, are critical to our formation of self-identity. Consequently, it is clear that the media (including games) play a role in how we come to determine our place in the world. As we have already touched upon, identity is not a fixed concept: it shifts over time as we have more experiences with the world, with other individuals, and with other groups. On top of these social interactions, the media stories that we experience can have a significant impact on how we define ourselves as individuals and how we understand others. In the age of mass communication and pervasive media, it could be argued that the fictional and factual stories that we engage with on a daily basis have a more powerful effect on our self-identity and our perception of other groups than at any point in history. It is precisely because media have such a massive influence on the discourse on identity that we ought to be prepared to analyze and critique representation within video games.

REPRESENTATION

While identity concerns how we come to form an understanding of who we are, representation concerns how certain aspects of identity can be depicted via media.

An individual has the ability to make sense of, communicate, and express his or her own identity. Although there are central aspects of identity—such as gender or nationality—that inform and interact with our development of self-identity, ultimately we are all individuals, and we all have the power to formulate our own self-identity. We all have our own unique narratives, and we are the ones who shape our own identities throughout our lives. By contrast, representation concerns how core aspects of identity can be defined, shaped, and communicated by forces external to the individual. By using media to broadcast ideas about identity, it can be argued that media content producers are in a position of power. They have the means and authority to depict gender, sexuality, race, age, or any other aspect of identity in any way they see fit. As consumers of media, modern audiences come to learn about and understand others through media such as films, television, and video games. We encounter different types of people in our daily lives, but the dominance and pervasiveness of media mean that much of what we think about other people is shaped by what we see in the cinema, on television sets, and on computer screens. Media representation can therefore be used to create meaning about the world. Every content producer engages with representation and makes meaning through the depiction of character, even if she is not explicitly aware that this is what she is doing. This is a particularly important consideration for video game character design and analysis, as there are notable issues with character representation in games.

One of the key ideas behind representation is that it is never neutral: that there is always some bias present, and that a completely objective take on representation cannot be achieved. Bias can be easy to identify within small projects, where one or two people might have complete authorial control. In these cases, the individual or group of creators will generate representations in line with their vision, and objective portrayals of reality are rarely their goal. Even on larger scale creative projects there is bias in terms of how representations are produced. Big-budget films and games might have hundreds of developers and producers working on them, and many of them might have a high degree of creative control. But character representations in these products are still biased by the collective decisions of the studio, the filtering of the managers and directors, the interventions by publishers and funders, and so on.

To take this further, even media that are purported to be objective are still considered to actively engage in the generation of representation. It might be suggested that, when characters are shown in factual media (such as news programming and documentaries), they are actually reflections of the world as it really is. In other words, the individuals or organizations responsible for creating the news have set out to objectively show people exactly as they exist in reality. This view, however, is not in line with how many theorists interpret the presentation of people in the media. Instead, what is shown in factual media is still considered a biased representation, which has to some degree been edited or generated so that the end product is a construction of the world, rather than a perfect reflection of it. Documentary filmmakers set out to make their films with an idea, message, or ambition in mind, and this will bias their representation of characters. News media tend to serve a particular political agenda, either explicitly (a news station declaring support for a particular brand of politics) or more subtly (a newspaper with no declared affiliation, but with an editorial team that evidently leans politically to the left or right). Even the simple fact that news programming is geographically situated (for instance the BBC in the United Kingdom) means that there is some unavoidable bias in its construction, as it is framed by (and for) a group of people from a particular culture who have much more exposure to and experience of a particular way of life. Regardless of whether the subject of study is a work of artistic expression or an allegedly unbiased report, it can therefore be strongly argued that all media content is built upon a system of representation. Subsequently, the characters presented in media are not a complete reflection of reality. Instead, they have been constructed, refined, and edited in order to modulate how we interpret and understand them.

In the following sections, we look at examples of representation in games in relation to aspects of identity that are commonly raised in critical discussion. While we only look at a limited number of identity categories and do not delve deeply into any one area, the goal is to consider the potential problems that character representation in games can create. In order to carry out an in-depth study of character representation—or indeed to more carefully design characters that are sensitive to the complexity of identity—it is essential to engage with further reading and research.

Gender and Sexuality

Arguably the most prominent aspect of identity discussed in relation to games today is the representation of gender. Given the historical view that games are designed for young male audiences—and made by only slightly older male game developers—the representations of gender and sexualities within video games are often seen as biased toward heterosexual male identities. For much of the early years of gaming, virtual characters were almost entirely presented as masculine and associated with ideas of masculinity. Female characters—if they appeared at all—would typically be some form of damsel character (such as Pauline in *Donkey Kong*) or an image of feminine sexuality. So embedded was the notion that game characters ought to be male that, as we discussed in Chapter 1, the presentation of a strong female in *Metroid's* Samus Aran was somewhat shocking.

Any discussion of gender in games is likely to look to feminist theory as a means of analyzing and interpreting gender representation. It is particularly important that the existence of multiple approaches to feminist theory be acknowledged here. Feminism has a long history of theory development, and there are multiple takes on how media representations of gender might be analyzed. It is also important to note that feminism is often misunderstood as an attack on men. This is usually due to ignorance of what feminism is really about: the strive toward equality for everyone within society, regardless of their gender or sexual preferences. Nevertheless, there are different forms of feminist theory, and it is essential that you identify the ideas that are of relevance to your design project or study.

For instance, one of the most commonly cited feminist theories is the idea of the male gaze, proposed by Laura Mulvey (1989). This psychoanalytical approach to film studies proposes that, in film, the primary characters are male, and we are often required to see the world through their eyes. This doesn't mean that we literally look through their eyes as with a first-person camera (although in games this is often the case). Instead, what is presented to us is a world as a heterosexual male might see it, with submissive female characters as the object of desire. Ultimately, this theory provides us with the tools to deconstruct the representation of gender and sexuality in games and question whether what is presented is biased toward the visual pleasure of the heterosexual male.

It is clear that some feminist theories draw particular attention to the existence of two sexes. But as we discussed in Chapter 1, sex is a biological component of a character, and not synonymous with gender. Other forms of feminist theory recognize the fluidity and multiplicity of gender identities. In other words, gender is not an aspect of identity that we are born with, but is instead a social role that we perform. We may identify ourselves as male or female at different points of our lives, but this identification is not tied to our biological sex. One of the key texts on this form of feminist theory is *Gender Trouble: Feminism and the Subversion of Identity* by Judith Butler (1999). Butler's work could be useful in analyzing virtual characters in terms of their gender performances. Additionally, it could be argued that our identification of gender cannot be dissected from our sexual orientation, leading to blurred lines between genders and sexualities. The various modes of gender and sexuality representation in games can be appropriately considered by drawing on queer theory. As David Halperin (1997, 6) has noted, "Queer is by definition whatever is at odds with the normal, the legitimate, the dominant." Queer theory therefore builds on the ideas of Butler by addressing not just gay and lesbian identities, but all forms of gender-sexuality identity that are perceived to sit outside societal norms. Sullivan's (2003) introduction to queer theory would be an excellent start point for a critique of gender and sexuality in games.

Masculine identity is another (and perhaps unexpected) aspect of gender representation in virtual characters that we ought to account for. This may seem like a strange oversight, but the fact is that men are often regarded as the general or default identity depicted in media. In his book *On Men: Masculinity in Crisis*, Clare (2001) highlights the fact that men are typically depicted as being dominant, aggressive, violent, antisocial, deviant, and even criminal. This representation of men can easily be seen in video games, where a disproportionate number of games center on this concept of masculinity. Emerging from critique of this masculine trope was the idea of a softer, gentler representation of men: men who are comfortable being the subject of female (or indeed male) gaze, and who are more likely to take on feminine attributes and downplay their masculinity. Often discussed as the *new man* (McNair 2002), video games are yet to demonstrate widespread representation of this softer and more ambiguous male gender, with the majority of male virtual characters (particularly leading characters) shown as being highly masculine.

Analysis of video games and game characters framed by gender and sexuality is a well-established research topic, no doubt a result of the prevalence of heterosexual masculinity embedded in games and gaming. Perhaps the most well-known feminist theorist to discuss the representation of female characters is Anita Sarkeesian (2013). Sarkeesian's analysis of female characters in games has received much attention thanks largely to her well-reported funding campaign and her use of online video to reach a wider audience. Sarkeesian's work is an excellent entry point for anyone new to feminist theory as applied to game studies. Analysis of virtual characters from the perspective of queer theory can also be identified in the literature, particularly with respect to character customization in online role-playing games and transformation in fan culture. We return to examples of gender and sexuality representation later, in the sections on customization and transformation.

With the breadth and depth of feminist and queer theory in mind, it is worth dwelling on some of the common issues that have been raised with respect to representation of gender and sexuality in video games. The damsel archetype—the central topic of Sarkeesian's (2013) analysis—is one of the most widely discussed and observed representations of female virtual characters. Presented as plot devices rather than as fully rounded characters, damsels in video games are typically ill-defined and shallow, playing a much less significant role than that of the archetypal male hero. In most cases a damsel is epitomized by her helplessness and her need to be rescued by the powerful male. Also, the damsel is often the lead (if not only) female character in a game. Famous examples include Princesses Peach and Zelda from the *Super Mario* and *Legend of Zelda* games, respectively, but this archetype appears in a vast number of games, including both AAA and indie titles today.

A further problematic representation of gender in games is the depiction of violence toward women, including sexualized attacks. Many female game characters appear as subordinate to male characters, to the point where they are shown to be attacked and even killed by male characters (including in some cases the player character, or PC). This violence may be used as a plot device to set up the narrative for a lead male character—such as the murder of the titular character's wife and daughter in *Max Payne* {Remedy Entertainment 2001}—or as a means to embody the agency and dominance of the male character, such as the simplistic choice to either save or murder the PC's girlfriend in *Far Cry 3* {Ubisoft Montreal 2012b}. In these cases, the violence toward women is effectively a means to focus on the development and importance of male characters.

In addition to examples of disempowered, weak, and victimized female characters, there is the long-standing representation of women as objects of sexual desire in games. In some respects, a gradual improvement in the complexity of female character roles beyond that of a sexual object can be observed. Lara Croft is a notable example of a character who has transformed from an object of heterosexual male gaze in 1996's *Tomb Raider* to a more realistic, less caricatured, and more rounded character in the 2013 reboot of the same name. However, there are still crude examples of sexual caricature in games, including the infamous *Dead or Alive Xtreme Beach*

Volleyball {Team Ninja 2003} that allowed the player to zoom and rotate the camera around its scantily clad and hypersexualized female characters.

Representation of lesbian, gay, bisexual, and trans identities are often difficult to find. Certainly, the representation of LGBT characters in video games is less developed than it is in other media, for example, film and television. This is in part a consequence of the hypermasculinized characters that are so embedded in gaming history and that continue to appear in the biggest games. LGBT characters can be identified in a range of games throughout gaming history, but representation of these identities is neither extensive nor center stage. Sometimes, an LGBT character is presented as an important NPC with which the player can interact. For instance, it is suggested that the character Reaver in the *Fable* series {Lionhead Studios 2008} is bisexual, through his flirtatious advances toward the player (irrespective of gender) and reflections on past history (see Figure 3.1). But

FIGURE 3.1 The character Reaver and a wedding ceremony from *Fable II*®. (Used with permission from Microsoft Corporation.)

the ambiguity surrounding his sexuality, the limited significance of the character (he is just one of many NPCs), and the fact that his sexuality is rarely discussed all serve to downplay this as an example of profound bisexual representation.

However, there are examples of games that have sought to grapple with the more focused representation of LGBT people. Anna Anthropy is one notable game designer who has embedded queer themes within her games, including personal reflections on hormone replacement therapy in the game *Dys4ia* {Anthropy 2012}. Attempts to break down barriers and bring representations of homosexuality into mainstream gaming can also be identified. A good example is *My Ex-Boyfriend the Space Tyran*t {Up Multimedia 2014}. This game contains a cast of gay characters and themes, and showcases homosexual representation in a humorous and overtly camp manner that clearly challenges the lack of LGBT diversity and openness in games. More often than not, though, the representation of LGBT identity in games is fulfilled through player agency. For example, game series such as *Fable*, *The Elder Scrolls*, *Dragon Age*, and *Mass Effect* have included releases that allow for character gender selection and the development of romantic and sexual relationships between player and non-player characters, with no gender constraints (see Figure 3.1). They have also featured key characters that were presented as bisexual, gay, or lesbian. Overall, it should be clear that (a) there remain some challenging questions regarding issues of gender and sexuality representation in virtual characters and (b) there ought to be more critical consideration of the design of LGBT, female, and indeed male characters.

Ethnicity, Religion, and Nationality

We have seen that gender and sexuality are complex and fluid aspects of identity, and that representation of these concepts cannot be simply reduced to male–female and gay–straight categories. When it comes to discussion of ethnicity, religion, and nationality, it should be plain that these aspects of identity are as multifarious as they are interactive. For example, when we are asked about our ethnicity on official forms, it is common to see overlap between ethnic and national categories, such as White-British and Asian-Pakistani. But these categories do not necessarily encapsulate what individuals might self-identify as. For instance, someone who technically belongs to a White-British group according to an official form might identify as neither White nor British. As we have discussed earlier, it is clear that self-identity on these matters is a deeply personal and individual construct, even if it has some basis in the geographical and cultural heritage of the individual. But again, use of language and representation in media can control ideas about ethnicity, about nationality, and about religion. Furthermore, as Spencer (2006, 35) identifies, the term *race* has, at various points in history, been used to categorize peoples based on a range of factors. In the last two centuries, concepts such as ethnic heritage, customs, cultural practices, religion, and nationality have all been considered part of the discourse on race. This shows us that we must demonstrate some caution in the use of terms when discussing matters of ethnicity, religion, and nationality. The complexity of the interactions and the variety of ethnic, religious, and national identities make it easy for both game designers and game analysts to misrepresent and misinterpret these challenging aspects of identity.

In preparing to understand and critique the design of virtual characters in terms of their representation of ethnic, religious, or national ideas, one of the key theories to be considered relates to the earlier discussion of *the other*. Said's (1995) theory of Orientalism argues that ideas about Asian (and specifically Middle Eastern) cultures are largely constructed by Europeans and North Americans. Through use of media control and power, representations of Asian culture are manufactured and spread by Western media producers and companies. Poems, literature, films, television, and video games all serve to massively communicate mistruths about Arabian, Iranian, Indian, or Chinese cultures. This can include the depiction of camels, oases, or exotic dress and music, all of which simplify and conflate ideas of Arabia, reshaping Arabian culture around the West's stereotypical views. At best, this can be seen as condescending and misrepresentative, with limited or no basis in fact or sensitivity to the multiplicity of ethnic, religious, and national identities. At worst, examples of Orientalism can actually set up an oppositional relationship between West and East, us and them, whereby Western culture is seen to be modern, rational, and civilized, and other cultures are shown to be primitive, emotional, and barbaric. While this theory specifically looks at an Eastern presentation by Western media, Orientalism and postcolonial theories of media in general are a useful means of analyzing and critiquing representation of ethnicity, religion, and nationality in virtual character design, particularly when considering games developed by Western game studios and publishers.

There are notable analyses of ethnic, religious, and national representations in video games. For example, Šisler (2008) examined how the portrayal of Arabs and Muslims in Western-designed games led to typologies of Middle Eastern representations. Said's (1995) Orientalism is applicable here, with Arab and Muslim characters reduced to modern stereotypes as enemies, terrorists, and extremists. This tendency in military games to reduce representations of nationalities, ethnicities, and religious groups to stereotypes has also been discussed by Höglund (2008). Another notable instance of problematic ethnic and national portrayal is in *Resident Evil 5* {Capcom 2009}. The game initially caused controversy when a trailer of the game, screened in 2007, depicted the killing of black enemies by a white hero in an African setting. In his analysis, Brock (2011) underlined the problematic portrayal of African villagers in the game and, of particular interest, the response of gamers. Many gamers highlighted that it was just a game, and that in the context of the horror genre the enemies were zombies to be killed: The color of their skin was irrelevant. Although seemingly stating the obvious, this tendency to write off issues of representation with the "it's just a game" defense fails to show a broader awareness of the connotations and history of ethnic and national conflicts. Regardless of whether the gameplay or narrative of the game series justified the portrayed scenes, the depiction of white brutality against black natives showed little awareness of the connotations that this imagery conjured.

Given the fantastical nature of many video games, and the drawing upon science-fiction and fantasy genres for inspiration, one interesting angle to analysis of virtual character design involves the examination of nonhuman characters and their potential racial connotations. Many fantasy and science-fiction games introduce and develop mythical or alien races that in turn are used to signify ethnic, religious, or national identities. These representations can offer an opportunity to explore historical and contemporary issues in a way that might be more problematic if a nonfantasy setting were used, and can allow developers more freedom to explore tensions between groups of people without being constrained by geographical or historical facts. However, there is also the risk that these representations can tap into cultural stereotypes. Poor (2012) offers an insightful analysis of elves as a race within fantasy games, and how they might align with real-world peoples. Through his examination of *The Elder Scrolls III* and *IV* {Bethesda Game Studios 2002, 2006}, *Dragon Age* {BioWare 2009}, *Everquest II* {Sony Online Entertainment 2004}, and *World of Warcraft* {Blizzard Entertainment 2004}, Poor discusses how elves have traditionally been depicted as an "other" in relation to humans, where the humans are typically seen as equivalent to White-European. Within his analysis, he shows how various types of elves have connotations with Black, Native

American, Chinese, and Jewish cultures, through use of objects, environments, and depictions of faith. Furthermore, he shows how the half-elf trope (typically an individual with mixed elven and human parentage) can serve to represent ideas of mixed-race identity. Looking at the fantasy genre more broadly, it is possible to identify these kinds of imagined representations of real-world identity. In the Tolkien tradition, for example, dwarves are often depicted with Scottish-like dialects and attire, and are associated with both negative and positive connotations of Scottish character such as greediness, dourness, and a high-spirited nature.

On the whole, racial representation—where race merges concepts of ethnicity, nationality, and religion—is arguably the most complex aspect of sociological identity that can be examined by game developers. Given the torrid history of relations between ethnic groups, religious institutions, and nations, there is always going to be some concern that a mishandling of representation could cause offense, demonstrate ignorance of racial diversity, or alienate groups of gamers. Ubisoft—the producers of the *Assassin's Creed* series of games—went so far as to present a disclaimer at the start of their games. The disclaimer from *Assassin's Creed II* {Ubisoft Montreal 2009} reads as follows:

> Inspired by historical events and characters, this work of fiction was designed, developed and produced by a multicultural team of various religious faiths and beliefs.

Given that the series deals with Jewish, Christian, and Muslim peoples—and later Native American peoples and issues of national identity in *Assassin's Creed III* {Ubisoft Montreal 2012a}—it is understandable that some sensitivity be shown toward the handling of representation. By making the disclaimer, Ubisoft are declaring that the series is not a Western-minded and stereotypical presentation of the Oriental, as Said (1995) warned. Instead, Ubisoft's worldwide studios and multicultural staff produced the game, and they are at pains to make this clear. Nevertheless, the fact that the disclaimer was made in the first place highlights the potential problems of representing ethnic groups, religion, and national identities with virtual characters.

Age and Social Class

While gender, sexuality, and ethnicity may dominate discussions of representation in games, depictions of age and class can be easily overlooked.

This in itself is somewhat emblematic. It is often the very young, very old, and very poor who are forgotten about in Western society, as they are not the ones who fill the jobs or positions of power. By extension, we could argue that representation of these groups in video games is limited because they do not represent the core of video game consumers. Young and (increasingly) middle-aged adults with money to spend are the ones who are consuming the most video games, and so representations of these groups are more commonplace.

Looking at representations of age in the first instance, it is worth noting the general perceptions of both the young and the elderly in the media and the negative connotations associated with each age group. Young people on the whole tend to accrue a negative response based on analysis of news programming. While young children can be represented as cute, innocent, and as victims, representations of older children and teenagers have been linked to violent crime and a threat to wider society (Wayne et al. 2008). Derogatory terms such as *chavs* or *hoodies* have been associated with young people in the UK, and the behavior of young people has often been linked to moral panics covered by the media. Conversely, the elderly are often portrayed as being in a state of dependency and as a burden (socially, economically, and physically) on society. Both groups are typically underrepresented in creative media. While mainstream media broadly target young adults and the middle aged, children and the elderly are more typically represented in media aimed at these groups (e.g., television channels that specifically serve children or the elderly).

In video games, the underrepresentation of young and old age groups has been demonstrated. Williams et al. (2009) showed that representations of adults as characters in video games was approximately 47% higher than the US population, while both children and the elderly were underrepresented when compared with the actual population. (Teenagers appeared roughly in line with their percentage of the US population.) With this in mind—and with the knowledge that the elderly are increasingly becoming video game players—it is worth contemplating how the young and old are represented in games, how often they appear as the main protagonist or as PCs, whether they defy stereotypes and offer a more realistic view on age, and whether or not these games are aimed at mainstream audiences or audiences that are in line with the age group being represented. One of the few examples of an authentic and humbling representation of an elderly virtual character is in Tale of Tales's 2008 game *The Graveyard* (see Figure 3.2). *The Graveyard* {Tale of Tales 2008} is a short experimental

FIGURE 3.2 Screenshot from *The Graveyard*. (©2008 Tale of Tales. With permission.)

game that places the player in control of an elderly lady walking through a graveyard, and it explores the theme of death. Although death might seem to be a simple theme to convey through an elderly virtual character, the manner in which both old age and death are handled encourages thoughtfulness and reflection.

When it comes to sociological issues surrounding class, Newman (2012) provides an extensive and in-depth discussion of representation, including discussion of status. His overview of sociological theory and social inequality is useful for a study of virtual character representation generally, but is particularly useful for anyone looking to research the depiction of social class. Looking at the wider media, Newman identifies the proliferation of expensive and luxury consumer goods—holidays, high fashion, and prestige cars—that are the focus of media attention. These items are beyond the reach of most of society. The stock markets and financial news are both prominent in the media, even though a small percentage of the more wealthy people can access and make use of this information. Furthermore, Newman highlights the problem of working-class demonization in the media. Depictions of poorer groups as a societal problem are not uncommon, and associations can be made with criminality, drug addiction and other vices, unemployment and dependency on welfare, single-parent families, and general social inadequacy.

While these issues might seem to be a problem for the news media—both broadcast news and newspapers—creative media like films, television, and video games must also be aware of the dangers of unfair representations of social class. Video games—as with film and television—have a tendency to overrepresent the middle classes and upper classes of society while underrepresenting the working classes. The reality of poverty is not something that is particularly well explored in video games, and there are few examples of genuine working-class characters. More often than not, characters are introduced as being from a privileged background to add to the allure and fantasy of their narrative. This is clear from games we have already looked at, from Ezio Auditore in *Assassin's Creed II* (an exemplar of middle-class wealth in Renaissance Italy) to Lara Croft in *Tomb Raider* (the English aristocrat adventurer who we return to in Chapter 7). Video games that do include PCs that represent working-class reality or experience poverty often fall afoul of stereotypes such as those discussed by Newman (2012). Consider Niko Bellic in *Grand Theft Auto IV* {Rockstar North 2008}. Niko is simultaneously a depiction of racial and social class "other." To an American and Western European audience, Niko is an Eastern European immigrant with low social standing and minimal wealth. Subsequently, the game depicts Niko as a stereotype of both immigrants and the poor: a violent criminal who wastes no time getting in trouble with the law and becoming immersed in the underworld. But what is more important here is what drives Niko. Like most games that place the player in control of a character who is impoverished or who has low social standing, the aim is to accumulate wealth and power. You might start off poor, but sooner or later you will become one of the wealthiest and most powerful figures in the game world. This escapist fantasy is understandable, and a game design that is based on dominance is a popular one (consider the board game *Monopoly* and the quality of the gameplay experience it provides). However, these characters do little to reflect or commentate on the gritty reality of life in the lower classes of society. Games that examine a more authentic and extended depiction of true poverty and social inequality are relatively rare, with the indie game *Cart Life* {Hofmeier 2011} providing one of the few examples.

Film and television can often struggle to examine age and social class without falling into the pitfalls of stereotypes, however, this is perhaps an even greater challenge for game designers. Consider that characters in games need to have complementary gameplay actions that correspond with or otherwise support the game narrative. The stark reality is that most games focus on characters that are fit and powerful, or characters that offer some form of escapism. It can be difficult to fully explore a realistic depiction of older or less privileged characters while also providing gameplay that engages gamers. One way that all aspects of identity can potentially be examined through fair and sensitive representation is to open up character design to modification by gamers, allowing them to customize appearance and abilities. In the following sections, we look at customization of characters within games, transformation of characters outside of games, and how player and fan agency can level the playing field of representation and push game developers to rethink their character design choices in future.

CUSTOMIZATION

As we have seen, representation of aspects of identity can be communicated via all forms of media, including but not limited to news publications, radio, television, film, theater, painting, and, of course, video games. However, when it comes to video games and interactive media, there is an additional consideration that is important to any discussion of character representation. That is the fact that, by definition, there is a degree of control provided to players. This may be very limited (such as simple interactions that they can perform with characters) or elaborate (such as full customization of appearance). But the potential impact on representation is substantial. As Frasca (2004) identifies, simulations are very different from linear media where representation is concerned. Describing them as a "kaleidoscopic form of representation," his key point is that interactive media can provide tools to change, customize, and interpret virtual characters in a multitude of ways. It is possible that video game players can impose aspects of their own identity onto virtual characters much more easily than is possible in more controlled media such as film and television. It is also possible that players can entirely dictate how aspects of identity are represented within the characters they play.

The ability to configure a character to match a player's preferences has its roots in the role-playing game (RPG) genre. As we discuss in Chapter 5 when we cover game genres, the RPG is largely defined by player configuration, predominantly through the allocation of stats and other attributes at the start of a game. These attributes can dictate how characters perform in a game world, how they develop and improve, and what roles they can fulfill. In addition to these statistics, common aspects of identity are often part and parcel of RPG character configuration: typically this includes sex, ethnicity, and age. With more advanced graphical power, the visual appearance of RPG characters—particularly characters in massively multiplayer online role-playing games (MMORPGs)—has become more customizable. From specific physical features of the face and body to dress, hair styling, and body modification, players of many RPGs can dictate exactly how they want their character to appear. Furthermore, RPGs have traditionally catered to players who wish to tell stories of their own. By providing tools that allow players to write backstories and customize the appearance of their characters after the start of the game, there are now examples of games that give almost unlimited power back to the players so that they can project their own identity (or an imagined identity) into the game world.

While character customization clearly does not apply in all cases, the prevalence of customization options in video games has grown substantially. Over time, there has been a gradual blurring of traditional game genres. Many of the games today are no longer neatly pigeonholed as platformers, sports, or shooters. Elements of the RPG genre—in particular the ability to configure, customize, and develop a character—are now mixed with other game genres. As such, there is a good chance that any game chosen for study, irrespective of its fundamental genre, could contain customization tools. When it comes to a study of identity and representation, then, potential customization is a key consideration. Let us look at some of the key elements of customization so that we know what to look for when studying a game character:

- *Customizing player and nonplayer characters*: First, consider the extent to which a player has the power to customize the range of characters within a virtual world. When we discuss character customization in games, more often than not we are insinuating customization of the PC or avatar. This makes sense, as players by and large want to have more control over their own character. It is through their character that the story is told, and in most games the PC is the sole agent of the player in the virtual world. The level of PC customization of appearance therefore determines the degree to which the players can project their identity into the game, and potentially allows them to experience the game as an individual they identify with. However, games can also allow for wider customization of virtual characters, including the many NPCs that can be encountered. It is unlikely that the level of control would be as detailed or complex as it would be for a PC, for obvious reasons. Nonetheless, the ability to create and customize groups of characters that the player interacts with and/or commands (as in *X-COM: Enemy Unknown* {Firaxis Games 2012}) or even other characters that the player will come up against (such as editing football players in *FIFA 15* {EA Canada 2014}) can provide a means of adjusting representation. As such, the first thing to consider when looking at customization is the range of characters that can, in some way, be customized by the player.

- *Physical details*: After identifying which characters have the capacity for customization, you must then consider in what ways they can be customized and what the impact might be on representation. The most obvious area of customization is physical appearance, and many games allow for this. At the most basic level, consider whether the player can customize the biological sex of a character. This is a very common design feature. We have already touched on one game series in this chapter that caters for sex selection: the *Mass Effect* series {BioWare 2007}. Beyond sex selection, many games allow for finer control over physical attributes. In terms of how this interacts with issues of representation, customization of physical features that can be associated with ethnicity (skin color, face shape, hair color and type, etc.) are commonplace in RPGs, sports games, and typically any game where the player is required to create his own avatar. This might be much less common in games where a designated lead character is assigned to the player.

- *Voice*: Some games allow for the voice of a character to be altered, which may enable an enhanced level of control over the presentation of a character. For example, in *Soulcalibur III*, *IV*, and *V* {Project Soul 2005, 2008, 2012}, the character-creation mode allows the player to pick a voice from a range of male and female voices. As the series progressed, more options for voice control were added, for example, allowing players to select from a wider range of voices and providing them with tools to adjust the pitch and tone. A tenet of this customization is that fine voice control can allow for the projection of more specific aspects of self-identity, including age and personality. Although voice customization is a less common aspect of customization, it can be very powerful and allow the player more creative control over representation.

- *Hair, dress, and modification*: Perhaps the most popular facet of any character-customization tool is the ability to customize the appearance of a character in terms of hairstyling, dress, and other forms of body modification. The more powerful the customization tool, the more scope for reflecting very specific aspects of self-identity in a character's appearance. At the basic level, selection of clothing and hairstyles can enable the performing of gender, as we touched on earlier in the chapter. While biological sex can give us a start point (whether a character is biologically male or female), gender and sexuality are aspects of identity that are too fluid and varied to be encompassed by a binary choice of sex. Dress and hair selection can allow for representation of masculinity and femininity irrespective of sex. Furthermore, depending on the level of control and the range of options, selection of hair, clothing, piercings, tattoos, and other adornments can enable players to express sexuality through their avatars. The expression of gender through avatars is something that has been well researched in MMORPGs, for example, in games like *World of Warcraft* (Schmieder 2009). As such, studies of representation in virtual characters that come from the perspective of feminist or queer theory are likely to be interested in customization tools.

- *Story and behavior*: Because we are concerned with presentation of virtual characters in Section I of the book, we are predominantly concerned with character customization that impacts on the way a character looks and sounds. The considerations described here can enable a player to fully customize the appearance of a character so that it more closely reflects an identity that they associate with. However, this does not necessarily mean that players will be able to tell the personal story of their character within the game or be able to make the character act in a way that they identify with. As we have already established, self-identity has a lot to do with storytelling. In evaluating character customization, we should therefore look to identify to what extent players can write, edit, and enact the story of their character. This can involve: the selection of personality attributes and affiliations, the creation of a written backstory, the capacity to speak freely within the game world, and the ability to customize how a character moves and behaves. In Section II of this book we focus on the performance of virtual characters, including discussion of story in games as well as the simulation and animation of behavior. However, the ability to customize a character's appearance clearly interacts with these aspects of performance, and as such it is essential that an analysis of character customization account for these additional facets of character presentation.

- *Statistics*: Finally, the most game-oriented aspect of character customization is ultimately the selection of statistics. In the RPG tradition, statistics tend to involve core attributes such as strength, agility, wisdom, intelligence, and luck, as well as a range of specific skills such as mining, crafting, and use of particular weapons. On the face of it, these may seem entirely ludological concepts, as their selection and use is related to gameplay, the character's abilities in a game world, and the balance of the overall game design. However, there is always scope for customization of statistics to interact with the more sociological aspects of a character's presentation and, thus, to make a connection to representation of aspects of identity.

With the increasing application of customization tools within games, it is particularly important that this aspect of virtual character design be taken into account when studying the representation of identity in interactive media. Games such as *The Sims 4* {EA Maxis 2014}, for instance, offer players the opportunity to manipulate physical appearance in intricate detail. However, customization within a game is always going to be constrained in some way, meaning that the player is never in full control over how characters are presented.

TRANSFORMATION

One final concept that is worthy of our attention when approaching virtual characters from a sociological perspective is transformation. In our discussion of representation and customization, we were focused on the presentation of characters and character-editing tools within the confines of a computer game. In other words, these characters are owned and controlled by the game developers, who have designed the appearance of a character and the rules by which a character may be customized. While some examples of customizable characters may provide a high level of potential for player editing, the characters remain under the control of the game system. But virtual characters can and do exist outside of the games in which they were originally presented.

The prominence and prevalence of fan cultures surrounding computer games has led to an increased interaction between games, game developers, and the fans who seek to imitate their favorite characters. The quality and subsequent popularity of some cosplayers (costume players) or transformative artworks has led to a two-way relationship between developers and fan communities. A good example is the cosplayer Anna Moleva, whose convincing imitation of the character Elizabeth from *BioShock Infinite* {Irrational Games 2013} led the developer to recruit her for the game's marketing (Levine 2012).

Transformation by fan artists can also be used to expose problems in virtual character design by taking tropes and stereotypes and subverting them. Often, these transformative works address key issues of representation that audiences have picked up on. For example, a digital artist interested in depictions of romanticized homosexuality famously used *Tomb Raider* as an inspiration for his transformative work, creating images that placed a male character in poses and attire more commonly associated with Lara Croft (Starr 2013).

Other notable examples of transformation involve game hacks: instances where fans or other individuals with game design knowledge have taken an original game and manipulated the design or code in order to alter how the game looks or plays. A popular trend involved playing with gender in classic games in order to change the sex of the playable and/or secondary characters. This included a hack of *Donkey Kong*, created by Mike Mika (2013) for his daughter so that she could play as Pauline (the original damsel) and rescue Mario (the original hero). In this example, Mika stated that he "didn't set out to push a feminist agenda, or to try to make a statement" but that he just wanted to keep his daughter (who had asked why she couldn't pick a female character in the game) happy. This was similar to a previous hack of *The Legend of Zelda: The Wind Waker* {Nintendo 2004}, which, it happens, was also made by a father for his daughter (Narcisse 2012). In this case, the hack acknowledged that the game by design allowed the player to name the PC whatever they wanted, meaning that both male and female names could be used. However, despite the name selection, the game still referred to the player as male, and so the hack changed the in-game text to ensure that the pronouns for the player were female.

Although transformative works such as those described here are derivatives of the virtual characters that are designed and presented in games, and as such are not directly part of the games people play, they are still part of the wider culture of virtual characters. As such, it would be an oversight to dismiss these works on the basis that they are made by amateur artists, not the game developers. Often, these works provide additional context for analysis, highlighting the desires of game players and providing a critical commentary on character representations in games.

SUMMARY AND ACTIVITY

In this chapter, we have discussed the relationship between virtual characters and our understanding of our society, our culture, and ourselves as individuals. We examined what is meant by identity and discovered that we do not define ourselves by simply attaching a label based on key statistics. Instead, we use a variety of biological, psychological, social, economic, political, and cultural factors to constantly assess and reassess who we think we are. Our identity is fluid, and our interactions throughout life impact on it in meaningful ways. We looked at representation: the notion that media construct ideas of identity and society using language and images. Common areas of identity and related representations were discussed, including gender, sexuality, ethnicity, and age.

With a specific focus on games, we examined how representation using virtual characters can often fall afoul of stereotypes. We saw that game developers (particularly in the West) have a tendency to design pivotal characters around notions of who the typical audience might be (white, male heterosexuals aged 18–35), while other identities can be presented as background characters with limited depth (if they are represented at all). We then looked at the interactivity of games and how this makes it possible to customize existing characters or even create characters from scratch. By providing a means to adjust the appearance of virtual characters, players arguably have a degree of control over identity representation in games that they do not have in other media. The amount of freedom character customization and creation afford fluctuates from game to game, but nevertheless this is an important criterion in an analysis of virtual characters. Finally, we considered how transformation of characters can take place outside the confines of the game world, empowering audiences to completely overhaul depictions of game characters through fan art, cosplay, and hacks.

It is worth reflecting that while an appreciation of the diversity of human identities and an awareness of the power of representation in games is essential for any intellectual discussion about the sociological impact of character design, there is always a danger of oversimplification. Specifically, a common misinterpretation is that characters can be categorized as if they align with audience types, and that simply swapping out a character norm (e.g., the white heterosexual male) for another character that might represent a marginalized group will broaden the audience, appeal, or sophistication of a game. As Shaw (2012, 39) notes in her paper on gamer identity:

The audience is an industrial construction, and these constructions shape how people approach media; however, simply adding diversity to games will not automatically make the gamer audience more diverse.

Instead, it is important that we take a much more measured and critical approach to character design and analysis and that we concern ourselves with the development of the medium as an art and narrative form. Identity and representation are key considerations for this development.

With this in mind, two exercises are proposed here. These exercises are based on a critique of virtual character design from a sociological perspective, taking into account issues of identity, representation, customization, and transformation. You may want to target your analysis and designs into one of these areas: for instance, not all case studies will reveal important information concerning transformation, and so this might not be relevant to your analysis. Or you may want to focus exclusively on how customization tools within a game serve presentation of identity. As identity is a complex concept, it is expected that you will have to read more widely around a specific topic in order to conduct an analysis involving identity and representation. This is reflected in the activity outline. The list of references at the end of this chapter provides a good start point for further reading.

Exercises

CHARACTER ANALYSIS

How are specific aspects of identity represented in the design of virtual characters for video games, and what potential issues do these designs present?

1. Identify the core topic to be addressed in your analysis (e.g., sexuality) plus any other aspects of identity that you feel should be covered in your study. This does not need to be limited to the aspects of identity we have discussed in this chapter: Be open to considering other ways in which people form self-identity.

2. Review the associated literature on your topics, in particular targeting published books and articles that discuss theories of identity and representation and that discuss games or visual media.

3. List criteria that you feel should underpin your analysis and subsequent discussion (e.g., dress, speech, body language, cultural references, preferences).

4. Identify a character or series of characters that provide an interesting case study for your selected topic.

5. Research existing publications on these characters and their associated games. Ensure that you have access to the games so that you can play them, and collect videos of gameplay for further analysis.

6. Play through the game(s) and take notes on virtual character appearance, actions, and dialogue.

7. Take screenshots of important observations and try to establish what the character appearances might signify.

8. Consider the degree to which available customization relates to the identified topic and criteria. What are the limitations? What key elements are missing?

9. Consider whether there are any interesting examples of transformative works in the fan community that highlight limitations or problems with the original character designs.

10. Write an evaluation of the character or characters, drawing on examples from your notes and screenshots to illustrate key points.

11. Aim to discuss the case study critically, making connections between your observations and the related literature, other media, and so on. Identify strengths and weaknesses in the character(s) you studied.

CHARACTER DESIGN

How might an existing character design be reimagined in order to explore aspects of identity that are less well represented in video games?

1. Identify a small number of player characters from popular video games that embody conventional or widely used representations (e.g., male, heterosexual, white, Christian/atheist, wealthy, etc.).

2. Develop concepts for transformative designs based on these characters, with the aim of creating characters that reflect less well-represented aspects of identity.

3. Be sure to thoroughly research texts and other materials that discuss the reality of the identities you are examining, and to iterate on your designs in order to avoid simplistic interpretations or stereotypical depictions.

4. Identify a genre of game that might typically be associated with a conventional character type (e.g., an action shooter based on themes of war that is commonly associated with male, white, American, straight character designs).

5. Proceed to design characters for this genre that explore alternative and less well-represented identities, again paying attention to the thoroughness of your research and the need to iterate and improve your designs.

6. In both of these examples, consider how you might design a range of customization tools for the characters, allowing players to manipulate presentations of identity.

7. In both examples, aim to avoid simply building designs that contrast with a perceived norm. Instead, consider how less well-represented aspects of identity enhance your character design.

REFERENCES

Brock, A. 2011. When keeping it real goes wrong: Resident Evil 5, racial representation, and gamers. *Games and Culture* 6 (5): 429–52.

Butler, J. 1999. *Gender trouble: Feminism and the subversion of identity*. New York: Routledge.

Clare, A. 2001. *On men: Masculinity in crisis*. London: Arrow Books.

Frasca, G. 2004. Videogames of the oppressed: Critical thinking, education, tolerance, and other trivial issues. In *First person: New media as story, performance, and game*, ed. P. Harrigan and N. Wardrip-Fruin, 85–94. Cambridge, MA: MIT Press.

Hall, S. 1966. Who needs identity? In *Questions of cultural identity*, ed. S. Hall and P. du Hay, 1–18. London: Sage.

Halperin, D. 1997. *Saint Foucault: Towards a gay hagiography*. New York: Oxford University Press.

Höglund, J. 2008. Electronic empire: Orientalism revisited in the military shooter. *Game Studies* 8 (1). http://gamestudies.org/0801/articles/hoeglund.

Lawler, S. 2008. *Identity: Sociological perspectives*. Cambridge, UK: Polity Press.

Levine, K. 2012. *We love our Bioshock cosplayers so much we hired one!* Irrational Games. http://irrationalgames.com/insider/we-love-our-bioshock-cosplayers-so-much-we-hired-one/.

McNair, B. 2002. *Striptease culture: Sex, media and the democratization of desire.* London: Gingko.

Mika, M. 2013. *Why I hacked Donkey Kong for my daughter.* Wired. www.wired.com/gamelife/2013/03/donkey-kong-pauline-hack/.

Mulvey, L. 1989. Visual please in narrative cinema. In *Visual and other pleasures,* 14–26. Basingstoke: Macmillan.

Narcisse, E. 2012. *Father hacks Zelda for his daughter, makes Link a girl.* Kotaku. kotaku.com/5958918/father-hacks-zelda-for-his-daughter-makes-link-a-girl.

Newman, D. M. 2012. *Sociology: Exploring the architecture of everyday life.* 9th ed. Thousand Oaks, CA: Sage.

Poor, N. 2012. Digital elves as a racial other in video games: Acknowledgement and avoidance. *Games and Culture* 7 (5): 375–96.

Said, E. 1995. *Orientalism: Western conceptions of the Orient.* Harmondsworth, UK: Penguin.

Sarkeesian, A. 2013. *Damsel in distress (Part 1) tropes vs. women.* Feminist frequency: Conversations with pop culture. http://www.feministfrequency.com/2013/03/damsel-in-distress-part-1/.

Schmieder, C. 2009. World of maskcraft vs. world of queercraft? Communication, sex and gender in the online role-playing game *World of Warcraft. Journal of Gaming and Virtual Worlds* 1 (1): 5–21. DOI: 10.1386/jgvw.1.1.5/1.

Shaw, A. 2012. Do you identify as a gamer? Gender, race, sexuality, and gamer identity. *New Media & Society* 14 (1): 25–41.

Šisler, V. 2008. Digital Arabs: Representation in video games. *European Journal of Cultural Studies* 11 (2): 203–19.

Spencer, S. 2006. *Race and identity: Culture, identity and representation.* New York: Routledge.

Starr, M. 2013. *Meet Lara Croft: If Lara were a man.* CNET. http://news.cnet.com/8301-17938_105-57591172-1/meet-larry-croft-if-lara-were-a-man/.

Sullivan, N. 2003. *A critical introduction to queer theory.* Edinburgh, UK: Edinburgh University Press.

Wayne, M., L. Henderson, C. Murray, and J. Petley. 2008. Television news and the symbolic criminalisation of young people. *Journalism Studies* 9 (1): 75–90.

Williams, D., S. Martins, M. Consalvo, and J. D. Ivory. 2009. The virtual census: Representations of gender, race and age in video games. *New Media & Society* 11 (5): 815–34.

II

Performance

IN THE PREVIOUS THREE CHAPTERS, we looked at factors that can impact on the presentation of characters within games and interactive media. From basic biological and artistic principles to issues of identity and representation, our concern here was primarily how we can display and interpret characters. In the following three chapters we move beyond visual appearance to consider how characters perform. First, we examine the psychological theories that can inform our understanding of character personality, emotion, and nonverbal expressions. We then consider the context in which virtual characters are placed, encompassing both narrative and game-design theories. Lastly, we look at how theories of acting, movement, and animation underpin the creation of the virtual character performances.

CHAPTER 4

Personality, Emotion, and Expression

W E SHOULD BEGIN OUR discussion of performance by first examining the psychological concepts that underpin human behavior and actions. If our goal is to design characters audiences can relate to and empathize with, then it's essential that we have some understanding of the nature of personality, emotion, and expression. From the overarching attitudes and traits that define how we behave to the short-term feeling states that affect our thought processes and immediate actions, an appreciation of both personality and emotion is vital for good character design. By extension, how we use nonverbal communication to express who we are, what we are thinking, and what we are feeling is fundamental to the creation of authentic and emotive performances.

Psychology is, of course, a vast subject domain, encompassing a range of research traditions and methodological approaches. It is beyond the scope of this book to comprehensively review and discuss the psychology of human personality, emotion, and behavior. Indeed, there are already a number of books and academic papers that specifically target a psychological discussion of character design, most notably the excellent book by Ibister (2006). For a broader and deeper understanding of psychological principles, it would be advisable for readers to start with Ibister's work before delving deeper into the literature to study human psychology. For now, the aim of this chapter is to specifically target concepts that will help us to both design and analyze characters in terms of their personalities and emotional journeys.

First, we look at three useful approaches to breaking down a character's personality: the five-factor model for personality measurement, the role of individual attitudes in defining personality, and the Nolan chart for plotting political views and beliefs. Moving on to emotion, we look at the psychobiological nature of emotions (what emotions are and what role they serve in an evolutionary sense). Finally, we consider how we communicate nonverbal information using our faces, bodies, and voices.

PERSONALITY

Personality Traits and the Five-Factor Model

Personality can be defined as the pattern of behaviors, traits, and characteristics that make any individual unique. Unlike emotions (which are short-term affective states), a person's personality is fairly stable throughout his or her life. Although environmental factors and significant life events might impact on an individual's personality, we can generally consider personality to be a long-term and relatively permanent state.

In psychology, researchers and theorists have made attempts to describe personality in terms of a small number of factors. As discussed by Digman (1990), the roots of this research in the modern era can be traced to the 1930s, with the following 50 years seeing a flurry of activity in the development of models based on personality factors. Digman stresses that there was general agreement on the notion that personality could be expressed according to just five factors, but notes that psychologists often had different opinions on the definition of these factors. For example, early research by Fiske (1949) lists the factors as *social adaptability, conformity, a will to achieve, emotional control*, and *intellect*. Other definitions include *surgency, agreeableness, dependability, emotionality*, and *culture* (Tupes and Christal 1961), and *power, love, work, affect*, and *intellect* (Peabody and Goldberg 1989). However, one of the most well-known and frequently used models is NEO-PI-R (or the Neuroticism, Extraversion, Openness Personality Inventory, Revised). This model was proposed by Costa and McCrae (1985) and can be useful in both the design and analysis of characters. While any validated model of personality in the five-factor paradigm could be valuable in your own research and practice, for now we focus on Costa and McCrae's model as a good and well-supported example.

The NEO-PI-R operates by measuring personality according to the factors of *neuroticism, extraversion, openness to experience, agreeableness*, and *conscientiousness*. These are subsequently broken down into six facets

TABLE 4.1   The NEO-PI-R Model

Factor	Facets
Neuroticism	1. Anxiety
	2. Angry hostility
	3. Depression
	4. Self-consciousness
	5. Impulsiveness
	6. Vulnerability
Extraversion	1. Warmth
	2. Gregariousness
	3. Assertiveness
	4. Activity
	5. Excitement seeking
	6. Positive emotions
Openness to experience	1. Fantasy
	2. Aesthetics
	3. Feelings
	4. Actions
	5. Ideas
	6. Values
Agreeableness	1. Trust
	2. Straightforwardness
	3. Altruism
	4. Compliance
	5. Modesty
	6. Tender-mindedness
Conscientiousness	1. Competence
	2. Order
	3. Dutifulness
	4. Achievement striving
	5. Self-discipline
	6. Deliberation

that help to shape and define each personality factor (see Table 4.1). All in all, the five factors and 30 facets provide a means of assessing the nature of a personality.

Neuroticism measures the extent to which someone is likely to become distressed, including whether she is freely anxious, has a tendency to experience anger and frustration, has a tendency to experience sadness and despondency, is shy, is impulsive, and is prone to becoming stressed. In binary terms, we can summarize either end of the neuroticism scale as *nervous* or *confident*. Extraversion concerns the level of energy an individual feels toward social interaction, including whether someone is interested in others, enjoys others' company, is forceful, is active, requires stimulation, and commonly experiences positive emotions. The two extreme categories of extraversion can be described as being either *solitary* or *outgoing*. Openness is a measure of someone's appreciation of experiences, including whether he enjoys fantasy and imagination, appreciates art and nature, is open to emotive experiences, is open to new experiences, is interested in the world, and is prepared to evaluate his own and others' values. The two extreme categories for openness are *curious* and *cautious*. Agreeableness concerns whether someone is compassionate or uncompassionate, including whether she believes others are sincere, are frank, are concerned for others, are compliant, are humble, and are tender. For agreeableness, we can consider someone to be either *friendly* or *cold*. And finally, conscientiousness encompasses persistence, control, and motivations, including whether someone has belief in his own abilities, thinks things through, feels a sense of duty, feels a need to achieve things, feels a need to complete tasks, and tends to think before acting. We might consider a conscientious person to be *organized*, while someone who is not conscientious is *careless*.

NEO-PI-R, as with other measures for personality, is clearly complex. Further reading into five-factor models and NEO-PI-R can be useful for those with a deeper interest in the psychology of personality. In the domains of character design and game studies, however, the information presented here can be sufficient to begin conceptualizing or analyzing a character in terms of its fundamental traits.

Individual Attitudes

The traits that we have looked at so far are fairly generic, in the sense that they can describe how characters might generally respond when interacting with others or being subjected to a given stimulus. While these traits can be useful for defining how a character commonly behaves, attitudes offer us a means of being a bit more specific about a character's reactions to particular situations. Furthermore, we have also identified that personality (strictly speaking) is a relatively fixed concept, in that traits tend not to change much or at all over time. A character's attitudes are arguably more susceptible to fluctuation.

As with most psychological concepts discussed in this chapter, there is not sufficient scope to explore attitudes in detail. Instead, we look to focus on some of the most interesting and pertinent ideas about human attitudes that could be used to frame our character designs and analysis. Readers who are interested in an in-depth overview of attitudes in psychology can look to Maio and Haddock (2009). Their book offers an insightful discussion of how attitudes are structured and what influences and shapes them.

Perhaps the best way to conceptualize attitudes is to consider them as a predisposition to evaluate particular objects, people, or concepts either negatively or positively. In other words, a character's attitudes inform how it would express an evaluative judgment. Judgments can be passed on fairly straightforward matters—such as a style of music or a type of cuisine—as well as issues of much more significance, such as feelings toward specific people or political ideologies (which we look at in the next section). In effect, we can think of virtual character attitudes as a means of listing objects of varying importance that a character might form an opinion on. Consequently, we can use this list to help us define how a character will behave in response to environmental and social factors within a video game world.

To do this, we ought to take into account both the elements that define a person's attitudes and the categories of objects on which they can form judgments. First, attitudes can be defined according to the following two factors:

- *Valence*: We might consider valence as the direction of the attitude. Simply put, a character can have an attitude toward an object that is positive, negative, or neutral. For every object considered in the design or analysis of a character, we can define whether that character expresses a liking for the object, a disliking for the object, or expresses indifference about the object.

- *Strength*: In addition to the direction of the attitude, we can also consider the strength of the attitude. Our judgments are rarely binary, in that we don't simply like or dislike something. We tend to show a degree of positivity or negativity toward it; that is, one person might only have a weak dislike of a film genre, whereas another person might express strong feelings of hate toward it.

As we have already identified, we can express an evaluative judgment of virtually any object we can imagine. This means that the attitude objects that are important to one character are likely to be very different from those of other characters, as every character will have its own list of objects that it has feelings about. In reality, we could define an individual's attitude toward thousands of different objects using the factors of valence and strength. Every individual will have objects that she holds positive or negative views on, with some objects inciting the strongest reactions. But even when an individual shows indifference toward an object, there is still the potential that this could be an interesting or even defining aspect of his personality.

For reasons of practicality, it is simply not feasible to design a character taking into account its attitudes toward all imaginable objects. Neither is it possible to identify a character's attitudes toward all objects through analysis of its performance. Instead, there is a need to prioritize the objects that you, as a designer or researcher, feel are most important and most interesting about a virtual character. What are the objects and ensuing attitudes that will be of significance to the character in terms of how it behaves and performs within a video game? In order to approach this task, we could look to break down all conceivable objects into broad categories, and use this as a starting point for defining key attitude objects for a given character. Objects can be

- *Physical*: This can be considered the most generic category. It includes any object—animate or inanimate—that exists in a form that can be detected by the senses; that is, it can be seen, heard, smelled, tasted, and/or touched.

- *Human*: As an extension of the physical, we can specifically consider individual humans as attitude objects, including both the self (a character's feelings about itself) and others (a character's feelings toward friends, family members, colleagues, celebrities, etc.).

- *Groups*: As an extension of humans, we can then consider groups formed by humans that are representative of some form of collective identity or ideal, for example, football fans, particular nationalities, religious groups, and so on.

- *Events*: We might also consider events to be objects that we have attitudes toward. These might be historical events of key importance or interest, current events such as sporting competitions, or future events such as an upcoming general election.

- *Abstract*: Finally, we can also hold attitudes toward abstract concepts ranging from emotional feelings to complex political ideologies.

Building on the five-factor model, we can use attitudes to paint a more detailed picture of a character's personality, enabling us to consider in depth who it is, how it behaves, and how it should perform. In particular, we might want to look more closely at a character's attitudes toward abstract concepts such as political ideologies, as political views can become a defining aspect of a character's personality and greatly inform its behaviors.

Political Views

When it comes to categorizing who we are, one of the most commonly used techniques is to define our political views in relation to a range of attitude objects and in relation to other individuals and other groups. Establishing our political stance helps us to express how we think people should respond to difficult social, cultural, environmental, and economic problems. By aligning with a particular political ideology, we are effectively stating what we think we would do if we were confronted with a tough choice or were tasked with making an important decision. Taking this further, we can see that political categorization can also be a means of understanding the attitudes and subsequent behaviors of a virtual character when placed into a complex situation or world.

There are many techniques and models that can be used to help define a political stance. Normally, these models are driven by a respondent's answers to a series of probing questions, which can then pinpoint the respondent's political stance along one or more axes. For now, we look at just one of the most commonly used political attitude models that underpins the thinking of core political parties and movements of the modern era: the Nolan Chart.

Developed by American Libertarian Party member David Nolan, the Nolan Chart aims to plot political views along two axes and subsequently place individual perspectives into five categories. The two axes relate to Personal Freedoms and Economic Freedoms. The former concerns the degree to which individuals should have the freedom to make their own decisions (about lifestyle, religion, sexuality, consumption of drugs and alcohol, etc.) free from government interference, while the latter concerns the degree to which markets should have the freedom to act without government intervention (e.g., laws regarding trade, manufacture, wages, taxation, etc.). This then creates the following five categories that more or less align with the main political philosophies that exist in modern democratic nations:

- *Conservatism*: The traditional right-wing conservatives favor economic freedom (i.e., free markets with no or limited government interference) over personal freedoms (for instance by introducing laws that define legal relationships that outlaw drugs and other vices, etc.).

- *Liberalism*: What is often described as the left wing and encompassing social democratic parties as well as socialist parties, liberalism is defined by a high degree of personal freedom but with restrictions on economic freedom. Liberals believe that governments should allow individuals to act with limited interference, but should intervene in the market in order to maintain control over the economy and protect individual rights.

- *Libertarianism*: Libertarianism can be considered a form of individualism with a preference toward a small government that has limited or no significant power to interfere in either the lives of individuals or in the market. This means that libertarians share views on the freedom of individuals with liberals and on the freedom of markets with conservatives. In the extreme, a preference for the removal of government can be considered a form of anarchism (a stateless society).

- *Statism*: Statism is the counter to libertarianism and is defined through the preference for large governments with control over both individual freedoms and market freedoms. In the extreme form, an all-powerful government can be considered to be authoritarian or totalitarian.

- *Centrism*: Finally, the centrist category is used to define political philosophies that balance the views of the four other categories. In reality, most mainstream political views and mainstream democratic parties are effectively centrist, even those parties that lean toward the other categories.

These categories might seem to be taking us on a tangent away from the design of virtual characters toward a discussion of sociology and ideology. However, there is value in understanding the overarching principles behind political stances. They offer well-established categories of human thought that we can use to shape or interpret character actions. This won't always be applicable, of course. Some video game characters have limited opportunities or requirements to perform in a manner that would be reflective of a complex series of political views (although we might argue that, on a basic level, even *Pac-Man* appears to be a libertarian!). Nevertheless, many virtual characters inhabit rich, multifaceted storyworlds that facilitate interactions, reactions, and performances that can be informed by the political philosophies outlined here and the related attitudes. Notable examples include the villains from the *BioShock* series, including Andrew Ryan of *BioShock* {2K Boston 2007}—an extreme rightist character driven by the ideals of modernism, objectivism, and Western capitalism—and Zachary Comstock of *BioShock Infinite* {Irrational Games 2013}—essentially an extreme nationalist totalitarian who exhibits a need to control both the economy and individual freedoms.

As such, the Nolan Chart and other political charts can be useful tools for both the design of original virtual characters (helping you to flesh out character descriptions, backstories, and their behaviors) and the study of characters in existing video games.

Balancing Personality Design for Virtual Characters

We have only scratched the surface of the psychological factors that impact upon personality and behavior, but we have established a sufficient base knowledge of how traits, attitudes, and political views can shape a character. Although the literature on personality is valuable for anyone with a vested interested in virtual characters, there is a vast amount of information out there, most of which is not targeted toward or even sensitive to the performance of characters in interactive media. Additionally, most of us who design and research virtual characters are neither psychologists nor sociologists, but artists, animators, directors, developers, or media theorists. As such, it is very easy to get lost in the density of psychological theories, the numerous models, and the unfamiliar language and terminology. At this stage, it would be more useful for us to consider how we might combine our basic knowledge of personality and behavior into a practical method for designing or deconstructing a character.

One way to do this is to divert from the psychological literature for a moment and instead look to the existing works on character design. Specifically, David Freeman's book *Creating Emotion in Games* (2003) offers perspectives on emotive and authentic character design that are underpinned by psychological theory but pitched in terms of creative writing, direction, and performance. Although there are many excellent books on writing for characters, including others that look at writing for video games, Freeman's book provides an easy-to-follow series of techniques that can help us to design and study virtual character performance. In particular, Freeman suggests a method for character design built upon trait selection: a method he calls the NPC Interesting Technique.

Fundamentally, the premise of this technique is that, to make characters interesting, designers ought to consider how they can create internal dynamics and conflicts by assigning "traits." To achieve this, a character diamond is proposed. The diamond diagram has four points, each of which symbolizes an attribute of the character (e.g., friendly, honorable, quick tempered, etc.). The first thing to note is that not all characters necessarily need to make use of a four-point diamond. Characters of lesser importance might be designed or deconstructed using a triangular diagram, whereas complex and major characters might even require a pentagonal diagram. What is important is that the character diagram—be it triangular, diamond, or pentagonal—should be used to define a character that is interesting. Characters that have predictable or clichéd combinations of attributes will inevitably have flat personalities: for instance, the hero who is brave, loyal, chivalrous, and just, or the antagonist who is wicked, conniving, vengeful, and power hungry. Some element of conflict is essential in order to make the personality of the character more unique, more distinctive from other characters and other narratives, and primarily to ensure that the character is interesting to the audience. For example, the hero who is arrogant and selfish while also ethical and brave could make for more interesting character development and interactions.

We could look to adapt this technique to help us utilize our knowledge of traits, attitudes, and political views in a practical way. Rather than conceiving of or analyzing these elements in isolation, we can instead unify them as core aspects of a given virtual character's personality: its fundamental traits, attitudes toward objects, and more fully formed views on human society and order. How we balance these can greatly inform how a character will ultimately perform. Figure 4.1 shows an example of how we might attempt to balance a character based on elements of the five-factor model, attitude objects, and political views. Here, we can see a concept for character that is not defined in terms of heroism, villainy, or even whether it is a protagonist or antagonist (topics we deal with in the next chapter). Instead, the focus is entirely on the high concept of the personality of the character. From the five-factor model, three traits are identified as most

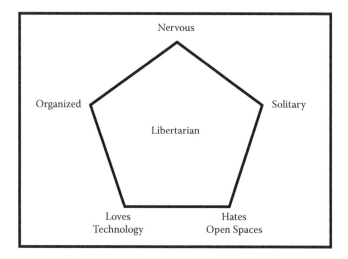

FIGURE 4.1 Proposed method for quickly visualizing a character's personality traits (five-factor model), attitude objects, and political views.

defining for this character: *organized, nervous*, and *solitary*. Two attitudes are identified: It loves technology but hates open spaces. And finally, in the center of the diagram, it is identified as being in the libertarian category of political views. There are no obvious or blatant contrasts here: contrasts for the sake of contrasts don't necessarily make a character interesting. But this balance of identified traits, attitudes, and views does tell us something. This is a character that appears to enjoy solitude and is probably nervous in social interactions or even fearful of others given the character's hatred of open spaces. The dedication to organization could overlap with the love of technology, while there is scope for conflict between the love of technology and libertarian feelings. If the character lives in an age of ubiquitous computing and cyber espionage, does a conflict arise between the desire to use new technologies and a possible hatred of secret intergovernmental surveillance interfering with individual liberties? At the level of the character arc, this could be the motivation for an unlikely hero: or, indeed, an unlikely villain. At the macro level, we can draw on these identified personality elements to define character performance style (e.g., twitchy, anxious) and gameplay mechanics (e.g., hacking, stealth).

While this example diagram is ultimately a simple overview of a character, it can provide us with the means to quickly prototype and iterate on character design concepts. It gives us an overview of the core aspects of personality (which we can subsequently explore in more depth once we have a firmer idea of the personality we wish to develop) and allows us to think more holistically (e.g., relating personality to how a character might fit into a narrative, how it might perform, how it will react to player interactions, or how it will feature in gameplay). It is highly recommended that those with a greater interest in personality development delve into the wider literature, including the suggested sources in the references at the end of this chapter. But for now, we are going to place personality to one side in order to focus on the psychology of character emotions.

EMOTIONAL STATES

Our discussion of personality placed emphasis on the fixed or long-term attributes of characters. In contrast, emotion is concerned with a character's short-term feelings and needs. In a virtual character performance, it is often the emotions of characters that players and critics pay the most attention to, given the immediacy of emotion and the potential for carefully designed emotional journeys to generate strong reactions in an audience. By experiencing, exhibiting, and acting on a series of emotions, a virtual character can generate feelings of sympathy or revulsion in audiences. A powerful emotional performance can leave a lasting impression. In the very best examples, the emotions exhibited by characters on screen can cause us to feel empathy: in other words, we literally share the emotions of the characters we are controlling, observing, or interacting with. Because emotions are part of human nature, and because most of us experience a range of emotions daily and throughout our lives, emotion is one of the more effective means of making a connection between a virtual character and an audience.

Before we can look a little more deeply at what emotions actually are, we should first seek to identify the types of emotions that are commonly experienced. One of the most widely recognized taxonomies of emotion is the wheel of emotion as described by Robert Plutchik (1994). A version of this wheel based on Plutchik's original diagram is shown in Figure 4.2. The wheel of emotions is often cited in studies of emotion and in emotional theory. Although greatly simplified in relation to the true complexity and variety of human emotional experience, this diagram is a useful way to conceptualize how emotions relate to each other. As the diagram shows, Plutchik proposed eight primary emotions (represented by the second ring of emotions from the center). These emotions are arranged so that four opposites are identified: joy and sadness, trust and disgust, fear

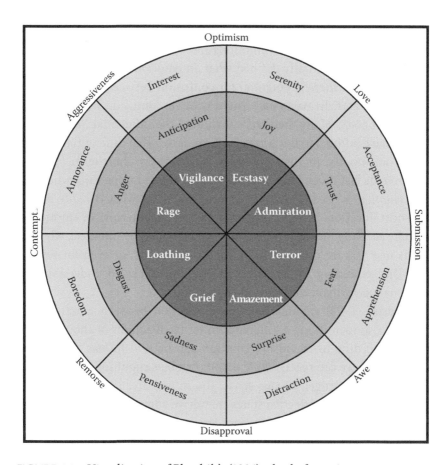

FIGURE 4.2   Visualization of Plutchik's (1994) wheel of emotions.

and anger, and surprise and anticipation. Furthermore, Plutchik provided names for varying levels of intensity for these emotions, with more intense varieties shown in the inner circle and less intense varieties in the outer circle. Finally, Plutchik identified terms for advanced emotion combinations, which are shown on the outside of the wheel (e.g., contempt as a combination of anger and disgust).

The wheel of emotions can be an excellent tool for planning and defining the emotions and emotional journeys that characters will experience. However, knowing the names of and interactions between specific emotions is unlikely to be sufficient for designing or analyzing an authentic character performance. In order to really understand how these emotions operate, it is important to consider what underlying processes occur when an emotion is experienced.

Emotions as Adaptive Behaviors

Although we have introduced emotions and attempted to categorize them, we have not as yet actually defined what an emotion is. This may seem a trivial point, but there is potential for confusion between different types of affective states. In particular, there is often confusion between emotions and moods. Many theorists—including the influential Paul Ekman (1994)—have pointed to duration as a main factor that differentiates emotions from moods, in that emotions are relatively short-term feelings, while moods last much longer. What is often missed (especially when the word *emotion* is used in art and entertainment) is what is *really* meant by a short duration. In psychological and biological terms, an emotion is typically a feeling that lasts for a few seconds (not many minutes), whereas moods may last for up to an hour, for several hours, or even for several days. Understanding the briefness of emotion is key to understanding emotional performance for virtual characters.

Davidson (1994) expands on this distinction between emotion and mood by also identifying a difference in terms of actions or thought processes. According to Davidson, emotion can be said to bias action (the different ways we can react), while moods can bias cognition (the way that we process knowledge). In this sense, the shorter-lived emotions can be seen as more intense affective states that drive someone to take action in response to a given stimulus. Longer-lasting moods, on the other hand, impact on our cognition and moderate our emotions. The mood that we are in may make it more or less likely that a particular emotion will be felt in response to a stimulus. For instance, someone in an irritable mood might be more likely to become angry.

According to Parkinson et al. (1996), a distinction can also be made in terms of the origin of emotional and mood states, in that an emotion typically has a clear stimulus, while moods do not necessarily stem from a specific eliciting event. This leads us into one of the first major observations that we should make regarding emotions: that they should be considered as biological responses to environmental stimuli. In other words, emotions are natural responses that help us to deal with events by taking some form of appropriate action. Plutchik (2002) describes emotion-driven actions as adaptive behaviors and relates these to specific emotional states. For instance, a stimulus such as a threat could trigger the emotional experience of fear. A feeling of fear coincides with raised awareness, more

TABLE 4.2   Adaptive Behaviors as Described by Plutchik (2002)

Stimulus	Cognition	Emotion	Behavior and Effect
Gain valuable object	Possess	Happiness	Repeat for resources
Member of group	Friend	Trust	Seek mutual support
Threat	Danger	Fear	Escape to safety
Unexpected event	What is it?	Surprise	Stop to observe
Loss of valuable object	Abandonment	Sadness	Cry for lost object
Unpalatable object	Poison	Disgust	Vomit
Obstacle	Enemy	Anger	Attack obstacle
New territory	Examine	Anticipation	Gain knowledge

frequent intakes of breath, and a raised heartbeat, all of which will help someone who is preparing to run from the threat. Table 4.2 shows a summary of adaptive behaviors in response to a range of primary emotions (Plutchik 2002). While this table seems to list primitive behaviors, it could be argued that these fundamental instincts underpin our emotional reactions to events in the modern day as well, that it is simply the *context* of the stimuli and responses that might be interpreted in different terms.

It can be contended that evolutionary theories of emotion dictate that emotional states are universal biological responses: in other words, that particular stimuli will elicit particular emotional responses irrespective of individual cognition. An alternative set of theories of emotion stipulates that cognition is a more fundamental component of emotion. Cognitive-appraisal theories of emotion instead place emphasis on the evaluation process. Rather than viewing emotion as a strictly automatic biological response that has emerged in modern humans through natural selection, appraisal theorists suggest that individuals will assess events, situations, and other emotional stimuli (consciously or unconsciously) in order to determine which emotional response is appropriate. The underlying principle of appraisal theory is that specific emotions are not inevitably experienced as a result of a particular stimulus. Instead, individuals assess how a situation or event affects their goals. Specific emotional states will be evoked, but different individuals will experience different emotions when presented with the same stimuli. Cognitive-appraisal theories typically constitute a series of criteria or dimensions that dictate how the process of appraisal is conducted, with variation in the nature and the number of dimensions, depending on the particular theory. The specifics of the dimensions of various proposed theories are not essential for us at this point, but

Scherer (1999) offers a comparison of different cognitive-appraisal theories for those with an interest in the specific criteria that can be applied.

Emotion and Virtual Character Performance

How can the previous discussion of emotional theories be of practical application to the design and analysis of virtual characters? As before, it is vital to stress that the intricacies of emotional theories can easily lead us too far from the task of building authentic interactive character performances. All we need to do at this stage is appreciate what emotions are, that is, bridging elements in a short-term thought process that leads from a stimulus event to a responsive action. How we choose to engineer or scrutinize the process can be informed by the theories and models of emotion that exist in the literature, such as those described by Plutchik (2002) and Scherer (1999).

How should a character behave in a given context? This might be a narrative context that is scripted, and thus relatively fixed. But it could also be a dynamic context where player action and choice determine the events that will take place. What if a virtual character witnesses a traumatic event, such as the death of the lead PC John Marston in *Red Dead Redemption* {Rockstar San Diego 2010}, as witnessed by wife Abigail and son Jack? By examining the adaptive behavior for loss and considering the more complex cognitive appraisals that these two characters might go through, we can establish what authentic, naturalistic responses could be demonstrated in their performance (and ultimately in their future motivations). Perhaps more importantly, though, consideration of adaptive behaviors and emotional processes can help us to devise systems for on-the-fly virtual character responses. When a player can interact with a character, having some means of rationalizing how it should respond is vital. What should a character do if you choose to hug it, insult it, steal from it, or even punch it? The experimental game *Façade* {Mateas and Stern 2005} provides opportunities for players to generate multiple events that effectively trigger adaptive behaviors and cognitive appraisal processes in the NPCs Trip and Grace (discussed in more detail in Chapter 9). While the aspects of personality that we discussed earlier in the chapter help us to shape and examine the overall performance of a unique character, it is how virtual characters handle emotions that is of more importance to dynamic and responsive performances.

EXPRESSION

Having discussed personality and emotion in terms of intrinsic character-istics and processes that determine how a character behaves and thinks, for the rest of this chapter, we turn our attention to how personality and emotion can be manifested through physical expression. Expression (or nonverbal communication) is often discussed in the character design lit-erature. In character illustration and animation, artists need to be able to communicate both simple and intricate ideas through a limited number of drawings. An audience should not have to work hard to understand what a character is feeling. If an audience fails to understand what the emotion or mood of a character is at a critical point in the narrative, this can undermine the quality of their experience or even their ability to fol-low the story. We come back to acting and animation concepts that can be used to evaluate the quality of an emotive performance in Chapter 6. For now we focus on key concepts of human expression that can be perceived in nature through the body, face, and voice. These nonverbal cues are inte-gral to the aesthetics of a virtual character, and being able to identify them will greatly enhance your ability to discuss expression as part of charac-ter performance.

Posture and Proximity

When it comes to nonverbal communication, the body is perhaps the most obvious channel for expression. Body expression can be a useful means of communicating the thought process, emotions, and personality of a char-acter regardless of the placement or orientation of the camera. In contrast, the finer details of facial expression may require a close-up to be easily recognized. Even when the camera is behind a character, it can still be possible to read and understand basic body expressions.

Knapp and Hall (2010) provide an in-depth discussion of the role of nonverbal communication, including the use of the body. This and other related literature should prove extremely useful when preparing to ana-lyze or design body expressions for virtual characters. For now we focus on two of the most important aspects of a character's body expression: posture, and proximity to other characters.

First, posture is the overall positioning of the body. Posture can be indicative of the emotional state, mood, or temperament of a character. We can simplify analysis of posture by considering the following scales:

- *Open and closed*: Probably the most widely understood aspect of posture is whether a person's body language appears to be open or closed. An open posture is typically perceived as friendly and positive, while a closed posture is seen as detached, threatened, or hostile. An open posture can be identified through open arms and legs, a straight back, a raised head, and a more expansive use of space. Conversely, a closed posture will appear more defensive, with crossed legs or arms and a less-expansive use of space (for instance a slouched posture or bent back). Open and closed poses are shown in Figure 4.3.

- *High energy and low energy*: The next consideration concerns the apparent presence of energy in a character's posture and movement. As with the open/closed comparison, high energy and low energy can be correlated with contrasting affective states—in this case, high arousal and low arousal. Higher energy can be observed through faster, bouncier movements and more dynamic posing, while low-energy postures will contain slow and sluggish movements and more-lethargic posing.

FIGURE 4.3   Examples of open and closed poses.

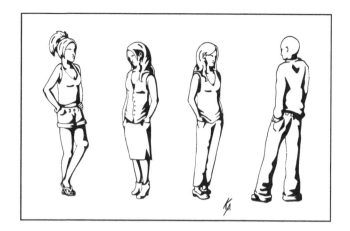

FIGURE 4.4 Examples of couples demonstrating opposition (left) and similarity (right).

- *Similarity and opposition*: Finally, in social groups, humans have a tendency to participate in imitation. This can be a strong indicator of the interpersonal attitudes between characters in any group. Higher degrees of similarity in posture suggest that characters are engaged in mimicry. It is a possibility that one character is dominant, and the other characters are imitating its pose. Similarity in pose can imply agreement, the presence of a bond, feelings of empathy from one character toward another, or simply an enjoyable conversation between the characters present. Where contrasting postures are shown, this can imply a reversed situation: that is, lack of agreement, lack of connection, lack of empathy, or feelings of dislike or disdain between characters. Both similarity and opposition are illustrated in Figure 4.4.

Variety in posing dependent on context can greatly enhance the presentation of a character to an audience. Without the need for dialogue or narration, posture selection can clearly communicate a character's thought process and attitudes, including attitudes toward other characters. For instance, the NPC Clementine in *The Walking Dead* {Telltale Games 2012} frequently exhibits low-energy and closed postures. This reflects her nervous and vulnerable state and subsequently encourages the player to protect her. In the *Assassin's Creed* series, the characters Shaun Hastings and Rebecca Crane are often shown imitating each other's poses. This helps to cement the fact that they are part of the same social group and that, despite stark differences in personality and temperament, they have a shared goal.

The other form of nonverbal communication using the body that we consider relates to the proximity between characters. *Proxemics*—the study of the use of space and the subsequent impact on interpersonal communication (Hall 1963)—is a useful framework to apply to the design and analysis of scenes that incorporate multiple virtual characters. The underlying principle that is of most relevance is the correlation between personal and social space. Breaking personal space down into bubbles, proxemics proposes that personal space can be described in terms of distances, with each distance mapped onto a social interaction or relationship between parties.

- *Intimate distance*: Where the distance between characters ranges from less than 6 inches (15 cm) up to 18 inches (46 cm), intimate distance suggests a very close relationship, and serves interactions such as touching, embracing, and whispering. Characters that are positioned within this range are likely to be presented as being romantically involved or as very close friends. More broadly, this distance suggests that the characters are intent on communicating within their own sphere, excluding others around them.

- *Personal distance*: From 18 inches (46 cm) to 4 ft (1.2 m) apart, personal distance is an appropriate distance for communication between allied characters that have an established personal relationship. At this range, subtle physical and vocal expressions can be detected that may not be easily picked up at a greater distance.

- *Social distance*: Social distance ranges from 4 ft (1.2 m) to 12 ft (3.7 m). As the name implies, this distance is more appropriate for characters that share a basic social relationship, for example, acquaintances or colleagues within a wider group, but characters that are not close friends or family.

- *Public distance*: Finally, public distance can be considered as 12 ft (3.6 m) to 25 ft (7.6 m) or more. This is a suitable distance for characters that do not have an established relationship and are instead engaged in an open and public conversation or interaction.

By applying these rules of thumb, it is possible to determine what relationships characters within a scene are depicting. Over the course of a

game, these ranges may well shift in order to depict a changing relationship between characters.

Facial Expression

As with the expressive body, the expressive face is complex. From an
anatomical perspective, the flexibility of the face and the large number
of facial muscles means that a vast number of unique expressions can be
shown. These range from subtle movements (known as microexpressions)
to broad and intense movements used in social interaction or states of
high emotional arousal. A detailed examination of all the permutations
would not be practical within the scope of this book. However, a good
working knowledge of the biology and psychology of facial expression is
very useful for anyone studying virtual characters, and there are a number
of practical (Osipa 2007) and theoretical (Ekman and Friesen 1975) books
that are well worth reading. For now we concentrate on the fundamentals of facial expression that might be of most immediate application to
your work.

To begin with, consider that the face can be broken down into two primary regions: the upper face (including the brows and eyes) and the lower
face. When studying a character's face, you will likely note actions taking
place in these two areas. The upper facial region is most typically associated with subtle movements that infer thought process, whereas the lower
face region is much more malleable and is normally capable of larger, more
intense movements. Research has shown that the upper face in particular
is key to creating believable expressions, as delayed or missing action in
this region can affect observer perception (Sloan et al. 2010; Tinwell et al.
2011). As such, it is suggested first and foremost that a character's face be
considered in terms of upper and lower facial appearance.

From here, one of the most straightforward things to take into account
is the presence of an emotional facial expression. As we discussed earlier,
there are many emotions, including those identified on Plutchik's (1994)
wheel of emotion. When it comes to emotional facial expressions, however,
there is a tendency to focus on a core six emotional expressions that are
commonly recognized as being culturally universal. In other words, these
six expressions are believed to be embedded in human nature, as people
from all over the world use and recognize them. The six universal expressions of emotion are commonly stated to be joy, sadness, anger, fear, disgust, and surprise (see Figure 4.5).

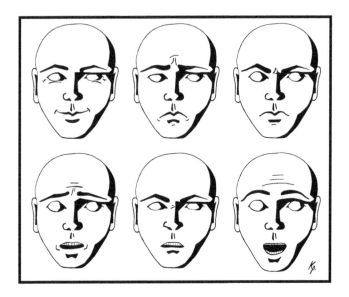

FIGURE 4.5 The six universal expressions of emotion. Top row: joy, sadness, and anger; bottom row: fear, disgust, and surprise.

Because these expressions occur in nature, typical audiences of all ages are capable of reading and understanding them. Identifying the presence of different emotional states can help the player to determine not only what the character is feeling, but also to judge whether the character's design is in keeping with the context of the game, narrative, and setting. For example, the smile of the happy expression is a feature that even very young babies will recognize and be comforted by. Anyone who has been around young babies will know that, within a few weeks of birth, they will not only recognize your smile, but also respond to it with a smile of their own. The appearance of the happy expression in itself incites a feeling of joy in the observer, and this is particularly powerful for babies and young children. As such, embedding the features of happy expressions into likeable or friendly virtual characters is a key consideration when designing for younger audiences. You will notice that most friendly characters in games that are aimed at younger audiences ought to have the ability to show happy expressions particularly well. Similarly, characters that audiences are supposed to identify as unfriendly typically make use of unmistakable negative expressions of emotion.

The key features of each of the expressions are listed in Table 4.3. You can look for evidence of these features in order to determine the type of expression being exhibited by a virtual character. For visually complex

TABLE 4.3   Universal Expressions of Emotion

Facial Expression	Description
Happiness	Raising of mouth corners, raising of cheeks
Sadness	Lowering of mouth corners, raising of midbrow
Anger	Brow lowered, lips pressed or teeth bared, eyes wide
Fear	Brow raised and knotted, eyes wide, mouth open
Disgust	Upper lip and cheeks raised, nose wrinkled
Surprise	Brow raised, eyes wide, jaw dropped

characters, expressions can be much more varied, making use of asymmetry, microexpressions, and facial wrinkles. In these cases, you can make value judgments about the exact nature and quality of an expression. For instance, you may detect different types of fear within an expression (anxiety, worry, terror), or you might observe a blending of expressions. Consider the facial regions when making these value judgments. The upper face may show one expression while the lower shows another. Or one region may be lacking in expression, impacting on the quality of its appearance. Ultimately you will have to rely on your observation and instinct to discuss a virtual character's facial expression more comprehensively, but aim to support your claims with reference to screenshots or comparisons with acted or naturalistic expressions. From expressions of unbridled joy in celebrations in *FIFA 15* {EA Canada 2014} to Vaas's expressions of menace, rage, and lunacy in *Far Cry 3* {Ubisoft Montreal 2012b}, the fidelity of expression can be vital to the quality of our experience of a virtual character.

Voice and Emotional State

While the visual performance of the body and face must take into account the use of posing and facial movement for nonverbal communication, the way that a character sounds is of great importance to expression. Setting aside the use of language to communicate vocally, the acoustic qualities of the voice can provide clues about the type of person a character is, the mood the character is in, and the emotions the character is experiencing. As such, design and analysis of virtual character performance ought to take into account the properties of the voice, drawing on what we know about the role of vocal expression in nature.

When considering vocal properties that can impact on audience identification of a character's affective state, key factors identified by Bachorowski (1999) can be useful in our analysis:

- *Fundamental frequency*: One of the most important factors is the fundamental frequency: the lowest tone of a harmonic series, and what we commonly perceive as the pitch of someone's voice. Research into vocal emotion often looks at the fundamental frequency, as this has been shown to vary with emotional state. For instance, emotions that correspond with higher levels of physiological arousal can be associated with an increased fundamental frequency (i.e., a higher pitch of voice). This can include happiness, fear, anger, and surprise. Conversely, the fundamental frequency will be reduced when a low-arousal emotion such as sadness is experienced. Fundamental frequency can also increase or reduce over time. For example, anger within a voice can be characterized by a decrease of fundamental frequency over time, while happiness can be characterized by an increase in fundamental frequency.

- *Jitter*: Vocal jitter is variation in the fundamental frequency during speech. This too can be linked to the type of emotion being experienced. High-arousal emotions such as happiness and anger can contain a higher level of jitter in the voice, whereas low-arousal emotions such as sadness or boredom tend to have a consistent frequency with no variation.

- *Amplitude and shimmer*: Vocal amplitude is the loudness of the voice, while shimmer is the degree to which the amplitude of the voice varies, with a high level of shimmer corresponding to regular fluctuation in the softness and loudness of the voice. Again, it is likely that high-arousal emotions would correspond with more shimmer, and low arousal with less shimmer. In terms of the amplitude alone, high-arousal emotions will typically correlate with a louder voice and low-arousal emotions with a softer voice.

There are other factors that can connect affective state with the sound of the voice, and further reading into voice research is strongly recommended if your study has a particular focus on character voices. However, the considerations presented here form a good foundation for any analysis of virtual character voice quality. In particular, it is important to note the degree of congruence between the vocal emotion contained within a character's speech and the emotional state implied by the narrative of gameplay. A mismatch between dialogue or context and the voice of a character can greatly undermine the aesthetic of a virtual character. Consider, for example, the infamous voice acting of *Resident Evil* {Capcom 1996}. Although the unexceptional dialogue did little to enhance the authenticity of the characters, the lack of alignment between the expected emotional states (particularly fear, anxiety, and stress) and the sound of the voice resulted in notoriously poor virtual character presentation that has become all the more apparent with age.

SUMMARY AND ACTIVITY

In this first of three chapters on the performance of characters, we focused on psychological and social principles that underpin personality, emotion, and expression. First we examined personality by looking at traits, attitudes, and political views. We learned that we can categorize a character's personality traits through use of the five-factor model, which measures neuroticism, extraversion, openness, agreeableness, and conscientiousness. While traits and personalities in general are typically considered to be fixed, we discussed how personality can also be shaped by attitudes toward a range of objects and how these attitudes may be more likely to shift over time. By extension, we looked at political views and how these can impact on the perceived personality of a character. Next, we discussed emotions. In particular, we examined how emotions form part of our cognitive processes. We saw that, in nature, an emotion can be conceived of as a biological response to a given stimulus that facilitates a course of action. In the sections that followed, we examined both nonverbal communication through the body, face, and voice expression as well as the ultimate impact of the physical expression on observer perception. We discovered that posing and discrete facial expressions can communicate affective states such as emotion, and this is found to be a vital consideration for a game character if it is to clearly communicate internal thought processes to the player.

Much of the focus of this chapter has been on theory, with limited discussion of applied examples. A lot of what has been discussed is also quite far removed from the creative fields that are commonly involved with interactive character design, which can make interpreting the language of the theories tricky at times. In order to place the theories we have discussed into a practical context, the following two exercises encourage you to take the knowledge you have gained in personality, emotion, and expression and apply it to both the creation and analysis of virtual characters.

Exercises

CHARACTER ANALYSIS

How can personality, emotion, and expression enhance the authenticity of nonplayer character performance in video games?

1. Identify a range of notable nonplayable characters in video games that are renowned or praised in terms of character complexity, emotion, or performance. Aim to select characters that have significant screen time.

2. Record gameplay footage that encompasses the performance and development of your characters, or obtain source videos of playthroughs that show the performances in full.

3. For each of your characters, aim to describe:

   a. The personality of the character as evidenced by their performance, considering traits, attitudes, and political views

   b. The key emotions that are frequently exhibited by the character

   c. The emotions performed by the character that clearly lead to an action or decision

   d. The use of expression through body language, facial expression, and vocals

   e. The potential for player action to impact on the personality and emotional performance of the characters

4. Write up short case studies for the most interesting of your examples. Aim to focus on a comparison of personality types, a comparison of emotion in relation to action, or a comparison of expressiveness.

5. Aim to discuss the case studies critically, making connections between your observations and the related literature in personality, emotion, and nonverbal communication.

CHARACTER DESIGN

How can consideration of personality, emotion, and expression inform the development of virtual character performance?

1. Take an existing visual concept for an interesting character: either one of your own or a piece of concept art for a character that you have sourced. This character should have limited biographical information. All you want is the image.

2. Using the image as a basis, begin to block out the following design considerations:

   a. What is the character's personality, in terms of the five-factor model traits?

   b. What key attitudes does the character have? Aim to develop both positive and negative attitudes, and include a range of different attitude objects.

   c. What political category does your character fit into, if any?

3. With the character personality defined, create a series of storyboards that show the character performing within gameplay. Some of these should be in response to player actions. In order to do this, consider the following:

   a. How does your character stand, walk, run, and rest? Consider the character's personality and how this might impact on the design of these core animations.

   b. How does your character perform when confronted by its attitude objects? Consider its use of body language, proxemics, and facial expressions.

   c. How does your character respond to basic interactions such as receiving a compliment, receiving an insult, being told bad news, or being attacked? Write out the emotions that your character would experience; state how this informs its thought process, and then visualize its performance.

REFERENCES

Bachorowski, J. 1999. Vocal expression and perception of emotion. *Current Directions in Psychological Science* 8 (2): 53–57.

Costa, P. T., and R. R. McCrae. 1985. *The NEO personality inventory*. Odessa, FL: Psychological Assessment Resources.

Davidson, R. J. 1994. On emotion, mood, and related affective constructs. In *The nature of emotion: Fundamental questions*. ed. P. Ekman and R. J. Davidson, 51–55. New York: Cambridge University Press.

Digman, J. M. 1990. Personality structure: Emergence of the five-factor model. *Annual Review of Psychology* 41: 417–40.

Ekman, P. 1994. Moods, emotions, and traits. In *The nature of emotion: Fundamental questions*, ed. P. Ekman and R. J. Davidson, 56–58. New York: Cambridge University Press.

Ekman P., and W. V. Friesen. 1975. *Unmasking the face*. Englewood Cliffs, NJ: Prentice Hall.

Fiske, D. W. 1949. Consistency of the factorial structures of personality ratings from different sources. *Journal of Abnormal and Social Psychology* 44 (3): 329–44.

Freeman, D. 2003. *Creating emotion in games: The art and craft of emotioneering*. Indianapolis, IN: New Riders.

Hall, E.T. 1963. A system for the notation of proxemic behaviour. *American Anthropologist* 65 (5): 1003–26.

Ibister, K. 2006. *Better game characters by design: A psychological approach*. San Francisco: Elsevier.

Knapp, M. L., and J. A. Hall. 2010. *Nonverbal communication in human interaction*. 7th ed. Boston: Wadsworth Cengage Learning.

Maio, G. R., and G. Haddock. 2009. *The psychology of attitudes and attitude change*. London: Sage.

Osipa, J. 2007. *Stop staring: Facial modeling and animation done right*. 2nd ed. Indianapolis, IN: Wiley.

Parkinson, B., P. Totterdell, R. Briner, and S. Reynolds. 1996. *Changing moods: The psychology of mood and mood regulation*. Harlow, UK: Addison-Wesley Longman.

Peabody, D., and L. R. Goldberg. 1989. Some determinants of factor structures from personality-trait descriptors. *Journal of Personality and Social Psychology* 57 (3): 552–67.

Plutchik, R. 1994. *The psychology and biology of emotion*. New York: Harper Collins.

Plutchik, R. 2002. *Emotions and life: Perspectives from psychology, biology, and evolution*. Washington, DC: APA.

Scherer, K. R. 1999. Appraisal theory. In *Handbook of cognition and emotion*, ed. T. Dalgleish and M. Power, 637–63. New York: John Wiley & Sons.

Sloan, R. J. S., B. Robinson, K. Scott-Brown, F. Moore, and M. Cook. 2010. Choreographing emotional facial expressions. *Computer Animation and Virtual Worlds* 21 (3–4): 203–13.

Tinwell, A., M. Grimshaw, A. Williams, and D. Abdel Nabi. 2011. Facial expressions of emotion and perception of the uncanny valley in virtual characters. *Computers in Human Behavior* 27 (2): 741–49.

Tupes, E. C., and R. E. Christal. 1961. *Recurrent personality factors based on trait ratings*. USAF ASD Technical Report AD 267778. http://www.dtic.mil/dtic/tr/fulltext/u2/267778.pdf.

CHAPTER 5

Context, Story, and Gameplay

N OW THAT WE HAVE ESTABLISHED a basic understanding of the psychology of personality and emotion, the aim of the current chapter
is to consider how characters can be designed to perform in creative contexts. Specifically, we look to examine a selection of narrative and game
design theories that can impact on virtual character performance.

In many ways, this is arguably one of the most important chapters on
theory in the book. The ideas that we discussed in previous chapters are
clearly of value to the design and analysis of characters: it is essential that
we know how to build visually appealing characters, that we understand
how to use and manipulate anatomy, that we aim to reflect the diversity
and depth of humanity in our designs, and that we create character profiles that incorporate our knowledge of personality and emotion. But why
are we designing these characters? We could be looking to create them for
use in isolation: to appear as illustrations or avatars that are devoid of a
setting. But it is far more likely that we are creating these characters to be
used in a given context. It is the context that really brings virtual characters to life. This is the environment in which they exist, the place where
their story is told, where they can form relationships and make enemies,
where they can act and perform, and where they can fulfill their destiny.
In essence, without a context, there is limited value to a virtual character.

There are two fundamental areas of theory that we really need to consider with regard to the context of virtual characters: narrative theory and

game design theory. These are obviously major areas of study, and there are many books that specifically discuss theories of narrative in relation to characters, theories of narrative in interactive media, and theories of video game design. We discuss some of the texts that touch on narrative theory and game design in this chapter, but further reading would be essential if you wanted to achieve a more comprehensive grasp of narrative theory for video games. The reference list at the end of the chapter offers a starting point.

In this chapter, we aim to apply some of the key ideas from narrative theory and game design to the creation and study of virtual characters. We consider the role of characters in narrative, including discussions of setting and backstory, archetypes and stereotypes, the problem of narrative point of view in video games, and the importance of thematic statements. We then discuss interactive storytelling, arguably one of the most difficult aspects of story creation for games. From there, we focus more on video game design in relation to characters, including discussions of the impact of gameplay on characterization, video game genres, and some of the main theories that can help us to scrutinize characters within a game. First, though, we consider a basic model of game design that we could use to encapsulate the entire context of any given game: the core-and-shell model.

CORE AND SHELL

One of the most-discussed topics in game studies—particularly around the turn of the twenty-first century—was the supposed debate surrounding the narratological and ludological natures of video games. Narratologists generally sought to examine games as a narrative medium, while ludologists argued that games were built upon rules and were therefore not comparable to narrative media. Although contemporary game criticism encompasses the study of both narrative and play, these early critical discussions about the video game form highlighted the complexity in reconciling storytelling and interaction. Traditional narratives are explicitly authored (or at least controlled by a narrator) with a fixed order of events and a carefully constructed development of characters. Linear narrative forms—particularly film and television—have heavily influenced video games. However, video games are also the digital descendants of traditional games: of board games, of card and dice games, of toys, and of sports. Here, the focus is on play rather than narrative. Play suggests freedom for participants to act within a given set of rules. And as many theorists have argued, the coexistence of play and narrative is not necessarily straightforward.

We do not want to be sidetracked into discussing how narrative and play interact, but we do need to acknowledge that there is an issue of balancing story and gameplay in relation to the design of virtual characters. As a means of kicking off the discussion in this chapter, we therefore consider the core-and-shell model as discussed by Mäyrä (2008). According to his model, we can conceptualize a game as being made up of two components: the core and the shell. The core contains the rules of a video game: the code that defines the physics of the world, how the world is drawn, how characters behave, what actions they can perform, what controls a player has access to, and so on. The core of a video game has its roots in traditional games and sports. On the other hand, the shell is concerned with representation rather than rules. The images, sounds, and stories contained within video games are all part of the representational shell. Characterization exists in its fullest sense within the shell. We can simulate the behaviors and actions of virtual characters within the core, but the shell is required to communicate these characters to a player. The shell might consist of basic graphics and bleeps like those used to represent Pac-Man, or it might contain explicit storytelling and visually complex characters.

In very simple terms, the core is focused on gameplay, while the shell is focused on representation, communication, and storytelling. We can consider the combination of core and shell to be the complete context in which a virtual character exists. Both the core and the shell are essential to the design of virtual characters for video games (and indeed for other forms of interactive media, too). Without the shell, we would have no means of representing virtual characters. If we didn't have a core, our characters would not be interactive.

This all seems fairly obvious, but the core-and-shell model can be very useful to us when we are seeking to achieve a holistic understanding of a virtual character's role and functionality within the context of a video game. We can seek to describe every character in a video game according to its core and shell components. We might approach our design or analysis from either direction (core then shell, shell then core), depending on the nature of the video game or the aim of the study. But ultimately, all virtual characters can be described and then discussed in terms of both the rules that govern them and the manner in which they are represented.

We can embed all of the ideas that we cover in this chapter into the core-and-shell model. Some are fundamentally about the core (such as the design of gameplay), while others are fundamentally about the shell (such as the communication of thematic statements). Others cross the boundary between core and shell. But we can take this even further by appreciating that all of the ideas that we have discussed thus far in the book can be mapped onto the core-and-shell model. Visual style, anatomical structure, expressions, animations, and representations of audience identity can all be situated in the shell. While personality, emotion, and thought processes can all be exhibited within the shell, they can also be programmed and simulated within the core, as can the capacity for players to customize virtual characters. As such, this particular model for the design and study of video games can also support our broader understanding of virtual characters. Reconciling play and storytelling is always going to be something of a challenge, but the core-and-shell model can help us to simplify a virtual character and make it easier for us to identify how its performance can be governed by both rules and representation.

With this in mind, we start our discussion of the context of virtual characters by first considering the narrative shell. In the second half of the chapter, we move on to discuss the gameplay at the core of a character's design.

NARRATIVE SHELL

Setting and Backstory

When it comes to establishing the context for a virtual character, there is a need to consider the game's setting early on in the research and development process. It would be easy to overlook this part of the process in order to proceed directly to fleshing out the specific histories, predicaments, and personalities of a character, but the setting tells us a lot about how a character should look, speak, act, and even think. Seger—who notes that "characters don't exist in a vacuum" (1990, 5)—provides extensive advice on the process of character design, including creating the setting and blocking out the backstory. Fundamentally, the setting can be said to combine three main elements:

- *Period*: What time period is the story set in? Answering this question could be fairly straightforward: you might have a specific year in mind or a more general idea of a decade or century. This could be in the past, present, or future. But identifying the period is just the first (and simplest) step. Once you know what time period a character exists in, you will need to undertake significant research to establish how this period impacts on your character's performance. Even if the character exists in the modern day, you will still need to identify how this impacts on your characters in terms of the way they speak, the events that have shaped them, and the challenges they could face. If your character exists in the future, there is a need to research anticipated developments in science and technology and to research the science-fiction genre.

- *Location*: By extension, you also need to identify and then research the specific location (or locations) within a narrative. The combination of period and location of origin can help to define the speech, mannerisms, and personal history of a character. The definition of a location has several levels: the country or state, the city or town, and the building or environment. For example, you might identify the location as being an inner-city high school in Birmingham in England, a scientific research institute in Geneva in Switzerland, or a dilapidated asylum in a remote village in Siberia. In order to understand your character deeply, you will need to carry out location research through analysis of historical and geographical texts, through viewing documentaries and news media, through visual research, by speaking to people from the location, or (if possible) through visiting the location yourself.

- *Culture and identity*: Beyond period and setting, we can consider the sociocultural context of your character(s). There is a range of cultural influences that can impact on your character design. You might start with some of the wider issues of social and cultural identity, such as those discussed in Chapter 3. National and religious contexts, for example, can interact with your chosen setting, impacting upon your character's experiences, challenges, and desires.

While the setting in terms of the period, location, and culture provides us with a broad context for a virtual character, there is of course a need to go deeper. Many writers stress a need to develop a more detailed outline as part of a character's backstory. For instance, you might consider the subcultures and associations that your character is a member of, which can in turn tell us a lot about its motivations and personality. You might also want to identify very basic profiling information, such as age, sex, and sexuality. All of these aspects of a character's identity ought to be considered in order to establish how a character will perform in a video game. One of the most commonly discussed approaches to backstory generation suggested by character creators such as Seger (1990), Kress (1998), and Tillman (2011) is to produce a detailed background for the character by addressing a wide range of questions. These questions are often broken down into three categories:

- *Physical questions*: Age, sex, ethnicity, height, weight, disabilities, and so on.

- *Social and ethical questions*: Education, occupation, hobbies, class, religious affiliations, political affiliations, moral standards, and so on.

- *Psychological and emotional questions*: Gender, sexuality, abilities, intelligence, temperament, motivations, fears, relationships, and so on.

Understanding the context of your characters in terms of setting and backstory can greatly inform the manner in which they perform. Consider the video game *Gone Home* {The Fullbright Company 2013}. Although the characters in *Gone Home* are never shown in an animated form, they are revealed in intricate detail through their notes, diaries, and material possessions. The authenticity of the characters in *Gone Home* is partly due to the deep consideration of context. The time period is very specific (June 1995), the setting is a new family home in the US state of Oregon, and the principal NPC is identified as being immersed in alternative rock culture (in particular the underground feminist rock movement known as *riot grrrl*). Extensive research into the period, setting, and culture—as well as careful consideration of personal history and experience—was essential to developing the context for this authentic character performance.

Archetypes and Stereotypes

Most books that address character writing and design identify archetypes as a means of categorizing characters. We can consider archetypes to be universal categories of character that repeatedly appear in the stories we tell. As a result of their recurring appearances in folktales, in poetry, in literature, in film and television, and in video games, audiences are familiar with archetypal characters, making it easier for them to understand who a character is and what its role within a narrative should be. In essence, they act as a simple form of character shorthand. But this simplicity can also have a less desirable consequence: the creation of stereotypes. In this section, we discuss a range of archetypes and the pitfalls of stereotyping in relation to virtual characters. As always, there is much more to this topic than we can feasibly address here. Further reading is advised for those designers and researchers interested in the application of archetypes to character writing.

The first thing we ought to note regarding archetypes is that there isn't a definitive list that we can simply refer to. Many character-design books identify what might be regarded as the most commonly applied archetypes within a given culture, society, genre, or medium. The reality is that a wide range of archetypes can be specified, and there isn't really a right, wrong, or comprehensive list to draw from. Carl Jung's work on archetypes is often cited as one of the most important sources for character writers. Jung (1959) proposed that archetypes existed within the collective unconscious: the universal pool of experiences and knowledge shared by humanity. In this tradition, Jung first identifies four major archetypes of the mind:

- *The self*: The self can be considered the complete personality of an individual, combining his or her consciousness and personal unconscious. In character design we could see this as a reflection of the audience: a character whose thoughts, attitudes, and motives we empathize with.

- *The shadow*: The shadow is the darker side of the self, symbolizing animal instincts, wildness, repressed urges, and personal flaws. In virtual character design, we could look to use the shadow archetype to frame the design of adversaries who challenge or otherwise conflict with characters that epitomize the self.

- *The anima/animus*: The anima and animus are, respectively, images of femininity from a male perspective and masculinity from a female perspective. In a very general sense, we could regard the anima as a male character developing an understanding of and connection to femininity, and the animus as a female character developing an understanding of and connection to masculinity. Combined, the anima and animus can inform the development of male–female couples: characters that develop a relationship by coming to understand each other's nature over the course of a narrative.

- *The persona*: Described as the social archetype, for Jung the persona concerned how we present ourselves in different situations using different *social masks*. While Jung focused on the psychological implications of personas that are fixed, flexible, or new, in character design we can align the persona with the playing of a social role: for instance, a character who is defined by its occupation or status.

While Jung identifies these four major archetypes, he describes many more archetypes that exist within the collective unconscious. These other archetypes tend to be the ones discussed most frequently in relation to narrative design. For instance, Joseph Campbell (1949) focused on archetypal heroes and discussed other archetypes that heroes encounter on their journey. It is within this wider range of common archetypes inspired by Jung and Campbell that we might encounter more familiar virtual character types:

- *The hero*: The hero is the champion who goes on a quest or journey. We can have variations on the hero, with the main variants being the ideal hero (the typical hero of fantasy literature) and the antihero (a hero with flaws, more commonly used in realistic fiction). Most PCs in video games tend to fall within a hero archetype.

- *The wise old man/woman*: Sometimes called the *mentor*, the wise old man or woman is the character that trains or guides the hero. Mentors are fairly common in video games, as they can provide a narrative context for tutorials.

- *The herald*: The herald is the character that initiates the quest, or the *call to adventure*, by saying or doing something that forces the hero to act.

- *The maiden*: The maiden is typically presented as a feminine character that symbolizes innocence and desire but is often dependent on others. Variations include archetypal princesses and damsels in distress. This is another example of a common but often-problematic archetype in games, as we saw in Chapter 3.

- *The trickster*: The trickster is a deceptive character that relishes breaking the rules and causing chaos for other characters. That doesn't necessarily mean that it has to act as a negative force: Tricksters can be allies of the hero.

- *The fool*: The fool is typically an optimistic, lucky, and innocent character whose attitudes and behaviors counter the hero's more level-headed or cautious approach. The fool often appears confused or causes unintentional chaos.

- *The mother*: The mother is a nurturing, accommodating, and protective female archetype.

- *The father*: The father is a stern, authoritative, and powerful masculine archetype.

- *The devil figure*: The devil figure is a villain who tempts the hero with power, knowledge, or wealth. The hero must be able to overcome the temptation in order to succeed in the quest. A devil figure that can be saved might be called a *redeemable devil*.

This is just a small selection of archetypes, and many more have been discussed in the literature. Jung also suggests that archetypes can be mixed or become overlapped. For instance, there is no reason why the hero cannot be a maiden or a trickster, or the mentor also a fool or mother/father figure. When further archetype lists are considered, it becomes clear that it is necessary to treat archetypes as a means of framing a character's design rather than defining it completely. For instance, Phillips and Huntley (2004) suggest a list of eight narrative archetypes that comprise two categories: driver characters and passenger characters. Within their structure, these archetypes are further broken down into four pairs. The driver characters are:

- *Protagonist*: The protagonist is the character that audiences will most closely identify with, who is most affected by the antagonist, and who is primarily responsible for driving the plot. We might expect that the protagonist would overlap with the self, while hero archetypes are also typically protagonists. But the protagonist could be framed by any of the archetypes we have identified thus far.

- *Antagonist*: The antagonist is the opposing force to the protagonist, providing the main obstacles that block the protagonist's journey. Again, we might see the shadow archetype as a typical antagonist (reflecting the darker nature of the protagonist) or for the main antagonist to be a devil figure. But looking to other archetypes can form more complex and interesting antagonists.

- *Guardian*: The guardian is the character that provides guidance to and protects the protagonist, similar to the description of the wise old man/woman or the mentor.

- *Contagonist*: The contagonist is an interesting archetype that acts as an opposite to the guardian. The contagonist misleads the protagonist and provides obstacles, but is not necessarily acting against the protagonist, and might even be on the protagonist's side. A typical contagonist might be a trickster or a shadow.

The passenger characters do not drive the story, and instead provide wider context:

- *Sidekick*: The sidekick is a loyal and supportive friend who provides the protagonist with confidence. The sidekick typically has differences or weaknesses that help to highlight the qualities and development of the protagonist. The sidekick is similar to other archetypes often mentioned in the literature, such as the fool, the companion, or the loyal retainer. Many games have made use of sidekicks to support the PC in gameplay.

- *Skeptic*: The opposite archetype to the sidekick, the skeptic is more pessimistic about the protagonist's chances. The sidekick and skeptic make for a useful duo of companions to the protagonist, with one making the case for hope and the other foreshadowing the potential for failure. In the *Assassin's Creed* series, the companions Rebecca Crane and Shaun Hastings serve as a sidekick-skeptic duo.

- *Reason*: The archetype of reason defines characters that are cool, levelheaded, and rational. They are organized and logical, and they oppose the emotion archetype.

- *Emotion*: Finally, the emotion archetype defines a character that is uncontrolled, passionate, quick to anger, but also more likely to empathize with others. The reason-emotion duo of characters is often used to reflect the practical and personal repercussions of the protagonist's decisions.

By now it should be clear that archetypes can be useful as a means of understanding who a character is and how the character fits into the game story. However, it should also be apparent that they can be incredibly limiting if they are treated as a one-size-fits-all solution. Archetypes are essentially just models for character roles and behaviors. In reality, most virtual characters ought to be more complex and should not be wholly defined by a single archetype description.

Perhaps the greatest pitfall of archetype application in character design is the risk of generating stereotypes. This is particularly prevalent when demographics are considered. While they can help us to design and balance a cast of characters in a way that will appeal to audience familiarity, they can also unwittingly lead to the creation of one-dimensional stereotypes of gender, age, sexuality, ethnicity, nationality, and religion.

Of all the virtual character stereotypes, the depiction of gender has arguably been the most problematic. This in part can be attributed to the young male bias of the early games market and the subsequent targeting of this market through several console generations. However, the concept of the young male gamer is somewhat of a stereotype in itself, as the games market is much more complex today. In consequence, gamers have demonstrated an increasing awareness of poor or underdeveloped female representation in games, as we discussed in Chapter 3. Archetypes have the potential to produce stereotypical female characters, for example, through the application of the damsel in distress archetype to the point where we repeatedly see stereotypical princesses deployed within game stories. Alternatively, archetypal villainesses can lead to stereotypical female antagonists that overpower the male hero through sexuality. One of the games we identified in Chapter 3 on representation, *Far Cry 3*, makes use of both of these female archetypes: the damsel in distress being Liza Snow and the sexual villainess being Citra Talugmai. If not handled thoughtfully or critically, these archetypes can easily turn into flat stereotypes.

In considering archetypes, it is therefore important that we acknowledge that they are a means of framing characters in terms of their narrative roles and behaviors, and that we should be cautious in attempting to use them as blunt instruments. The context of the game cannot be ignored when considering archetypes. Some video games that focus on an archetypal hero's journey—those that have a strong emphasis on fantasy or that are presented in a cartoon style for younger audiences—can make excellent use of archetypes in their simplest form. But an increasing number of video games seek to present more complex narratives with difficult or challenging themes, historical settings, and realistic characters. Here, unintentional stereotyping can undermine the authenticity of characters and generate regressive representations of identity. More fundamentally, stereotypical heroes and villains can also lead to dull and uninteresting video game narratives.

Interactive Plot

It is clear that setting, backstory, and archetypes are all important to the definition of a character within a narrative. However, as most writers will identify, backstories and characteristics alone do not make for interesting or compelling characters. It is what characters *do* that makes them interesting. This is why the relationship between character and plot is often stressed in the literature on narrative theory. Archetypes really underline this point. They define how a character should behave and the role a character should play within a narrative arc. There are many excellent texts on plot and character, including those in the reference list of this chapter. For now, we need only focus on how plot is affected by the inherent interactivity of video games and, subsequently, what impact this can have on virtual character design.

Typically, we can simplify interactive plot structure into three types. Meadows (2002) identifies these types as follows:

- *Nodal plot*: A linear plot structure that has one beginning, one narrative path, and typically one ending (although multiple endings could be available). The nodal structure offers the most control over the telling of the narrative. When applied in video games, the nodal plot can support a carefully crafted dramatic arc and explicit character development through a fixed series of events. Players will typically have agency within sections of gameplay, but will have limited agency in terms of changing the direction of the story. Many single-player first-person shooters make use of nodal plot structures, sometimes with a limited ability to choose a slightly different path or access an alternative ending.

- *Modulated plot*: Modulated plot structures typically have one start point that can lead to one or a series of endings, but with much more flexibility in terms of path selection. Players might be able to divert from the main narrative path and explore other stories, to jump between narrative paths by making key decisions, and to control how their character(s) behave and evolve. Many role-playing games make use of modulated plot structures.

- *Open plot*: Unlike nodal and modulated plot structures, open plot structures are less concerned about start or end points than they are with the journey itself. Indeed, there might not even be an ending. Players will typically be granted much greater control to determine how a story is told, with designers seeking to build narrative devices that can facilitate open storytelling rather than implementing an explicit narrative. Many massively multiplayer online games make use of open plot structures.

These three plot structures (visualized in Figure 5.1) are clearly not fixed options that designers are forced to choose from. They are best considered as archetypal interactive structures. An open plot structure can embed nodal plots, for example, a quest series within an open-world video game. The narrative of a video game might also be broken into different

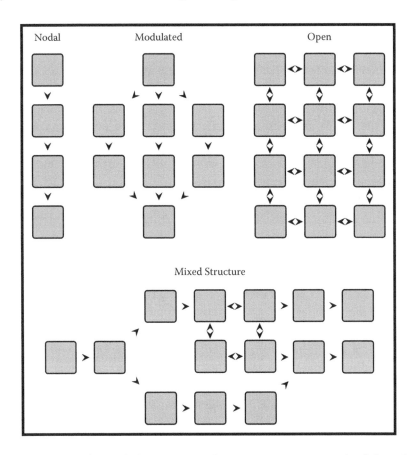

FIGURE 5.1 Archetypal plot structures for interactive narratives (nodal, modulated, and open) along with a mixed structure that might be more representative of a video game's narrative.

sections that are nodal, modulated, and open. A hypothetical example of this is also shown in Figure 5.1.

With regard to virtual character design, consideration of the three structures can help us to establish to what extent a character's story is fixed by the designer or open for manipulation by the player. As designers, we can look to map out any given character's story according to the key events that it can experience. A theoretical ideal would be the open plot structure, granting the player limitless agency to act and transform the narrative. This would lead to an infinite number of plots that could emerge from player action. Players would therefore experience a different plot every time they accessed the game. But in reality, there are not an infinite number of good or effective plots. Not every sequence of events is a compelling story. Most of the events that occur in the real world, in our daily lives, do not make for interesting narratives. As such, some form of system for monitoring events and generating plausible new directions that a player can take—a drama management system—would be needed. Open plot structures of this kind are explored in theory by Murray (1997) in her seminal book *Hamlet on the Holodeck*, but in practice most video games that allow for open-world interaction tend to downplay complex and deep narratives in favor of environmental exploration, role-playing, and gameplay. This is the case in many MMORPGs, such as the *Everquest* series of games. These games feature some rudimentary plots that can be accessed by players via quest lines, but in general players spend most of their time developing their characters, exploring worlds, and interacting with other players. When designing virtual characters for open-world plots, it therefore becomes important to consider the degree to which players can customize and develop their characters, that is, how they can use their characters to express themselves and tell their own stories.

Many more games focus on modulated plot structures as a means of presenting an interactive series of narrative events. Games such as the *Grand Theft Auto* series, for instance, allow for some open-world exploration and grant the player the ability to access events in different orders (or indeed to ignore events altogether) before culminating in one or a limited number of conclusions. In these games, PCs tend to accommodate some customization of appearance and scope for forming a limited identity, but this is balanced against the need for PCs to be more fully formed with distinctive personalities, backstories, and dialogue. The majority of single-player games still tend to favor a nodal structure. But even when a very tightly controlled nodal structure is used, it is still important to provide some illusion of meaningful player choice. In *Wolfenstein: The New Order* {MachineGames 2014}, for instance, the player takes on the role of William Blazkowicz, an American war veteran fighting against the Nazis in an alternative 1960s. Early on in the video game, the player is forced to choose which one of two colleagues will be saved, condemning the other to death. Blazkowicz clearly agonizes over this, and the brutal murder that follows makes the choice feel all the more pivotal to the narrative. And yet the choice is a false one. Although the colleague who is saved will reappear later in the video game, the choice does not set in motion an alternative set of events. The narrative events are primarily the same either way, with the only real difference being a minor gameplay modification. Nevertheless, the choice presented to the player helps to provide a sense of agency in the storyworld (even if that agency is actually limited) without sacrificing the quality of character development that is best achieved by a nodal structure.

Narrative Mode

One of the aspects of narrative theory that strongly overlaps with the design of virtual character performance is the use of narrative mode. The narrative mode essentially defines how the plot is narrated through consideration of three main components:

- *Narrative point of view*: The narrative point of view identifies the perspective from which the story is being told. There are three points of view that can be utilized: first person (I, we), second person (you), and third person (he, she, they).

- *Narrative voice*: The narrative voice is the manner in which a story is told. For instance, third-person voices can be subjective (in that the character's thoughts are revealed, common in many novels), objective (in that events are described without revealing characters' thoughts, common in many films), and omniscient (in that the narrator has oversight of many events and characters, common in narratives that have many characters). Omniscient voice can be subjective or objective.

- *Narrative time*: Narrative time concerns whether a narrative is told in the past, present, or future tense. Future tense is uncommon in most narrative forms.

Studies of narrative and characters within novels, comics, film, and television can reveal the strengths and weaknesses of specific narrative methods in different media. In our current focus on video games and interactive media, it is important that we try to understand narrative mode as applied to the design and performance of virtual characters.

First, we can obviously identify overlap between narrative point of view and camera point of view in video games. Most video games involving characters are typically presented in either first-person view (seeing through the eyes of a character, as in the *Half-Life* or *Call of Duty* series) or in third-person view (observing the character directly, as in the *Tomb Raider* or *Assassin's Creed* series). Many games also make use of mixed perspective, allowing the player to switch point of view (as in *The Elder Scrolls* {Bethesda Game Studios 2002, 2006, 2011} or *ARMA* games {Bohemia Interactive 2006}) or pulling out of a first-person view for cutscenes (as in the *Halo* series {Bungie 2001} or in *Wolfenstein: The New Order* {MachineGames 2014}). In all of these instances, the player takes on the role of a particular character, and so arguably the narrative point of view would be first person (the player *is* the protagonist). But this assumption can make our design and analysis of virtual characters quite problematic.

In video games, it is perhaps most appropriate to equate narrative point of view (and by extension, narrative voice) with the agency of the player, rather than simply the type of camera used. This can seem a little odd at first, but consider that we are asking the player to experience the narrative either from his own perspective (I am running; I am jumping; I am interacting with this NPC) or from an external perspective (he is running; she is jumping; they are interacting with this NPC). In the former, we might assume much more player control when it comes to acting in the world. If a PC begins to demonstrate some autonomy—such as speaking or making decisions that are predetermined and beyond the control of the player—then player unification with the character breaks down. The alternative to this unification of player and character is not strictly a third-person narrative point of view. While films and novels tend not to make use of second-person narrative point of view, the video game medium is actually much better disposed to this unusual perspective.

Many video games are built upon a narrative point of view that is somewhat balanced between player-as-actor and player-as-spectator. In some instances, the player is dictating what is happening with the character that she is controlling, similar to how we might control a puppet (you jump; you run; you enter this door). This happens during typical gameplay. In other instances, the writer has much more control over the characters in terms of the way they act, the things they say, and the decisions they make. Here, the player is more of an observer of the action, and thus we can equate this with a third-person point of view (he says this; she walks down that corridor; they make this decision).

In this sense, the camera point of view cannot be taken to mean the same thing as the narrative point of view. A video game that is presented entirely from a first-person camera does not necessarily equate to a first-person narrative point of view. The narrative can still be presented to the players from a third-person narrative point of view: in effect, they observe the action through the eyes of a character, but their experience is not the same as reading a novel written from a first-person narrative point of view. Characters that players control in first-person camera view can act autonomously, saying or doing things that the player does not command them to do. An example is the PC Booker DeWitt in *BioShock Infinite* {Irrational Games 2013}. This creates a distance between the character and the player, and our experience of Booker is closer to a third-person narrative point of view when he acts of his own accord (Booker is saying this; Booker is doing that). Extending this, we can see that narrative voice also plays an important role when it comes to establishing the relationship between the player and the PC. In virtual character design, subjective voice is commonly used to help players by allowing them to hear the thoughts of the character that they control. These thoughts can provide clues to help the player solve a puzzle or tips on how to tackle an obstacle. Alternatively, they might simply help to provide emotional context. However, a consequence of the use of subjective voice is a distancing between the player and the character. For players to achieve a full sense of unification with a character, they need to feel a sense of control over not only their actions, but also their thoughts.

While the use of narrative mode in video games is a tricky topic to cover here, we can note a couple of important points that impact on virtual character design and analysis before we move on to the next section. First, the presence of a narrator within interactive media is itself quite a difficult concept to grasp. The negotiation between play and narrative, as we identified in the introduction to this chapter, means that our understanding of narrative for linear media forms cannot be simply transferred and applied to virtual characters and interactive narratives. We need a unique take on narrative theory for video games and, as such, our understanding of how narrative point of view works in video games ought to be different from literature or film. The second thing to note is the use of narrative time in all of the examples we have identified. While novels and films are relatively free to play with tense, video games—if they are to maintain player agency within a narrative—are essentially locked into the present tense (I am doing this; you are jumping; she is talking to him, etc.). Cutscenes can allow for transportation into the past or future: to show virtual characters prior to or after the narrative time the player occupies. But as soon as the player is provided agency to control a character in the past or future, he needs to time travel. The past or future becomes a new "present" for the player, because gameplay can only ever occur in the present tense. It is important not to confuse time period (discussed earlier in the chapter) with player time: even if a game allows for character control in multiple time periods, the player always controls characters in the present tense.

As we show in Section III, narrative mode can have a clear impact on how we perceive and control characters. The selection of either first-person or mixed second–third-person narrative points of view can lead to subtly different experiences with virtual characters. The former can be considered a form of role embodiment—the player becomes the character—while the latter can be considered a form of role fulfillment—the player gets to control a character that also has some autonomy of its own. Meanwhile, the decision to make use of multiple PCs can be related to use of a third-person omniscient voice and support the use of co-protagonists in virtual character design.

Thematic Statements

Theme is often discussed as one of the major components of a narrative. Generally, we tend to talk about theme as if it were something that can be described in one word. For instance, the core theme for a narrative might be courage, honor, love, friendship, loyalty, betrayal, deception, honesty, or any of a number of ideas that provide the basis for an interesting human story. However, the theme of a narrative is typically something that cannot be conveyed in just one word. A core theme could be *love*, which would provide us with expectations of how characters will behave and how relationships between characters will form, but this basic theme is quite limited in scope and not particularly remarkable. It is more akin to a genre of narrative. But if this theme is extended, we can have a much clearer understanding of how and why characters act in a particular way. A theme of "love endures" suggests that characters will demonstrate a strong, unbreakable bond through adversity: that some form of antagonist will challenge the love between characters, but that the antagonist will be defeated by love. Alternatively, "love is fleeting" would indicate a different set of character actions and behaviors, whereby characters experience short-term love before coming to a realization or otherwise losing each other. "Love fades" is similar, except that this theme could be embodied by characters who experience strong love for each other but who see the nature of their relationship change over many years. Ultimately, a theme expressed in two or more words allows for a more precise interpretation of the moral of the narrative.

However, while these extended descriptions of themes provide more interest, they still do little to communicate a specific meaning or moral. To achieve more clarity we should look to identify or develop a thematic statement. This takes the grand concept of the core theme and makes it much more explicit. Robert McKee offers us a means of discussing the thematic statement, using what he calls the *controlling idea*:

> A controlling idea may be expressed in a single sentence describing how and why life undergoes change from one condition of existence at the beginning to another at the end (McKee 1997, 115).

McKee is keen to stress that the notion of a one-word theme is not useful. Indeed, he goes further than merely extending this into a two-word thematic statement such as "love endures" or "love fades." McKee's controlling idea is based on the notion that a theme ought to comprise two key components: a value and a cause. The value is effectively the central notion, positive or negative, that is conveyed by the narrative. Here, "love fades" can be considered the value, but without a cause it is not yet a thematic statement. The cause is the reason why the characters have come to experience the value. To progress "love fades" to a full thematic statement, it is necessary to explain why love fades. So, "love fades when lovers put career before family" is a thematic statement, as is "love fades when lovers want different things." These thematic statements provide a much more comprehensive explanation for the actions of characters within a narrative and help us to understand and critique how they behave and perform.

When it comes to analyzing a virtual character in relation to the narrative of a game, consideration of the thematic statement has become increasingly important. If we look to the history of games, we can identify many examples of character backstories, archetypes, dynamic plot structures, and different narrative points of view. But as games have matured, the desire of game designers (and consumers) to use the medium to convey more complex ideas has grown. Many video games embed thematic statements into their narrative design. Subsequently, the actions that virtual characters take and the consequences they face become much more meaningful and emotional for players. *The Last of Us* {Naughty Dog 2013}—a game we revisit in Chapter 8—is a prime example of a game that explores many complex themes that engage audiences on different levels. On the one hand, as a game centered on the collapse of society and the struggle for survival in a violent, anarchistic world, we could suggest that its core thematic statement is: "In order to survive, we must become the monster." Playing as Joel (the main PC), the player carries out many violent and brutal acts. And yet Joel is framed as a regular guy who simply wants to be left alone to survive. On a deeper and more personal level, we can suggest a thematic statement of: "To overcome the grief of personal loss, new meaning to life must be discovered." This is something we explore in more detail in Chapter 8, when we discuss the dependency between *The Last of Us* characters Joel and Ellie.

GAMEPLAY CORE

Video Game Genres

As we progress through the shell toward the core of game design, it would be useful to consider how video game genres can inform the design of virtual characters. We have already mentioned several game genres throughout the book, and it is likely that many readers will already be familiar with genres such as action, adventure, and RPG. Nevertheless, genres tell us a lot about the fundamental design of a game and, by extension, of the characters that might appear in a game. As such, it is important that we spend some time discussing the common game genres, and that we consider how these genres might impact upon virtual character gameplay.

As with any taxonomy of design, it is perhaps best to look to genres as being descriptive rather than prescriptive. Video game genres tell us something about the types of gameplay and game objects that will be involved in a game: the common mechanics and play styles. In practice, however, video games tend not to be so easily allocated to a single genre. Since the turn of the millennium, we have seen a gradual bleeding of genre boundaries, the combination of genres, and even the emergence of new genres and subgenres.

There are many common genres of video game, some with long histories that predate digital games and others that are relatively new and unique to modern video gaming. Rollings and Adams (2003) provide an excellent overview of the standard video game genres. Not all genres impact on character design in a meaningful way: indeed, some genres downplay the importance of characters (racing simulations, for example). In order to maintain our focus on virtual character design within the context of play, the following list identifies some of the overarching genres that are most likely to tell us something about the roles of characters:

- *Action*: Action games are fundamentally "twitch" based, in that players are required to respond quickly using skill-based actions. Actions tend to be simpler than in other genres due to the emphasis on response and skill. Common forms of action gameplay are shooting, running, and jumping. These forms of gameplay might even underpin subgenres of the action game, such as first-person shooters (FPS), space shooters, fighting games, and platform games. Typically, characters in action games are physically empowered or skilled (strong, fast, agile, etc.).

- *Adventure*: Adventure games, in their traditional sense, do not contain simulation or competitive gameplay, and instead place a strong emphasis on the narrative. In the '80s and '90s, graphical adventures such as *The Secret of Monkey Island* {LucasFilm Games 1990} were very popular. These games involved interaction with characters in order to progress the story, and they featured a lot of dialogue compared to other genres. Today, the adventure genre is more often seen integrated into other genres, particularly action and RPG genres. Dialogue choices and scene exploration are key features of the genre, both of which concern storytelling (through characterization or the environment). Exploration games such as *Gone Home* {The Fullbright Company 2013} and *Proteus* {Key 2013} are among the purest contemporary examples of the adventure genre.

- *Role-playing game (RPG)*: RPGs emphasize configurable characters (players can pick from different types of preset character and/or customize the skill sets and attributes of characters) and strong narratives. RPGs often provide a lot of scope for character customization, and characters typically develop skills and collect more advanced items as they progress through the game. Additionally, RPGs tend to feature large casts of characters that the player can interact with. Elements of RPG design are common within many modern action and adventure games, particularly character design features such as customization and skill development.

- *Strategy*: Strategy games involve complex and difficult choices, and as such tend to rely less on reactive play. Some strategy games might even make use of turn-based play. Strategy games typically emphasize themes of exploration, trade, and conquest. Although many archetypal strategy games focus on a society or empire with limited focus on individual characters, the strategy genre requires a high degree of balance between large numbers of character types. The abilities, powers, and attributes of characters must be balanced, because their design underpins the difficult decisions that players are required to make in gameplay (i.e., players are often tasked with deciding which characters to use in a given context).

- *Simulation*: Simulation games focus on the management and maintenance of a process. They are similar to strategy games in that complex and informed decisions need to be made, but a greater emphasis is placed on management of resources and construction. Also like strategy games, simulations tend to lack an explicit focus on characters, but *The Sims 4* {EA Maxis 2014} is a prime example of a heavily character-based simulation game. We discuss the simulation of characters in *The Sims* in Chapter 9.

- *Sports*: Sports games are essentially a specific form of simulation, in that the vast majority of sports games are simulations of real-world sports (although fictional sports games are also fairly common). Depending on the sport, there is likely to be a mixture of action and strategy gameplay. In terms of characters in sports games, there is a need for a degree of authenticity not only in presentation, but also in the experience of play, given that the idea behind sports characters is that they are a simulation of real athletes. This is discussed in terms of flow in Chapter 7.

- *Massively multiplayer*: Although the MMO is not so much of a genre in its own right (as massively multiplayer games still need to be defined through another genre such as RPG or first-person shooter), it is important to note the impact that online play has on the design and performance of virtual characters. MMOs—due to the sheer number of players involved—need to allow for open narratives. Additionally, they need to provide a level playing field: In a single-player game, the player can be the all-powerful hero, but this is not a practical option in an MMO. It is also worth noting that the boundaries between single-player and online multiplayer games have started to blur, with opportunities for players of "single-player games" to interact online. *Journey* {thatgamecompany 2012} is a remarkable example of online interaction between virtual characters in a video game that at times feels much more like a single-player experience.

This is by no means an exhaustive list, and as we have identified, it is far more common for today's video games to mix and match genres, invent and subvert genres, or even defy categorization. But when it comes to planning, balancing, or interpreting gameplay types in relation to virtual characters, it is important to understand the major genres of games and how these genres impact on the style of play.

Gameplay Design

Having briefly considered video game genres and the impact on virtual character design, we now shift our focus toward how characters are affected by the design of gameplay. Many authors have published on the practice and theory of game design. Some of the most notable books on the design of gameplay include Salen and Zimmerman's seminal text *Rules of Play* (2004), Schell's *The Art of Game Design: A Book of Lenses* (2008), and Fullerton's *Game Design Workshop* (2008). Readers who wish to learn more about the theories and concepts that underpin rules, play, and interaction design will find these books to be an excellent starting point.

The game designer Sid Meier famously stated that games could be conceived as a "series of interesting decisions," a suggestion that ultimately led to much discussion about what gameplay actually is. But this broad premise does offer us two important pointers: that gameplay requires players to make decisions (or else all notion of play is lost) and that these decisions really ought to be "interesting." That may sound vague, but by "interesting" Meier simply means that the player ought to have a reason to make a decision and that the consequence of making a decision should be a notable impact on the game. This could be a major decision that ultimately impacts on the path a player will take for the rest of the game, or a minor decision that only has a short-term effect. Either way, the game is responsive to the decisions that the player can make.

When it comes to virtual characters, these gameplay decisions can impact on both the shell and the core of the character design. First, let's consider how the shell might be affected. Take a common fight-or-flight decision, for example. If the player chooses to fight, he might risk injury (which subsequently leaves a permanent scar on the character) but might also end up saving another character that will continue to participate in the narrative. Running away might maintain the PC's appearance but lead to the sacrifice of another character that can no longer feature in the story. The interesting decision to run or to fight can therefore impact on both the visual presentation of the character and on the narrative. With regard to player decisions impacting on the game core, one of the most common decisions that will manipulate gameplay for a character involves character progression and allocation of skills. For instance, a player decision to focus on building up defensive skill points might make a character more heavily armored and better equipped to dodge enemy attacks, while a decision to focus on offensive skill points might make it more lethal with weapons but more likely to take damage in a fight.

Fable is an excellent example of a video game series that relates player decisions to the performance of a virtual character. In the *Fable* games, the player takes control of a somewhat anonymous hero. Over the course of the game, the player is forced to make a series of moral and ethical decisions that will see her PC evolve to reflect those decisions. Both the shell and core are affected by these decisions: The PC is given an appropriate appearance to match her choices, while the manner in which NPCs will interact with the PC will depend on their actions in the game world.

While conceptualizing gameplay as a series of meaningful decisions provides us with a basic foundation for discussing a virtual character's design in relation to player interaction, a more detailed model of gameplay design would be useful. One approach suggested by Kremer (2009) in his book on level design is to consider gameplay in terms of design goals and level hierarchies. Kremer suggests that designers ought to have goals that they want to achieve when designing a game and, specifically, when designing game levels. He suggests goals such as empowering the player, teaching the player, maintaining suspension of disbelief, providing a sense of achievement, rewarding the player for exploration, and providing fun gameplay. These are fairly broad goals, but they can frame a gameplay design hierarchy:

- *Goal*: Identify the goal for the level: What do you want the player to experience?

- *Scenarios*: Identify the specific types of gameplay scenarios that can exist within the game and that will help to satisfy the stated goals. For example, if the goal is to provide a sense of empowerment, then scenarios that allow the player to tackle and defeat a wave of enemies could be appropriate.

- *Moments*: Scenarios can then be broken down into scripted moments that make the scenarios more exciting, dynamic, and rewarding. For example, if the scenario is to tackle a wave of enemies, then this might comprise moments such as enemies bursting through the floor unexpectedly, enemies grabbing and holding down the PC, or enemies using the environment against the player.

- *Actions*: Finally, we have the specific actions that the player can perform in order to meet the challenge presented in gameplay moments. In the given example, this might involve mechanics such as punching, kicking, throwing objects, using weapons, and so on.

Not all games involve explicit challenges (as we saw in the previous section), but this hierarchy can be useful for framing how gameplay impacts on the design of a virtual character. Fundamentally, we can consider what direct actions a character can perform in relation to the moments and scenarios that exist within a game, regardless of whether the game is a standard first-person shooter or an abstract exploration game. The problem that often arises is a disconnect between gameplay design and the wider context of the game. On the one hand, there might be no logical relationship between the narrative the characters are participating in and the gameplay that is presented, which can make it very difficult to empathize with the characters. Or perhaps more problematically, we might find that gameplay contradicts the wider narrative: for example, gameplay that is excessively violent might be at odds with the story, genre, themes, or character personalities. Violence in gameplay is a common issue in gameplay design, and even when context is provided within the narrative—as in games such as *Far Cry 3*, *The Last of Us*, and *BioShock Infinite*—the resultant death toll can still seem implausible and excessive.

An ideal for gameplay design in relation to virtual characters could be considered to be "meaningful play." Salen and Zimmerman (2004) discuss that, on the one level, meaningful play concerns cause and effect: when a particular action is performed, there ought to be a logical and consistent effect. But they also argue that, for meaningful play to exist, gameplay actions (and the outcomes of actions) should be integrated into the wider context of the video game. The gameplay should relate to the characters in terms not only of their abilities, their identity, and their personality types, but also to the narrative themes of the game. This is arguably one of the most difficult challenges in game design and the design of virtual characters, and the prevalence of gameplay mechanics that are combative in nature can be directly linked to the prevalence of games that explore themes of war, conflict, and survival (and the shortage of games that explore comedic or romantic themes).

Mechanics, Dynamics, and Aesthetics

As we look to draw this chapter to a close, we consider two final concepts that have proven useful to the design of gameplay experiences. The first of these—the MDA framework—extends the ideas behind Kremer's (2009) hierarchy into a more formal model of game design. Proposed by Hunicke, LeBlanc, and Zubek (2004), the MDA framework provides us with a concise yet thorough methodology for constructing or deconstructing a game. The three core components of the MDA framework are identified as mechanics, dynamics, and aesthetics:

- *Mechanics*: The mechanics are the fundamental components of the game in terms of data, rules, and algorithms.

- *Dynamics*: The dynamics are the behaviors that emerge when mechanics and player actions interact at runtime.

- *Aesthetics*: In the MDA framework, the aesthetics are considered to be the emotional reactions of players as they encounter dynamics.

Described as a formal approach for understanding games, the MDA framework is based on the premise that all video games are purposefully designed artifacts that are consumed by audiences, and that this therefore means that two main stakeholders are involved: the designer and the player. We can consider the mechanics, dynamics, and aesthetics to be categories that exist on a continuum. At one end of the continuum sits the designer, whose primary concern is the mechanics. At the other end of the continuum is the player, whose experiences of the game are the aesthetics. In other words, the designer is fundamentally concerned with creating game mechanics, extending these into game systems (or dynamics), and ultimately achieving a particular aesthetic response in the player, whereas the player's first contact with the game is his aesthetic reaction to gameplay, which is invoked by encounters with video game dynamics, the root of which are the core mechanics. Hunicke, LeBlanc, and Zubek suggest that a good approach for either design or research is to first consider the player's perspective in terms of the desired aesthetics, and then work backwards to define the dynamics then mechanics.

To achieve this, a taxonomy of eight aesthetic categories is defined. It is stressed that this list is not exhaustive, but it does cover much of what a player is likely to experience when engaged by a video game:

1. Sensation (games as sense-pleasure)

2. Fantasy (games as make-believe)

3. Narrative (games as drama)

4. Challenge (games as an obstacle course)

5. Fellowship (games as a social framework)

6. Discovery (games as uncharted territory)

7. Expression (games as self-discovery)

8. Submission (games as pastime)

We can first consider the aesthetic qualities that we want a video game to achieve. Then we can surmise what dynamics might support this and, in turn, identify what mechanics would be required to support these dynamics. For example, a video game that is intended to induce an aesthetic such as *challenge* could comprise dynamics such as twitch gameplay, accurate movement and timing, and competition against the clock and other players. In turn, we might expect mechanics such as shooting, setting traps, character maneuvering, and character movement to support these types of dynamics. Ultimately, the MDA framework suggests that the particular nature of the mechanics and the dynamics they support should be determined by consideration of the desired aesthetics to be experienced by a target audience.

The MDA framework applies to game design holistically, but we can target it more specifically at the design and analysis of virtual characters.

All characters in video games will, to some extent, serve intended aesthetic qualities as identified by the MDA framework. PCs and primary characters are likely to have a wider range of desired aesthetics, but even background characters should support at least one aesthetic purpose. Starting at the most basic level, then, consider that background characters will typically support qualities such as fantasy (in that their audiovisual design helps to flesh out a deep fantasy world), narrative (in that they provide a means of contextualizing the world through interactions such as conversation, trading, or issuing quests), or challenge (in that the player interaction with the characters centers on the need to defeat them through use of skill or intellect). We might easily dismiss these minor, nonplayable characters as being of limited importance, but the MDA framework reminds us that all game elements (including all characters) can impact on a player's emotional engagement.

When we then extend our application of the MDA framework into major characters—including key protagonists, antagonists, and playable characters—it becomes clear that we should anticipate a greater range and depth of supported aesthetic qualities. A PC in a massively multiplayer online game, for example, could support any or all of the listed aesthetic qualities with varying degrees of importance. Is sensation the key quality, so that the character's primary role is to act as a virtual object of beauty? Perhaps fantasy and expression are more important, in that the character should represent fantastical ideas and worlds while also allowing for a high degree of customization and evolution? Given the multiplayer emphasis of the game design, fellowship is undoubtedly an important aesthetic, as the character will interact with, cooperate with, and support other player avatars in the game world. But narrative, challenge, discovery, and submission can all be equally important qualities for this character type. By applying the MDA framework, we can seek to design or deconstruct any virtual character by first determining the range and importance of aesthetic qualities, then tracing these back to the core mechanics that will ultimately determine whether those aesthetics are realized.

Flow

Lastly, we consider the concept of flow and how this relates to both game design and the subsequent design of virtual characters. Flow, as defined by Csíkszentmihályi (1990), is a state of complete immersion in a given activity. In its purest form, a person experiencing flow would be totally focused on the task at hand, lose track of time, and even fail to notice other stimuli.

Although the theory of flow is fundamentally about human psychology, it has been readily applied to discussion of individual-performance sports, education, and employment. Game designers have also taken it on board: most notably thatgamecompany (TGC) founder Jenova Chen (2007). Working from Csíkszentmihályi's original research, Chen identifies the following factors that affect the experience of flow:

- The presentation of a challenging activity that requires skill

- The merging of action and awareness

- The setting of clear goals

- The provision of direct and immediate feedback

- Concentration on the task at hand

- Sense of control

- Loss of self-consciousness

- An altered sense of time

In game design, these components of flow would certainly appear to be useful, although Chen does stress that it is not necessary to achieve all of them in a game's design for a player to experience flow. In particular, Chen defines the need to achieve a balance between the difficulty of the challenge and the player's own ability to overcome the challenge. If the challenge is too difficult, then the player will become anxious and frustrated, but if the challenge is too easy, then the player will become bored. A good balance between challenge and ability can be termed the *flow zone*.

We could look to evaluate the quality of a game by applying the components of flow and determining whether players become immersed in the experience of gameplay. More specifically, though, we can also consider flow in relation to the design of playable characters. When a player takes control of a character (or series of characters) in a game, she should ideally experience a feeling of flow when guiding her character through gameplay. There should be clear goals to achieve and challenging activities to carry out, a strong sense of control with quality feedback, and complete immersion in the action. In order for this to work, there is a need to consider everything about the user experience, from the control scheme and responsiveness, to the audio and visual performance of a character, to the level design and the associated challenges. Certain game types are utterly dependent on a strong sense of flow, such as sports simulations or platform games. We look at specific examples of flow in character design later in the book, when we come to discuss playable character types in Chapter 7.

SUMMARY AND ACTIVITY

In this extensive chapter, we have sought to discuss the context of virtual characters in terms of both narrative and play. We started by addressing the need to identify the setting in which a video game takes place, encompassing the time period, the location, and cultural factors. We then extended this by looking specifically at the backstories of characters and blocking out physical, social, and psychological profiles. From there, we moved on to discuss the use of character archetypes in storytelling and the danger of creating stereotypical characters. We discussed points of view in storytelling and video games, and saw how thematic statements can help us to shape the design and performance of characters. In terms of the unique attributes of interactive media, we examined the potential plot structures that can be used in media such as video games, before looking more closely at the design of characters in relation to gameplay and game genres. Finally, we discussed theories of game design and immersive play that have the potential to inform our approach to virtual character design, specifically the MDA framework and the theory of flow.

As we identified at the start of the chapter, theories of narrative and game design are difficult to capture within the space of a single chapter. Indeed, it would be a challenge to discuss how narrative and game design interact even if we were to dedicate the entire book to this topic. A wide range of books and academic papers have explored these questions, and the references listed at the end of this chapter represent a very small sample. What we have tried to attain in this chapter is a basic understanding of how the wider context of a game world can impact on the design and study of virtual characters. Through consideration of story and gameplay, we can define who characters are, what they can do, why they do it, and ultimately how this impacts on audience interpretation of meaning. We may have only scraped the surface of narrative theory and game design, but the key concepts discussed in this chapter should enable us to more closely scrutinize how characterization, story, and gameplay impact on the performance of virtual characters.

Exercises

CHARACTER ANALYSIS

Can you identify examples of playable characters whose actions within the narrative and within gameplay are complementary? Conversely, can you identify examples of characters whose gameplay actions are at odds with the character's role in the narrative?

1. Select a range of playable characters within games that have a clear narrative. Aim to select characters from a range of different video game genres.

2. For each game, try to establish the core themes of the narrative. Can you propose a central thematic statement for the game?

3. Identify the archetype(s) of the characters you have selected. Then write a brief backstory and biography for the characters based on information that can be extracted from the game or related materials.

4. Establish whether player decisions affect the plot. What kind of plot structure is used? If player decisions do affect the plot, are the decisions and consequences consistent with the narrative, with the character, and with the themes of the game?

5. Establish what the core gameplay entails, taking into account the variety of actions that the character can perform (or cannot perform). To what extent do these gameplay actions correspond with the nature of the character and reflect the themes of the game? Does the gameplay seem at odds with or distinct from the narrative of the game?

CHARACTER DESIGN

Can you design virtual characters whose gameplay actions are both: (a) consistent with the video game genre and desired aesthetics and (b) complementary to the narrative design, including the use of archetypes, narrative mode, and thematic statements?

1. Select a range of video game genres or combined genres. Use these genres as a starting point for establishing the basic gameplay.

2. For each genre, write a high concept for the narrative. Identify the main thematic statements and list the key characters based on archetypes such as the protagonist, antagonist, sidekick, skeptic, and so on.

3. Develop the design of the player character by applying the MDA framework. (Start with the desired player aesthetics and then determine (a) the potential dynamics that would be appropriate for the context and (b) the core mechanics.)

4. Compare the gameplay mechanics that you have devised to the narrative themes, the use of narrative mode, the use of archetypal characters, and the use of interactive plot. Do the mechanics seem consistent with the overall narrative design? What potential inconsistencies or contradictions can you identify?

REFERENCES

Campbell, J. 1949. *The hero with a thousand faces*. New York: Bollingen.

Chen, J. 2007. Flow in games (and everything else). *Communications of the ACM* 50 (4): 31–34.

Csíkszentmihályi, M. 1990. *Flow: The psychology of optimal experience*. New York: Harper & Row.

Fullerton, T. 2008. *Game design workshop: A playcentric approach to creating innovative games*. Burlington, MA: Elsevier.

Hunicke, R., M. LeBlanc, and R. Zubek. 2004. MDA: A formal approach to game design and research. *Proceedings of the challenges in games AI workshop, Nineteenth National Conference of Artificial Intelligence*. Palo Alto, CA: AAAI Press.

Jung, C. 1959. *The archetypes and the collective unconscious*. Princeton, NJ: Princeton University Press.

Kremer, R. 2009. *Level design: Concept, theory & practice*. Natick, MA: AK Peters.

Kress, D. 1998. *Dynamic characters: How to create personalities that keep readers captivated*. Cincinnati, OH: Writer's Digest Books.

Mäyrä, F. 2008. *An introduction to game studies*. London: Sage.

Meadows, M.S. 2002. *Pause and effect: The art of interactive narrative*. Indianapolis, IN: New Riders.

McKee, R. 1997. *Story: Substance, structure, style, and the principles of screenwriting*. New York: Harper-Collins.

Murray, J. 1997. *Hamlet on the holodeck: The future of narrative in cyberspace*. New York: Free Press.

Phillips, M. A., and C. Huntley. 2004. *Dramatica: A new theory of story*. Special 10th anniversary ed. Burbank, CA: Write Brothers.

Rollings, A. and Adams, E. 2003. *Andrew Rollings and Ernest Adams on game design*. Indianapolis, IN: New Riders.

Salen, K., and E. Zimmerman. 2004. *Rules of play: Game design fundamentals*. Cambridge, MA: MIT Press.

Schell, J. 2008. *The art of game design: A book of lenses*. Burlington, MA: Elsevier.

Seger, L. 1990. *Creating unforgettable characters*. New York: Henry Holt.

Tillman, B. 2011. *Creative character design*. Waltham, MA: Focal Press.

CHAPTER 6

Acting, Movement, and Animation

W HEN WE FIRST STARTED DISCUSSING character performance back in Chapter 4, our focus was on the psychological principles that underpin human behavior and perception. We examined personality, emotion, and cognitive processes, and went on to look at nonverbal communication through body language, facial expression, and vocal cues. Our emphasis was explicitly on the psychology of natural human performance—how we act in social interactions and how we react to stimuli—rather than on what we might consider to be the creative process of an actor. In this final chapter on the theories of virtual character performance, we look to extend our understanding of the psychological principles of human behavior into a discussion of acting, movement, and animation theory.

In the domain of character design and animation, it is clear that acting theory ought to be one of our most important influences. Indeed, animated characters in film and games have often been called actors, with terms such as *synthespians* or *vactors* (virtual actors) used to describe them. Although these terms seem somewhat dated today (if not outright cheesy), they still make an apt connection between the design and development of virtual characters and the creative field of acting. What we ultimately hope to achieve in video game design and other forms of interactive media entertainment is not so much the simulation of "real" humans, but the creation of emotionally engaging acted performances by believable virtual actors. In this sense, our earlier discussion of the psychology of human behavior might seem a little dry by comparison. However, as we show, this initial examination of personality, emotion, and thought processes is a crucial foundation for any discussion of acting.

We begin this chapter by looking at principles of acting that advance some of the ideas we have discussed in the previous two chapters. We show how personality, emotion, and character context all feed into the internalization of an acted character performance. Essentially, we discover that acting theories can help us to build upon earlier character design work in order to direct the final performance of a virtual character. From the internalization of a character, we then look to consider the externalization of the character through theories of movement. This discussion encompasses Laban movement analysis (LMA) and the celebrated principles of animation.

Finally, we proceed to discuss the application of theory to virtual character implementation. We note how important it is to have a strong understanding of a character's personality, emotions, expressivity, narrative role, gameplay role, and interactivity before a final animated performance can be produced. A range of methods is examined, and then we close the chapter by considering what the overarching aesthetic qualities of a virtual character performance might be.

THINKING AND ACTING

In order to bridge a gap between psychology and animated performance, an excellent place to start is the work of Ed Hooks (2000). In his acclaimed book *Acting for Animators*, Hooks emphasizes the connection between emotions and thinking, and ultimately how our empathy for characters stems from their capacity to exhibit both a cognitive process and emotional experience. In particular, Hooks notes that "we are all different, but all of us have certain traits in common. We all think, and we all experience emotions. Emotions come from thinking" (Hooks 2000, 3). This piece of acting advice—aimed at animators who want to bring their characters to life—echoes the cognitive appraisal processes we discussed in Chapter 4. In other words, in order to achieve a believable performance, we cannot treat emotions solely as an element of an adaptive behavior. Instead we must consider how emotions are formed as characters think, evaluate, and draw conclusions.

Hooks goes on to lay down his seven essential acting principles:

1. Thinking tends to lead to conclusions, and emotion tends to lead to action.

2. We humans empathize only with emotion.

3. Theatrical reality is not the same as regular reality.

4. Acting is doing; acting is also reacting.

5. Your character should play an action until something happens to make him play a different action.

6. Scenes begin in the middle, not the beginning.

7. A scene is negotiation.

To fully appreciate the contribution of Hooks's advice to the animation of virtual characters, it would be highly recommended to pick up his book. It will serve as an excellent and practical guide to the creation of high-quality animated performances. But we can certainly draw some important conclusions from his essential acting principles that will impact on our approach to virtual character animation. In particular, the first of his principles provides us with a process for determining how a virtual character should perform in response to any given context:

- *Thinking*: The first stage is the thought process of a character in response to an event or an action performed by the player or another character. Given the context, what is the character likely to think in response? This could be predetermined, and so part of the larger narrative. But consider that this can also be a real-time procedure, in that a character needs to be able to "think" in response to a range of events that could happen.

- *Conclusion*: The outcome of this thought process is a conclusion of sorts: an ethical value judgment. We could potentially derive this from the design of the character's personality, as we discussed in Chapter 4. What kind of conclusions is a character likely to draw when the context is compared against its personality?

- *Emotion*: The emotion is an automatic response, as discussed in Chapter 4. Given the context, what emotion or emotions is a character likely to experience? Again, this could come down to design factors that we have discussed over the previous two chapters.

- *Action*: Finally, there is the action: the performance itself. What physical action will the characters take? This performance will be driven by both their ethical conclusion and their emotional reaction.

These cognitive and emotional steps toward action offer us a basic means of conceptualizing the process behind a performance. We can imagine how this could be proceduralized: that computer programming in combination with personality design, script writing, and animation could lead to the production of interactive performances, where character action is driven by a simulated thought process.

STANISLAVSKI'S SYSTEM

Hooks's advice on acting for animators draws on the larger body of twentieth-century acting theory, most notably the work of Constantin Stanislavski. A Russian actor and director, Stanislavski is widely credited as one of the leading influences on modern acting theory. His development of acting techniques and his subsequent publication of books on acting greatly impacted on the practices of actors. Stanislavski's work also influenced the Ukrainian-born American Lee Strasberg, who went on to create method acting: the American adaptation of Stanislavski's system. Method acting is likely to be a familiar term to many Western readers, who will associate it with the development of emotional realism in stage and screen acting, and with the emergence of prominent screen actors such as Robert De Niro and Al Pacino. Stanislavski's system clearly relates to the main points raised by Hooks, in particular the need to consider thought processes and objectives. Perhaps more importantly, however, is the connection that can be made between Stanislavski's ideas about acting, the psychological theories of personality and emotion that we discussed in Chapter 4, and the ideas about backstory and context that we discussed in Chapter 5.

Stanislavski's work is extensive, including several of his own books as well as many other books about his work produced by other authors. It is of course important to read more about the system to expand your knowledge of acting theory, and Moore's (1960) book about the Stanislavski system is a recommended resource. In this section, we look at just a few aspects of Stanislavski's system that we can immediately apply to our design and analysis of virtual character performance:

- *The "magic if" and the "given circumstance"*: A cornerstone of the system, the *magic if*, asks actors to consider what they would be thinking if they were in the current situation. This does not ask the actor to "be" the character, but to place themselves into the context and ask themselves what their thought process would be. By extension, the *given circumstance* is integral to the *magic if*. The actor is required to believe in the circumstances fully, as if they were true. The circumstances encompass everything from the events, conditions, setting, and time period to the creative elements such as the writing, direction, production design, and costumes. Fundamentally, the *magic if* stresses a need to reduce the storyworld, gameplay, and narrative down to the combined impact on the discrete thought process of a character.

- *Imagination*: We can relate *imagination* to the need to flesh out a character backstory. Acknowledging the limitations on what can be presented to an actor as a character backstory, Stanislavski encouraged actors to imagine a backstory and fill in the blanks. By extension, these questions should help an actor to formulate what it is that drives a character. Asking questions such as "Where did I come from?" and "What do I want/need?" will help an actor to understand a character's motivations, which should then inform how a performance is delivered.

- *Communion*: Another important consideration for the actor is to fully understand the relationships between the characters. For Stanislavski, this was about communication between actors and rehearsal of dialogue to ensure a communal understanding of the characters and their interactions. In terms of virtual character design, we could consider communion to be an important step in the fleshing out of character thought processes: to really consider what they think about each other, how they behave around each other, and how they respond to the needs, wants, and actions of others.

- *Emotion memory*: A fundamental aspect of Stanislavski's s system, the notion of *emotion memory*, concerns the stimulation of the actor's own general memories of emotional experience in order to enhance the character's emotions in response to the given context. In terms of virtual character design, this clearly impacts on the writing and, more importantly, the voice acting and animation of a character. It also impacts on design and engineering, with a need to plan for and implement authentic emotions based on realistic emotional memory rather than rudimentary emotional responses such as those identified in Chapter 4.

We can think of these aspects of Stanislavski's system as a strategy for designing the internal thought processes of a virtual character. For character design and analysis, these steps can be used to stimulate discussion about what a character thinks and feels, helping us to construct authentic, humanlike performances. However, there are two further aspects of Stanislavski's system that are of great value to character design:

- *Objectives and units of action*: The objectives of a character within a given unit of action (or beat) should be considered. The objective is essentially the short-term desire of a character. What is it that it wants to attain or achieve in the given frame of reference? Units of action are used to describe the current activity of a character, and they are completed once an objective is resolved. There will likely be obstacles that hinder the completion of an action. By breaking down a script into units rather than acts or scenes, more emphasis is placed on the actions of a character and how this relates to its motivations.

- *Superobjective and through-line of action*: The superobjective is the objective of a character that persists throughout the narrative and that may link many of the objectives together. We should consider that a character's actions throughout a narrative relate to this superobjective.

Although Stanislavski's system is clearly geared toward the practice of an actor and how he prepares for a role, the end result essentially concerns the authenticity of an acted performance in the eyes of an audience. By considering Stanislavski's system, actors can work toward a more realistic emotional performance and ensure that suspension of disbelief is maintained. The designers of virtual characters also seek to suspend the disbelief of gamers. Actors (voice and physical), animators, writers, and programmers all contribute to the final performance of a virtual character:

a performance that is likely to be at least partially interactive or adaptive. While Stanislavski's system can help an actor to connect to and embody a role, it can also be used to help design adaptive performances. When virtual characters are required to adapt to whatever decision a player chooses to make, some means of describing how a character should respond to these decisions is essential. The plot structures we examined in Chapter 5 could help us to plan for the different directions a character performance can take, but they do not help us to define the internal thought processes of a character as the plot twists and turns. Stanislavski's system, in contrast, offers us a series of considerations that can inform the design of a living, emotional character.

MOVEMENT

Where Stanislavski's system focuses on acting as an internalized process—how characters think, feel, and act—we can also look to discuss the outward performance of a character. We have already looked at movement from a psychological and anatomical perspective in Chapter 4, when we discussed theories of posture, proxemics, and facial expression. However, these theories tell us little about the creative or artistic role of movement within a character's performance. We might be able to imply the emotions and social relations of characters through animation of facial expressions, poses, and use of space, but what about the broader aesthetic qualities of human movement?

One of the most prominent theories of movement that can be applied to virtual character is Laban movement analysis. Developed by Rudolf Laban, a dancer and choreographer from Bratislava, Slovakia, LMA has been applied not only to dance, but also to acting, sports, and exercise. In this section, we look to summarize some of the core concepts that we can apply to our discussion of virtual character performance.

LMA can be broken down into four main categories: body, effort, shape, and space. The body category concerns the structure and movement of the body, in terms of which parts of the body are moving and how these discrete movements relate to each other. The effort category describes the nature or dynamics of movements, in terms of timing and strength. The shape category more specifically describes the shape that a body takes and how shapes change during a performance. The last category, space, concerns movement in relation to the environment. All of the categories can be seen to overlap, but they combine to provide a powerful means of describing and evaluating the aesthetic qualities of bodily movement. To understand how we might use LMA in virtual character design, we look at just the body and effort categories for now. Further reading is of course recommended, as LMA is an extensive method that we can't discuss in detail here. Authors such as Newlove (2004) provide an in-depth description of all aspects of LMA.

First, patterns of body movement are identified that can be related to stages of development (from simple to more complex organisms) and expressive ideas:

- *Breath*: This focuses on the performance of breathing as the most simple of animal movements. This contained movement can express solitude, oneness, self-reflection, empathy, and self-esteem. In a virtual character performance, consider opportunities for limited movement that can draw attention to breathing. Typically, this might be in an idle animation that is used after exertion, showing tiredness. But in what other ways can exaggeration of breathing be used within gameplay and narrative sections to help express the ideas listed here? Consider when characters are at rest or when player opportunities for movement or action are limited.

- *Core-distal*: The core-distal category applies to radiation of movement out from the navel to the limbs, typically involving movements outwards and back in toward the center. These movements can express a tentative reaching out into the world and highlight relationships between a character and the environment. In gameplay, these movements can be pleasing when performed with fluidity and in relation to intended movement and action. For example, consider a character running through an environment, reaching out with their legs to make jumps before retracting back in to the center on impact, reaching out with their arms to reach ledges or ropes before pulling back in. The flow of movement is important to achieving a sense of authenticity and immediateness. The core-distal category gives us a means of describing and evaluating the aesthetic qualities of these movements.

- *Head-tail*: Similar to the core-distal category, the head-tail category describes movements where the head and coccyx expand away from each other and contract back together. This wormlike movement can express ideas such as playfulness, curiosity, and exploration. In virtual character performance, you can consider how head-tail movements are used when a character is moving slowly, tentatively, cautiously, or stealthily. Crawling and sneaking actions, particularly with an ability to peek at or scan an environment, can make excellent use of this type of movement.

- *Upper-lower*: With the upper-lower category, the patterns of movement become more complex. The upper and lower body can be considered as two distinct areas of movement that work in contrast to each other, expressing ideas such as power, strength, endurance, or survival. Within a virtual character we will commonly see upper-lower patterns in action or physical gameplay. Consider the stability of a strong, grounded lower body in contrast to the wielding of weapons or casting of spells in the upper body, or the speed of movement in the lower body contrasted with a sheltering of the body and head when fleeing a threat.

- *Body half*: The left- and right-hand sides of the body contrast against each other, emphasizing ideas such as opposition, alternatives, or dualisms. We will see this type of movement a lot, given that arms and legs ought to swing in opposition to each other when a character is moving through space. More subtle application can help to draw attention to the ideas discussed here, however. For example, consider how a character might simultaneously seek to attack with one half of the body while also attempting to protect another character with the other side of the body.

- *Cross-lateral*: Finally, cross-lateral movements are diagonal connections that express the most complex type of developmental motion. This can involve twisting, rotating, and spiraling through space, suggesting achievement, triumph, skill, and intelligence. The balancing of diagonal movements—for example, making connections across from the left leg to the right arm—will help to showcase the power and abilities of a virtual character. With a player character in particular, the application of cross-lateral movements in response to player commands can help to reinforce a sense of authority and control.

While the body category helps us to describe what parts of the body are moving and how these movements can be connected into patterns, it does not help us to describe the nature of the movement. For example, we discussed how a head-tail movement could be applied to show a character slowly peeking out from a hiding place before retracting. However, a devastating uppercut delivered in a fighting game can also make use of a head-tail pattern of movement. In other words, the effort is very different. Let's quickly consider how we can break down our descriptions of movement in relation to the effort category of LMA:

- *Space*: This subcategory concerns the attention and thought process behind the movement. Spatial movement can be considered either direct (very specific, focused, pinpointed action) or indirect (overlapping or multiple focuses, taking in all of the environment).

- *Weight*: Weight can be light, limp, strong, or heavy. Lightness is an active use of weight that is fragile and delicate, while limpness is a more passive giving up or relinquishing of weight. In contrast to these, strength is an active use of weight that is immovable and powerful, while heaviness is a passive use of dead weight.

- *Time*: The timing of movements can be considered sudden (movements that are quick, rapid, or hurried) or sustained (movements that are lingering, that are prolonged, or that take time to develop).

- *Flow*: In terms of LMA effort, flow can be considered as either free flowing (an open, uncontrolled, and fluid movement) or bounded (rigid, contained, and iterative movements).

Although LMA is most practically applied to physical rather than virtual performance, it can be useful to us when we are planning and deconstructing virtual performances, particularly performances that are intended to demonstrate a degree of authenticity and human realism. Nevertheless, virtual characters are not constrained by the same physical properties as human performers. Neither are they necessarily critiqued according to the same aesthetic ideals. As such, it is important that we consider representations of movement as well as physical movement in the real world. Most notably, we should consider the fundamentals of animated movement.

ANIMATION PRINCIPLES

In the 1930s, the animators of the Walt Disney Company were working tirelessly to come up with a method for producing more realistic animation. Up until then, animation was either greatly simplified and avoided the use of lifelike motion, or followed an established style that was at odds with our understanding of physical reality. Rubber-hose animation is a well-known example of a style that was used in this early era. This distinctive type of animation made use of rubberlike limbs and append-ages, a convention that helped animators to work around the problems of accurately representing the rotation of joints. For Walt Disney—who was determined to see more authentic movement in his studio's animated characters—the lack of a proven process for generating realism in anima-tion was not acceptable. Consequently, the animators working for Disney practiced and iterated upon a range of animation techniques, with the outcomes closely scrutinized by both the animation teams and Disney himself. The culmination of these efforts was a revolution in animation quality, leading to the release of the first feature-length animated film—*Snow White and the Seven Dwarfs*—in 1937. And yet the principles of ani-mation that were developed by the Walt Disney Company were not widely promoted for more than 40 years. In their famous book *The Illusion of Life: Disney Animation*, Disney animators Thomas and Johnston (1981) finally made explicit the 12 basic principles of animation that were used to create believable movements in Disney productions. Today their book remains highly regarded in the field of animation, and is recommended reading for anyone involved with the design or study of virtual characters.

Although by no means the only theory of animated movement (there are of course variations in terms of studio and cultural style and of differ-ent artistic interpretations of realism), the 12 basic principles of animation are a cornerstone of animation production and are essential knowledge for anyone seeking to create animated characters. The 12 principles as listed by Thomas and Johnston (1981) are:

1. Squash and stretch

2. Anticipation

3. Staging

4. Straight-ahead action and pose-to-pose

5. Follow-through and overlapping action

6. Slow in and slow out

7. Arcs

8. Secondary action

9. Timing

10. Exaggeration

11. Solid drawing

12. Appeal

These principles offer guidance on how to create animation that is grounded in reality but that is also a form of augmented or selective mimicry. Rather than seeking to replicate reality, the idea was to produce a creative and expressive imitation of reality that would suspend audience disbelief. We can relate this to the point we made earlier regarding the distinction between theatrical and physical reality. While the principles of animation are sensitive to physical rules and how these can be accurately represented, they are also concerned with a perceived authenticity in the medium of animation. The complexity of movement in the real world can be difficult for an audience to decipher. The lack of direction and clarity can make it hard to interpret, while the lack of a strong contrast between subtle and amplified movements can result in uninteresting or even tedious performances.

Although the principles were originally produced for application in cel animation, they provide a solid framework for the design and critique of virtual character movement. As such, we go through the definition of each of the principles and attempt to place them into the context of virtual characters:

- *Squash and stretch*: This principle defines the need for the flexibility of materials to be represented through the squashing and stretching of an object under pressure, for instance a rubber ball being bounced. This can be applied in a comedic sense to provide a caricature of force applied to a character's body. In a realistic scenario, the most important point is the need to maintain a consistent volume (i.e., an object should not appear to gain mass when stretched or lose it when squashed, which can happen inadvertently when characters are manipulated by animators or animation systems). It is also important to note that audiences expect character bodies and clothing to appear organic, which implies squashing and stretching. The lack of this seemingly rudimentary motion can make a virtual character seem rigid or plastic—a problem that can easily arise in game engines when severe limitations are placed on character rigs or on the complexity of animation that can be implemented. As such, a capacity to represent squash and stretch in all the relevant areas of a virtual character rig ought to be considered.

- *Anticipation*: Anticipation (shown in Figure 6.1) is the performance of an initial movement to prepare for a main movement (e.g., the bending of the knees, hunching of the back, and noticeable intake of breath before a jump). The lack of anticipation can make a character appear unrealistic, particularly if it is implied that the character would know what was going to happen next. The lack of anticipation can also make it more difficult for an audience to follow the action. This could be useful in some instances where shock or surprise is required, but in a video game, a character ought to be able to anticipate much of the animation that is played. Consider a player character running and fighting its way through a city: every crouch, jog, sprint, jump, climb, punch, kick, dodge, and change of direction should be anticipated by the character. This creates a conceptual problem for characters under direct player control: an anticipatory animation cannot be played *before* a player chooses to carry out an action. As a result, there is a need to consider balancing the immediacy of action (an action happens the instant a button is pressed) with the authenticity of motion (a delay occurs between button press and final action, during which an anticipatory motion is performed).

- *Staging*: More of a directorial consideration than an animation-specific one, the principle of staging states that any important element in the scene ought to be clearly staged so that the audience can notice it and accurately interpret the intended meaning. For a virtual character, this could mean a key aspect of its personality being shown, an emotion being expressed, or an action being performed that is critical to the gameplay or narrative. Good staging relies on more than just the quality of the animation of the character: there is also a need to consider placement of cameras, scene layout, and use of lighting. In a video game, this makes for a complex problem, given that most games allow for player control over the camera. This is particularly difficult when a game is played from a first-person point of view, or where the player is accustomed to having comprehensive control over a third-person camera in typical gameplay.

FIGURE 6.1 Examples of the principles of animation. From top to bottom: arcs, anticipation, and follow-through.

Nevertheless, staging is essential if the intention is to ensure that the player picks up on an important idea within the performance. This is why many games still use cutscenes where all player control is ceased, or restricted cutscenes where the player retains some control. Techniques such as forcing a player character to walk during character interactions (as in the *Assassin's Creed* series) or providing the player with a button that focuses attention on an element (as in *The Last of Us*) offer a middle ground between enforced staging and retention of player agency.

- *Straight-ahead action and pose-to-pose*: This principle has limited application to digital animation, and in particular to game animation. In early precomputer animation, there were conceivably two approaches to the animation process: the animator would start with the first frame and then progressively draw each of the consecutive frames (the straight-ahead approach), or the animator would draw the key poses first and then fill in the blanks by drawing the in-between frames (the pose-to-pose approach). In computer animation, the pose-to-pose approach is by far the most dominant method for animation production. The vast majority of animation software packages provide tools that assist pose-to-pose animation, and it is typical that the process of in-between animation is automated. The argument is that pose-to-pose is more accurate and efficient, while straight-ahead action provides more fluent and dynamic animation. However, the spirit of the two approaches does continue in virtual character animation today. While most animators are likely to work with the pose-to-pose approach to build animation loops and reusable sequences, other animation methods such as motion capture (animation generated by actors) and procedural animation (animation generated by code) align with the straight-ahead action approach. We come back to animation methods shortly, but bear in mind that the use of contemporary animation methods can be related back to this original principle of animation.

- *Follow-through and overlapping action*: These two concepts are paired as one of the 12 principles due to the fact that they are closely related. Follow-through (shown in Figure 6.1) states that loose elements of an object should continue to have momentum after the object itself has stopped moving before being pulled back to the object's center. For example, a loosely tied sash around a character's waist would continue to move forward after a character has ground to a halt, falling to rest moments afterward. Overlapping action states that different elements of an object that can move independently are likely to move at different rates rather than uniformly. In this case, we might expect to see a character moving its hands, feet, and head at different rates. Otherwise, a mechanical effect is produced. In character design, it is common to create characters with looser elements (scarves, hats, belts, attached weapons, etc.) not only because it makes for a more interesting visual design, but also because it supports follow-through and overlapping action (and therefore more interesting movement). As with squash and stretch, the lack of follow-through and overlapping action can give the appearance of rigid, unnatural materials and appendages, but at the same time more complex skeletons and character rigging might be required to support these movements in a game engine.

- *Slow in and slow out*: This is another principle that has more to do with the drawing process than contemporary practice in computer animation, but its application is still important to the production of authentic virtual character performance. Slow in and slow out (or ease in and ease out) refers to the gradual buildup of momentum as an object begins to move (its acceleration) and the gradual slowdown when it stops moving (its deceleration). This is typically an automated element of computer animation when poses are blocked out, but animators will manipulate how many frames are dedicated to both acceleration and deceleration. Aesthetically, manipulation of slow in and slow out can convey not only a physical sense of the characters (whether they are light/fit or heavyset/unfit), but also a sense of their personality and current emotional state (for instance whether they are confident or nervous, or whether they are happy or sad).

- *Arcs*: The principle of arcs (shown in Figure 6.1) concerns the natural roundedness of movement. If you imagine a moving object tracing a line through the space on the screen, a more natural, easy-on-the-eye movement would be arched rather than linear or jagged. As such, the arcs principle suggests that all movements should be intentionally and clearly rounded to maximize this natural effect, unless there is a good reason to negate this effect. When looking at or planning to create virtual character animation, you should consider how arcs are being used. For the average humanoid or animal character, an audience will expect to see the character moving through space in arcs and also to see arched internal movements in the limbs, head, waist, and so on. If a character feels uncanny, it may well be that the flatness of movement is undermining the naturalness of the performance. The principle of arcs could be negated specifically to achieve an unnatural effect, for example, in robotic or zombie characters.

- *Secondary action*: You could consider secondary action to be a principle that builds upon follow-through and overlapping action, in that it concerns adding asynchronicity to a character to create a more interesting performance. Secondary action is the animation of a secondary element of a character in support of a primary movement. The purpose is to complement the primary movement, rather than draw attention away from it. A prime example can be the use of facial expression to complement the more dominant use of the body. In *The Last of Us*, for instance, Joel exhibits a series of subtle facial expressions that convey anger, passion, and exertion while engaged in close combat. These secondary actions add to the overall authenticity and realism of his performance, making the combat much more emotional and gritty. This is a human engaged in a fight for his life, rather than a representation of a character carrying out combat moves. Lack of quality secondary action can ultimately make a performance feel flat, and so there is a need to consider how it can be implemented. This isn't always easy, given the restrictions on game engines and also given that subtle movements might not be easily read when the player has control over primary movements and the camera.

- *Timing*: In traditional animation, timing referred to the number of drawings used to show a character movement. In virtual character animation, we might use the equivalent of drawings for a two-dimensional (2D) character contained within a sprite sheet. But most characters in video games are not comprised of drawings and are instead driven by internal skeletons. As such, it is better to think about timing in terms of the speed of complete movements and how this communicates the status or personality of a character. This is similar to slow in and slow out, which applies to the start and end of movements. Good timing should convey a strong sense of the weight and mood of a character. Good timing should also convey a sense of physical laws and realism in character movement. When the timing of a movement is too fast or too slow, it can give the impression that a character is defying the physics of the world that it is in. In games we often see timing issues in relation to movement of a character across the ground, with footsteps out of sync with the speed at which the character is actually moving. This problem commonly arises when a virtual character's animation system is unable to deal with a player's insistence on running up steep hills or into walls, but it can be rectified by placing limitations on animation playback or forcing other animations to play under certain circumstances.

- *Exaggeration*: In some ways, we might consider exaggeration to be the most important principle of all, as it can be readily applied to all of the other principles and lies at the heart of traditional animation practice. While this of course relates to the application of caricatured movement in cartoon animation, it is more broadly defined as realistic movement that is amplified to an appropriate degree. For virtual character animation, a lack of exaggeration could ultimately disrupt staging or make it difficult to detect use of anticipation, followthrough, overlapping action, and the like. In particular, exaggeration is important when it comes to the animation of key sequences or gameplay maneuvers. Unlike movie audiences, game players can watch the animation of just one character for many hours. A lot of these animations will be repetitive loops, such as walking sequences. When a player executes moves that are fundamental to the game— such as the powerful finishing moves performed by Batman in the *Batman: Arkham* series of games—then some exaggeration is needed to make these animations stand out and to provide the player with a satisfying dynamic performance.

- *Solid drawing*: We could argue that solid drawing is the principle that has the least relevance to the animation of virtual characters, the vast majority of which are produced using digital production methods. Essentially, the principle of solid drawing concerns the need for animators to understand the presence of forms in three-dimensional space, and to practice their ability to represent three-dimensional (3D) forms in their drawings. While virtual characters tend to be developed using computer animation software that assists with 3D representation, we should bear in mind the importance of anatomical knowledge to character visual design (as discussed in Chapter 2). This anatomical knowledge is also essential to the design and analysis of performance. As such, we should consider the solid-drawing principle as a reminder that character bodies need to perform in 3D space in an authentic manner that at least appears anatomically accurate.

- *Appeal*: Finally, the principle of appeal is, in fact, an aspect of character design that we have already addressed in the book. We can equate this with the personality or charisma of a character: what it is about them that captures the audience's imagination. We considered this in terms of balancing personality traits and attitudes in Chapter 4, but we also considered the audiovisual appeal of characters in Chapters 1, 2, and 3. The principle of appeal reminds us that the quality of a virtual character performance cannot be solely derived by the way it moves or acts. An excellent performance emerges from the culmination of a range of design factors, including those that we have covered up until this point.

As we discussed earlier, the principles of animation as described by Thomas and Johnston (1981) fundamentally concern traditional or cel animation, but they have had a massive impact on animation production more broadly. Where subtle differences arise in production methods, adaptation of the original principles can be appropriate. For example, John Lasseter (1987), the chief creative officer of Pixar, wrote about the principles of animation as applied to 3D computer animation. What we have tried to ascertain in this section is the relevance and value of the original principles in the context of interactive character animation for virtual characters. Not all of the principles will have equal weight and meaning for every video game—or even every character in one particular video game—but it is clear that they provide an excellent framework for guiding the development of authentic virtual character performance.

ANIMATION METHODS

So far in this chapter, we have discussed theories of acting, movement, and animation. Before we can take this knowledge any further (in terms of either implementing a virtual character or deconstructing a performance exhibited in a video game), there is a need to consider the practicalities of creating animation for interactive media. Although technologies will change and practices will evolve, a general understanding of the process of virtual character animation will greatly improve your capacity to plan for and interpret dynamic character performances.

When it comes to animating virtual characters, there are three approaches to animation production that will typically be used:

- *Key-frame animation*: Key-frame animation is the process whereby an animator (or a team of animators) creates animation by hand by blocking out all of the frames of animation. The key frames are the frames of animation that define the beginning/end point of a transition. Other frames are added between key frames to create the illusion of movement. These additional frames can be added by hand or automated by software. Key-frame animation as an overarching term can be used to describe how traditional (hand-drawn and painted), stop-motion (photographed models), or computer (digital 2D and 3D) animation is created.

- *Motion capture*: Motion capture is the process of tracking movement in the real world using cameras or sensors and then using this data to drive the animation of a virtual character. The intricate body movement of one or several actors can be tracked, most commonly by using trackers that are picked up by cameras. Even complex facial movements can be recorded and used within the animation pipeline. Motion capture is often shortened to *mo-cap* and is sometimes called *performance capture* to emphasize the creative input of the professional whose movements are being recorded.

- *Procedural animation*: Procedural animation concerns the simulation of movement by a computer. Movements are calculated at runtime in order to generate character performances that can be manipulated by any number of variables. The most typical variables are physical (such as the effects of gravity, wind, or collisions) or based on player input (e.g., issuing commands that impact on how a character moves).

These three approaches can be aligned with different types of game development professionals: the character animator, the performance-capture actor, and the animation programmer. It is clear that there are strengths (and also limitations) to each of the approaches.

The character animator has a strong appreciation of animation theory and is a trained craftsperson who knows how to design and then piece together emotive performances that suspend the audience's sense of disbelief. Key-frame animation is not limited to the physical movements of a real actor and can be highly imaginative. There is also scope for breaking physical rules in order to show abstract or impressionistic movements. However, key-frame animation is a lengthy process. Despite advancement in animation tools that speed up the animator's workflow, this approach will typically take a great deal of time (and therefore money), particularly if highly complex and realistic movements are required.

This is where motion capture becomes immensely useful. Using state-of-the-art technology, almost all of the intricacies of real human movement can be captured and translated to a virtual character, including subtle facial movements. Furthermore, motion capture enables a direct connection between the intentions of the actor and the movement of a virtual character. While a key-frame animator must build a performance step by step, the actor's performance is instantaneously captured. Multiple takes can be recorded, allowing for a series of full-character performances to be generated, viewed, and scrutinized by an animation director immediately. On the flip side, motion capture is not without its costs. The technology (particularly the most accurate technologies) remains expensive to buy or rent. Even if the costs are reduced over time, there is still a need for a large-enough physical space. Actors are required, and not all actors will be well trained in motion-capture acting. It's also unlikely that actors will be embedded in a development team long term (certainly not in the same way that animators are likely to be), making it difficult to change or add more animations at a later date.

Procedural animation has the massive advantage of enabling new animations to be created at runtime. In other words, the animations seen on screen can adapt to conditions that neither a character animator nor a motion-capture actor can be fully prepared for. In theory, by incorporating all manner of environmental factors into an animation system, procedural animation can lead to the creation of thousands of unique and authentic movements that align with the context of play. Procedural animation could also be used to manipulate the movement of a character based on its internal state, for example by using simulated emotion to drive the way a character walks. However, there is a notable jump from simulating physical forces to simulating character thought processes and mapping these onto intricate movements. The complexity of the programming makes this a somewhat daunting task, and it is far more practical to make use of key-frame animators or actors when it comes to creating believable and emotional character performance. Full procedural animation also presents the problem of removing the human creative aspect from the process. We might be able to program a computer to generate visuals or imitate the art style of a famous painter, but art is fundamentally about human expression.

MIXED-METHODS ANIMATION

With all this in mind, the most sensible solution is not to treat these as independent approaches to be used in isolation, but as a complete toolbox of methods that can be combined to generate authentic, dynamic character performances. In many productions it is common for an animation director or lead animator to oversee the integration of all three methods, particularly for productions that feature 3D human or humanoid characters. By doing so, it is possible to draw on the strengths of key-frame animation, motion capture, and procedural animation while negating at least some of the individual disadvantages.

Perhaps the most-established methodology for the creation of virtual character performance involves building a library of animations. The library methodology has its roots in the earliest video game animation, before motion capture had been established and before procedural animation was adequately developed. Today, the library methodology can be used to incorporate animations created using any or all of the three main methods.

Although the implementation of a library methodology has varied over time and can continue to vary between development companies, the fundamental concept is consistent. The premise of the library methodology is to break down all conceivable character movements into just the base elements. These elements might be physical in nature, for example walks, runs, and jumps. They might be broken down by application, for example animations to play when a character is idle, when it is fighting, or when it is dying. It's possible to consider animations at a macro level, allowing for a greater number of combinations, for example animations that apply to just the arms, legs, or face. Or animations can be more complete, for example full performances to be used in narrative segments. The number and nature of categories will be dependent on the design of the video game and the requirements of a given character. Consequently, much of what we discussed in Chapters 4 and 5 impacts directly on the planning of a character's animation library.

Typically, you would expect a library to comprise animations generated through motion capture and animations generated through key-frame animation. Some of these may be mixed, that is, motion-captured animations that have subsequently been augmented by key-frame animation. Procedural animation can then be applied to the animations as they are called at runtime. This might be as simple as constraining the orientation of the head and eyes while playing an idle animation, or as advanced as independently manipulating all of the joints in a character rig during a run animation. Procedural techniques can also assist with blending between animations. Swapping between large numbers of preset animations without any blending would create a jarring effect, with characters suddenly switching between animation loops. Efforts can be made within animation planning to alleviate these jumps, but real-time blending between animations can make for much smoother transitions, accounting for character momentum, orientation, leg placement, and so on.

In terms of character movement, then, we can imagine an aesthetic ideal for a virtual character performance. Given the contributions that can be made through key-frame animation, motion capture, and procedural animation, we should expect the following qualities to be evident:

- *Structure*: If a virtual character's range of animations is well planned and well executed, there ought to be a comprehensive set of animations suitable for all logical contexts in which the character could be placed. Animations should be created for individual parts of the character rig, thereby allowing for the combination of animation loops.

- *Adaptability*: A virtual character's performance is consistent when placed under direct or indirect control by a player or when subjected to social and environmental interactions. Animations should flow seamlessly to adapt to changes. A quality animation structure is enhanced through the implementation of adaptability.

- *Authenticity*: The quality of the animation is authentic and believable in the context of the character and the story world. There ought to be clarity and accuracy within all movements, including those that are subtle or intricate. A quality animation structure is enhanced through authenticity.

- *Continuity*: Characters should exhibit emotional and factual memory. Previous events in the video game—both in narrative and in gameplay—should influence how a character performs in the future. Key decisions made or actions performed by the player should leave a lasting impact on characters affected by them.

When designing and analyzing virtual character animation, these aesthetic qualities should be considered. However, it must be remembered that these are ideals: there will always be compromises in video game development. We can reflect that the structure and adaptability principally concern the implementation of a library-based methodology, while authenticity and continuity relate to the ideas we have discussed throughout Chapters 4, 5, and 6.

SUMMARY AND ACTIVITY

Over the last three chapters, we have looked at the theories that underpin our design, development, and study of virtual character performances. In this chapter, we considered both the relevant theories of artistic performance—from acting, to movement, to animation itself—and the practicalities of actually building interactive character animation. First, we made a connection between acting theory and the psychological principles of personality and emotion that we visited in Chapter 4. We saw that actors seek to flesh out our characters by trying to understand their thought processes and emotions, and that they link emotional experience to direct action. In particular, we looked at how Stanislavski's system emphasizes the actor's need to fully understand a character's personality and intentions, to imagine what he would think and feel if he were in the character's situation, and to tap into his own personal and emotional memories to bring life and realism to the character performance. From the conceptual performance, we then moved on to discuss the extrinsic performance, first by taking into account Laban movement analysis (LMA). We saw that LMA can give us a language to describe how the human body moves. The principles of animation were then examined, providing us with a series of guidelines on how to produce more-authentic movement in the animated form. Finally, we discussed how virtual character animation is actually built, taking into account the animation pipelines (key-frame animation, motion capture, and procedural animation) and the method of combining animations to create adaptive performances.

This is the last chapter that seeks to introduce theoretical concepts that can inform our character designs and frame our research. For the remainder of the book, we look to discuss specific qualities of virtual characters supported by short case studies. Before that, one final pair of activities is suggested to help us to reflect on the ideas that we have discussed in this chapter.

Exercises

CHARACTER ANALYSIS

Can you identify examples of nonplayer character movement that reflect internal thought processes?

1. Identify a range of nonplayer characters that feature prominently in video games. These characters should exhibit a sufficient amount of animated movement for you to study.

2. Play through the games, interacting with the characters that you have identified. Record gameplay footage of the characters' animated performances and take notes while playing.

3. Select examples of animated performance for each of your characters and aim to describe:

    a. What you believe their thought process was within the given segment, considering Stanislavski's system

    b. The extent to which this thought process was interactive (Was it in a cutscene? Was it within gameplay? Were you able to make a decision that impacted on the character's thought process?)

    c. The movement of the character, framed by both LMA and the principles of animation

4. Write up short case studies for each of your characters and comparatively analyze them according to the qualities discussed in the final section of the chapter (structure, adaptability, authenticity, and consistency).

CHARACTER DESIGN

How can consideration of a player character's thought processes inform the design of an animation library?

1. Select a player character concept that you have already developed, for example a character that you created as part of the Chapter 4 or Chapter 5 design exercises. At a minimum, you should have an idea of the character's archetype, backstory, personality, and gameplay actions.

2. Using Stanislavski's system, imagine yourself as the character in the context of the game. Who is this character? How does it think? What emotions will it experience? What relationships does it have? Try to list the most important points about your character.

3. Continuing to use Stanislavski's system, identify the character's superobjective. From there, list what you think will be the character's main units of action (in gameplay and in cutscenes). Consider what the character's objectives will be for each unit.

4. Develop an animation library structure for your character. The library should account for all of the movements that you think your character will have to perform, based on the character's thought processes, objectives, and gameplay actions. Try to break your library down into categories and subcategories.

5. Within your structure, list all of the animations you think your character will need. For some of these animations, produce short storyboards that show how the character should move, taking into account LMA and the principles of animation.

REFERENCES

Hooks, E. 2000. *Acting for animators*. Portsmouth, NH: Heinemann.
Lasseter, J. 1987. Principles of traditional animation applied to 3D computer animation. *Computer Graphics* 21 (4): 35–44.
Moore, S. 1960. *The Stanislavski system: The professional training of an actor*. New York: Penguin Books.
Newlove, J. 2004. *Laban for all*. London: Nick Hern Books.
Thomas, F., and O. Johnston. 1981. *The illusion of life: Disney animation*. New York: Disney Editions.

III

Practice

THROUGHOUT SECTIONS I AND II, we were concerned with the development of critical frameworks that could be used to aid analysis and discussion of virtual character design. This covered domains as diverse as biology, psychology, sociology, visual art, narrative design, gameplay design, acting, and animation. In the final three chapters, we shift our focus from theory to practice in order to examine specific examples of virtual characters. These case studies aim to provide some insight into the aesthetics of virtual characters in different applications. Chapter 7 examines the aesthetics of player characters; Chapter 8 discusses the design and performance of the wider cast of characters in video games; and Chapter 9 focuses on the performance of characters within complex, hyperreal worlds.

Control

The Aesthetics of Playable Characters

W HEN DESIGNING VIRTUAL CHARACTERS, arguably one of the most difficult challenges is devising characters that will be controlled by players. Player characters not only require a significant amount of development time (on the basis that they are likely to be the most heavily featured and most interactive of all the characters in a given product), but also pose more conceptual problems. These characters need to be likeable and understandable to a wide audience, which raises sociological issues of identity and representation. They need to play a clear and central role within a video game narrative, but if they are too tightly authored and unresponsive to player agency, then players might feel detached from them. Ideally, both their presentation and their performance should reflect the intentions and aspirations of the player. But this high level of flexibility makes it exceptionally difficult for a developer to impose a coherent narrative structure or character identity. Above all, they need to be fun, exciting, and inspiring to play. And that, most certainly, is not an easy task to accomplish.

In the following case studies, we look at four types of player character and examine their aesthetic qualities. In other words, we seek to identify the features of these character types that make them appealing, pleasurable, and meaningful to control.

ROLE EMBODIMENT

A common design approach with PCs is to use the concept of a "character without a voice." This applies literally (in that these characters rarely, if ever, express verbal sounds, including in cutscenes) but also more metaphorically: they typically demonstrate less in the way of personality traits, moods, or emotions than other characters in the same game. These characters have on occasion been labeled as *empty vessels*, drawing on the expression that "empty vessels make the most sound." This is a fairly negative phrase when the meaning is considered: the implication is that those who are lacking in wit, intelligence, or spirit tend to be the loudest and noisiest people. One of the most famous uses of the phrase, in Shakespeare's *Henry V*, exemplifies this point: "I did never know so full a voice issue from so empty a heart: but the saying is true—the empty vessel makes the greatest sound." However, when we recontextualize this phrase to video games, a new meaning can be inferred: that characters that are sufficiently "empty"—those that are essentially shells that a player inhabits—have the potential to give the player an expressive voice in a video game world. An alternative description could be to describe these characters as shells, emphasizing their role as character skins or avatars. A more positive expression that we could suggest, however, is that these characters are roles that we as players can embody. In other words, they are designed so that we can place ourselves into a defined role within the storyworld without excessive conflict between the player's agency and the character's performance.

Many games that embrace a character aesthetic of role embodiment opt for as high a level of immersion as possible, and thus favor a first-person camera view (as discussed in Chapter 5). This isn't always necessary, and some games aim to create shell characters that are visually presented through third-person camera views in gameplay, cutscenes, or both. However, this can have a detrimental effect on the level of immersion, as the player is no longer seeing through the eyes of the person they are meant to be. Additionally, third-person camera views of shell characters can disrupt suspension of disbelief, as the character's performance can come across as lifeless (particularly when compared to other characters in the same game) due to the fact that its performance is greatly dictated by player agency. A problematic example of a third-person shell is the character Link in the *Legend of Zelda* series of games. Link is a highly regarded character, but his visual lack of thought process makes him appear detached and somehow uncanny in relation to other characters in the games. As such, we focus on case studies of two renowned first-person-camera games that make use of role embodiment: *Half-Life 2* and *Portal 2*, both developed by Valve {2004, 2011}.

In *Half-Life 2*, the player takes on the role of Gordon Freeman, a scientist with a PhD in theoretical physics. In the first game in the series, Freeman finds himself caught between US Marines and hostile aliens after a scientific experiment inadvertently open up seams between dimensions. *Half-Life 2* takes place 20 years after the events of the first game, and involves Freeman siding with a resistance movement in a fight against a dystopian empire. Gameplay combines environmental puzzles with typical first-person-shooter elements. The PC of *Portal 2*, Chell, is less defined. Occupying the same storyworld as the *Half-Life* games, Chell has very little backstory when compared to Freeman. Chell is a test subject in a scientific facility, where a menacing and malicious AI (artificial intelligence) called GLaDOS forces her to progress through a series of increasingly difficult test chambers. The gameplay in *Portal 2* is more puzzle-based than *Half-Life 2*, and most of the gameplay involves the player tackling environmental puzzles through the use of a gun that can open up teleportation portals.

In both games, we could argue that not only is a first-person camera used, but also the main PCs make excellent use of a first-person narrative voice. By purposefully limiting the extent to which Freeman or Chell can express themselves through either vocals or actions, *Half-Life 2* and *Portal 2* encourage players to willingly suspend their awareness of the characters as virtual others. In other words, players are not subjected to independently minded PCs who speak or act in ways that they cannot empathize with. Instead, the roles of Freeman and Chell are made available to players, who step into the shoes of these characters and imagine themselves as the protagonists in the narrative. To an extent, this type of PC makes it easier for players to take on the role of a character whose identity is unfamiliar or somehow distinct from their own personal experience. For instance, it is certainly difficult for most players to imagine what it means to be a scientist with a PhD in theoretical physics, and yet they willingly accept this as part of their role when becoming Gordon Freeman.

More seriously, in comparing these two similar games, we can make an observation of the use of gender in a PC. Players know that Freeman is male and that Chell is female, and gender pronouns are used within the games. But no significant gender performances are enforced on the players. Players are subtly introduced to the roles of Freeman and Chell but, when playing the games, the use of first-person immersion can lead to a fusion of the player and the player-character. Regardless of the identity of the player, they can literally become Freeman when playing *Half-Life 2* and become Chell when playing *Portal 2*. Players immersed in gameplay and in the game narrative can more easily interpret actions that are executed by Freeman or Chell as first-person actions. In other words: I am running down this corner; I am fighting these monsters; I am solving this problem; I am leaping through this portal, and so on. By extension, it becomes easier to break down any potential sociological barriers between PC roles and players' own sense of identity. Placing oneself in the role of a different gender and conceptualizing this role in the first-person voice is an excellent accomplishment in *Half-Life 2* and *Portal 2*, particularly when you consider that the vast majority of games create distance between the PC and the player and make more explicit use of second- or third-person narrative voice techniques (i.e., players see the PCs as characters that they are controlling, rather than seeing themselves *as* the PCs in the game world).

Another design feature used in both games is the deployment of pivotal NPCs as a means of developing the story of the PC. If we accept that Freeman and Chell are empty vessels that players embody, then their inability to act independently of player intent makes it very difficult for their emotions, personalities, and attitudes to be formed. As soon as Freeman or Chell express their thoughts or feelings, the value of the empty-vessel design technique is lost. To rectify this, Freeman is balanced against resistance fighter Alyx Vance, and Chell against the AI GLaDOS. Although other notable NPCs help to flesh out the roles of Freeman and Chell—in particular the sidekick-cum-antagonist Wheatley in *Portal 2*—it is primarily Vance and GLaDOS that reveal and flesh out the characters Freeman and Chell. Vance serves as a companion or sidekick archetype for Freeman and, despite the fact that Freeman is mute, speaks with him frequently throughout the game, providing narrative context for the storyworld and establishing an emotional bond. In her speech and actions—and in particular in her subtle use of nonverbal communication in her animation—Vance effectively tells the story of Freeman, showing the player the type of man Freeman is and revealing his personality and attitudes by proxy. In effect, Freeman becomes a more defined character through Vance: a character design technique that neatly avoids the need to make Freeman speak or act independently. Similarly, in her role as an antagonist, GLaDOS tells us much about Chell. Notably, in *Portal 2*, GLaDOS undergoes her own character arc. More than an antagonist, GLaDOS is first presented as a devil figure (with an element of a menacing and twisted mother figure), but over the course of the narrative is revealed to be something of a redeemable devil, who even plays a sidekick role for one portion of the game. The performance of GLaDOS over the course of the narrative directly reflects the role of Chell, who is subjected to her maleficence and conflicting expressions of care and cold contempt.

Despite the fact that we rarely see any visual presentation of Freeman or Chell—we mostly know what they look like through promotional art or glimpses of their appearance through portals—these are two roles that players have become enamored with. Role embodiment through the suppression of PC voice, the promotion of the sense of first-person narrative voice, and the use of expertly written NPCs make the visual design of a PC much less important.

ROLE FULFILLMENT

On the other hand, many games make use of PCs whose appearance and performance are integral to their success. Where role embodiment in games such as *Half-Life 2* and *Portal 2* can lead to limited communication of a PC's personality, games that seek to appeal to an audience's sense of adventure often approach PC design by presenting more independent characters with clearly defined and acted personalities. While this evidently degrades the quality of the synchronicity between a player and a PC (establishing a more likely use of second- and third-person narrative voice in gameplay and cutscenes, respectively), this approach offers an opportunity for role fulfillment. In other words, these are virtual actors—often presented as archetypal heroes—who we get to "play as."

Genre and setting are usually crucial to the development of these types of PCs. Not only should the characters be more rounded in terms of having more explicit personalities, mannerisms, emotions, and dialogue, but they should also represent the chance to fulfill the role of the archetypal hero in a given narrative. These narratives tend to borrow heavily from film, television, and comics, appealing to an audience's understanding of genre and setting. For example, war narratives in historical, alternative-history, contemporary, or futuristic settings are commonly used in game design, offering players the chance to fulfill the role of the soldier or general fighting against oppressive armies, terrorists, or mercenaries. Games such as *Call of Duty: Black Ops* {Treyarch 2010} reference cinema and draw heavily on historical events and real settings to add to the authenticity and familiarity of the experience. Players come into these games with some understanding of the narrative context, allowing them to focus on fulfilling the roles of Special Forces and CIA agents in the context of the Cold War in the 1960s.

Let us examine two examples of third-person-perspective action-adventure games that present PCs as a means of role fulfillment: *Red Dead Redemption* {Rockstar San Diego 2010} and *Tomb Raider* {Crystal Dynamics 2013}. These games look to established genres and archetypal heroes within these genres. First, *Red Dead Redemption* casts the player as John Marston: an antihero with a history of criminality who is now seeking to atone for his past. In this Western-themed game, Marston's role is a familiar one from the genre, in particular the Westerns of the latter half of the twentieth century. Beyond the antihero archetype, his rugged, unkempt appearance and distinctive accent are familiar to anyone who has seen a Spaghetti Western. Similarly, in the role of Lara Croft in *Tomb Raider*, the player comes into the game already understanding the role that he or she is going to fulfill. Not only is there a history of the character and the narrative from the previous *Tomb Raider* games, but there is also the understanding that Lara Croft is an archetypal adventurer. The most obvious similarities can be drawn from the *Indiana Jones* films, with Croft presented as the adventurer who solves puzzles, fights off adversaries, and hunts for treasure in exotic locations. In both games we therefore see the overwhelming importance of setting and genre conventions to the success of the PC role. Without the saloons, the panoramic desert scenes, and the sunsets, the role of Marston is not as appealing to the player who wants to step into a Western. Without the jungles, mountains, caverns, traps, and fantastical elements, Croft loses much of her character. To fulfill these roles, players need familiar and conventional worlds in which to perform.

Beyond the narrative context, there is a need for gameplay design to support the genre. A disconnect between narrative design and gameplay design can undermine a player's sense of role fulfillment. The prevalence of war-themed games can be connected to this need for continuity between gameplay and narrative design. Shooting mechanics and action gameplay work well in video games. Games such as *L.A. Noire* {Team Bondi 2011}, which is heavily influenced by the film noir genre, recognize the need to relate gameplay to expected character development within the selected genre and setting. In this case, *L.A. Noire* is not a run-of-the-mill action-shooter game, but instead makes use of gameplay that supports film noir conventions (suspect and witness interrogation, for example). The MDA framework (see Chapter 5) is useful when it comes to making this connection between genre and gameplay: we can consider the conventions of a film or television genre and align these with the different types of suggested aesthetics. In *Red Dead Redemption*, we could suggest that the important aesthetics are sensation (the sense-pleasure of the Western environment), discovery (given that the Western genre is largely categorized by the expansion of Western civilization into a new world), and, of course, narrative. *Tomb Raider* could also be considered in terms of the narrative aesthetic, but arguably the aesthetics of fantasy (given the importance of myths and legends within the adventure genre) and challenge (in that the hero often faces obstacle courses which he needs to navigate) are more important here. And in both games, we see mechanics designed to support dynamics that lead to these aesthetic experiences. For example, Croft is frequently placed into obstacle courses in *Tomb Raider*, running (and regularly falling) through collapsing buildings and down mountainsides in increasingly action-packed sequences. The gameplay dynamics in *Red Dead Redemption* and *Tomb Raider* underpin aesthetics that relate to the selected narrative genres, which in turn greatly enhances the quality of player experience when fulfilling the roles. In other words, the experience of feeling like you are in a Western or adventure film is achieved.

A recurring pitfall is, of course, the potential for archetypal heroes of recognizable genres to slip into stereotypes. This has been an issue historically in video games, but one that has been gradually addressed over time. Looking at Croft as the example, it is clear that there were issues of hypersexualization in her earlier incarnations. All of the games in the series have presented the player with an adventurer role to fulfill—making connections to the adventure genre and using exotic settings and appropriate gameplay. But Croft was often presented as a sexualized object rather than a strong character in her own right. This viewpoint has eroded in more recent games, and in the 2013 version of *Tomb Raider* we see a much more realistic, authentic, deep, and emotional portrayal of a female hero. Some could argue that the creep of the male gaze still exists within *Tomb Raider*, notably during sequences where Croft twists and turns to maneuver her body through tight crevices under the watchful eye of the camera. But there is certainly a marked improvement in her personality, emotions, and realism as a character no longer defined by her physical appearance. In many ways, Croft has evolved from something that more closely resembled an empty shell (given her previous lack of character depth and performance) to a more fully fledged and likeable personality: an adventurer role that players are keen to fulfill.

ROLE PROJECTION

Characters such as Lara Croft and John Marston eschew the empty-shell approach to provide players with roles that are carefully written to fit within a structured plot. They minimize opportunities for the player to see themselves as the PC in return for delivering more crafted performances. However, there are other types of playable character that provide the player with much more control. As we discussed in Chapter 3, games and interactive media can allow us to define a character's appearance and identity through the use of customization tools. Some games explicitly target customization of PCs as a central feature of the game design, to the point where we might describe these characters as avatars (virtual representations of the player) rather than virtual actors (preset characters that the player controls). We can consider this a form of role projection: PCs that are molded to the player's preferences.

Over time, character customization tools have not only become more advanced, but also more prevalent. Many different types of video game now include character customization tools, allowing players to create representations that align with their desired virtual identities. One game that is notable for its advanced character creation tool is the action-adventure game *Saints Row IV* {Volition 2013}, which is one of the games that we examine in this section. Best described as an open-world, third-person action game with elements of both science fiction and comedy, *Saints Row IV* casts the player as a nameless character (referred to simply as The President). *Saints Row IV* is by no means unique in its use of intricate character creation tools and a nameless protagonist. Other single-player games such as *The Elder Scrolls V: Skyrim* {Bethesda Game Studios 2011} also attach a title to the protagonist (the Last Dragonborn) and allow a high degree of flexibility in character creation, enabling the player to project her own identity or creativity into the game world. Nevertheless, *Saints Row IV* does make for an interesting case study due to its wealth of creation tools.

While single-player games have increasingly integrated character creation and customization into their design, the MMORPG genre provides some of the most well-known examples of role projection in virtual worlds. Most MMORPGs allow for a high degree of visual and even audio customization from the start, with continued customization and upgrading of appearance occurring throughout the game. We could look at any popular MMORPG as a case study, but Sony Online Entertainment's 2003 release, *Star Wars Galaxies*, makes for a particularly interesting example. One of the most anticipated MMORPGs in gaming history, *Star Wars Galaxies* allowed gamers to play a role within the fabled *Star Wars* universe, choosing from a range of races and professions and settling on a number of recognizable worlds. *Star Wars Galaxies* in its original incarnation (prior to a gameplay design overhaul some years after release) could be considered more of a sandbox game than a typical RPG: players did not necessarily have any clear goals, with the emphasis being more on assuming a minor role within a large storyworld and participating in a collective narrative.

First, we can consider the extent to which visual and audio appearance can be customized in games. *Saints Row IV* has arguably one of the most detailed creation tools of any game, in part supported by its use of comedy and science-fictional genres. As with most character creation tools, *Saints Row IV* allows players to start by choosing attributes such as sex, ethnicity, and body shape. Initially, we can liken these settings to the concepts we discussed in Chapter 1, that is, the base biological aspects of the character. Sex is binary, and fundamental body shape can be fine-tuned on a slider between three extremes: strength, fat, and skinny (or, respectively, mesomorph, endomorph, and ectomorph extremes). Unlike many other creation tools, *Saints Row IV* provides an accurate slider for age that visibly adjusts the skin texture to reflect signs of aging. Face and body proportions can then be adjusted, allowing players to create very precise appearances. These adjustments can be compared to our discussion of sex differences in Chapter 1, as the effects of testosterone and estrogens can be imitated to create more or less masculine or feminine appearances.

Beyond these core settings, however, more detailed and unique representations can be created. Specific details such as dimples, freckles, and scars can be added, allowing players to more carefully craft an appearance that they feel matches the personality and backstory of the character they wish to play. Through subsequent selection of a vast number of hairstyles and colors, facial hair, skin tones (including nonhuman tones), body markings, piercings, costumes, and voices, players are able to create characters that cross not only a range of gender, sexual, ethnic, and age identities, but also visual styles and genres. Given that the protagonist is nameless and open for interpretation, players are encouraged to engage with a high level of playfulness and creativity. They can choose to design a character that maps onto their original ideas, or they can choose to more accurately reflect their real-world appearance. Perhaps most interesting of all in *Saints Row IV* is the ability to change appearance during play. While character creation tools at the start of a video game can allow us to select an identity for our avatars, the ability to adjust and manipulate identity during play is notable. In Chapter 3, we discussed the fluid nature of identity—that our perception of ourselves shifts over time. In-game customization of appearance reflects this important aspect of identity formation.

While the initial character creation tools in *Star Wars Galaxies* were not as advanced or intricate as those in *Saints Row IV*, the game as a whole was effectively designed as a means of player expression in a massively multiplayer context. As with most MMORPGs, players selected a race (including humans plus a range of recognizable alien races from the *Star Wars* universe) and a sex before being permitted to adjust aspects of the character appearance based on these core choices. But the initial selection of an appearance was effectively the tip of the iceberg as far as role projection was concerned. Once in the game world, players were provided with a range of options that could be used to define a role within the *Star Wars* universe. One of the major choices was profession, which—unlike in most other RPG games—was not limited to a small selection of archetypal adventurer classes (such as warrior, priest, or mage). Instead, players were tasked with training in basic professions before specializing in advanced professions. The basic professions covered classic RPG classes (brawler, marksman, medic, and scout), but also included more social options (artisan, entertainer, and politician). Advanced professions either built upon one basic profession (advanced marksman professions included carabineer, pistoleer, and rifleman, for instance) or required training in two basic professions.

What was remarkable about the original profession system in *Star Wars Galaxies* was its sheer flexibility. Players could train in over 30 professions, were not required to follow any particular profession development tree, and could leave professions to retrain in other areas. Professions weren't balanced for more compelling gameplay, as is the case in most MMORPGs. They were created to allow as much room for creativity and self-expression as possible. Some professions clearly had a role in action gameplay, such as the combat medic, the ranger, or the squad leader. Some allowed players to fulfill roles like those seen in the films, including bounty hunter, smuggler, and (the initially rare) Jedi. And yet many professions were chiefly concerned with creativity (chef, droid engineer, tailor, bioengineer) or with social interaction (musician, dancer, image designer, merchant). Through a unique approach to character professions, *Star Wars Galaxies* allowed players to project virtually any role they could imagine for themselves into a complex and detailed storyworld. Professions were designed with gameplay design in mind, but with much more concern for the wider narrative context and the desire of players to represent their own identities and stories in the *Star Wars* universe. They supported the building of player homes, cities, and economies. And ultimately, the profession system of *Star Wars Galaxies* demonstrated that many players could be content roleplaying as background characters in universes most commonly affiliated with archetypal heroes, mentors, damsels, and villains.

CHARACTER FLOW

In Chapter 5, we introduced the concept of flow: a state of complete immersion in a given activity. We looked at a number of factors that influence flow, and also noted the importance of maintaining a balance between the difficulty of the challenge and the player's ability (known as the flow zone). Flow is such a crucial aspect of virtual character design—particularly for action-oriented video games—that we ought to consider flow as one of the key aesthetic qualities of a PC. Where the previous aesthetic qualities we have examined in this chapter have focused on the role of a character in relation to narrative design or player identity, the authenticity and satisfaction of manipulating and controlling a character is more a matter of good interaction design and, ultimately, designing for player flow. In order to examine flow in character design in more detail, we compare two video game series that arguably induce excellent flow experiences: the parkour-inspired action-adventure series *Assassin's Creed* and EA's long-running soccer simulator *FIFA*. For clarity, in this section we refer specifically to the games *Assassin's Creed IV: Black Flag* {Ubisoft Montreal 2013} and *FIFA 15* [EA Canada 2014}.

The fundamental challenge of both games concerns the skillful navigation of characters in order to achieve goals that are fairly simple for players to understand. In *FIFA*, the goal is literal: manipulate your team of characters in order to place the ball in the opponent's goal, or manipulate your team of characters in order to prevent the opposition from placing the ball in your goal. In *Assassin's Creed*, the goal is driven by a core set of mission types. These predominantly involve elimination (assassinate another character, destroy an object), retrieval (steal or collect objects), or speed (reach a target before another character or before the time runs out). The relative simplicity of the goals in these games is modulated by the dynamics (discussed in Chapter 5 as part of the MDA framework). Recall that dynamics are the runtime behaviors of the game, or the interaction between mechanics and player inputs.

In *FIFA* games, the ambition of the developer is the creation of an authentic soccer experience. A large part of this comes down to the overall presentation of the package, which reflects real-world broadcasting styles and commentary, and includes sporting details such as press conferences and player management. But as a sports simulation, the aim is not only to simulate the real-world systems of soccer, but also the experience of being a soccer player. To that end, a great deal of effort is placed in the capturing of realistic animation using motion-capture techniques and the development of authentic procedural animation that allows for dynamic performances based on player and AI actions (as discussed in Chapter 6). An individual soccer player can execute a wide range of maneuvers, moving in any direction at different speeds. This alone is difficult to map onto a typical controller. But sports simulations like *FIFA 15* make use of teams of PCs that can be controlled by one or multiple players. In this sense, the most advanced sports simulation games are often an excellent place to look for examples of flow. The control schemes are often unforgiving for first-time gamers, but for those with more experience of using complex controllers with multiple buttons, a sense of flow and creativity can be experienced. In *FIFA 15*, the level and accuracy of control over characters was taken to an advanced level, with characters mirroring the styles of real-world players and physics playing a crucial role in terms of character-to-character and character-to-ball contact.

In the *Assassin's Creed* games, the challenge emerges from the combination of simulated NPCs and environmental obstacles. The player might be focused on the simple goal of moving with stealth toward an assassination target. However, the challenge is increased through the need to move through a crowd that contains a number of different NPC types: allies that can help the player to blend into the crowd, citizens that will bump into the player and make the character more noticeable, peasants that will draw attention to the player by aggressively begging for coins, and soldiers that might recognize the player and follow or attack him. At the same time, environmental mechanics such as hiding places, climbable walls, and ledges can help or hinder the player as he tries to remain focused on the goal while maintaining stealth. Being identified by adversaries can shift the player's priorities from stealth to speed or survival: the player can choose to quickly move through the environment in order to achieve the goal using any means, or to fight off assailants and flee the scene. In *Assassin's Creed IV: Black Flag*, the iterative development of character animation systems and environmental navigation over the course of the series is clear to see, with intuitive control and rapid movement through complex spaces, even including moving ships.

In both games, we see a strong reliance on the underlying animation technology. We also see the need for robust and intuitive control schemes that will not confound the player. Often, when character flow is broken in sports simulations or action-adventure games, it is down to either a lack of connection between player input and the resultant PC action or a glitch in the animation system. A game that is too difficult can break the sense of flow. Given the complexity of control schemes in sports simulations such as *FIFA 15*, a means of adjusting game difficulty is therefore essential. But often the action that a player wants a PC to perform simply cannot be achieved, either because it doesn't work well or doesn't exist at all in the design. Consequently, extensive user testing is crucial to games that aim for a strong sense of flow. The fine balancing between motion capture, key frame, and procedural animation also poses technical challenges for developers, and visual flaws in movement can break suspension of disbelief.

In both the *Assassin's Creed* and *FIFA* series, it is clear that there are roles to be fulfilled. There are even opportunities for role embodiment and projection in *FIFA*, through creation of unique characters that can be developed using RPG mechanics and the ability to exclusively control one soccer player. But the experience of being a soccer player or being an assassin in these games is as much down to the success of character flow as it is the quality of the character roles.

SUMMARY

Through the case studies in this chapter, we have started to apply some of the theories we have discussed in the book to the examination of existing PCs. As we have seen, PCs are often the most complicated virtual characters to design, not only because they are the most prominent characters in a game, but also because of the difficulty in balancing character personality and narrative with player agency and gameplay design. We considered four potential ways of categorizing our aesthetic experiences with these characters. First, we discussed role embodiment, where characters lack an independent voice, thereby allowing players to step into the role and impose their own personality and agency onto the character. With role fulfillment, we saw that many PCs are presented as archetypal heroes from familiar genres, providing players with an opportunity to take part in adventures and narratives that appeal to them. Role projection was discussed as a means of customizing PCs to the point where they are a reflection of the player's creativity and identity within a virtual world, rather than a defined character role. Finally, we considered the importance of the feel of PCs, with emphasis on the reasons why a sense of flow is important to suspension of disbelief and player reward when directing a PC through the game world.

It is important to bear in mind that these aesthetics of player characters are not mutually exclusive. They are merely descriptive categories for the types of experience we might have when taking control of a virtual character. A PC might clearly fit into one of these categories. But given the breadth of game design approaches and the tendency for game developers to seek innovation in their products, it's more likely that they will fit into multiple categories. Or alternatively, a PC might not really fit into any of these categories. The list is not exhaustive, and should be considered merely a starting point for the design and analysis of PCs in video games. From here it would be a good idea to start developing your own concepts for character design within and across these categories, or indeed developing your own categories for PC aesthetics that you would like to test through the design or analysis of characters.

CHAPTER 8

Cast

The Aesthetics
of the Virtual Ensemble

$\mathbf{I}$N THE PREVIOUS CHAPTER, we considered the aesthetic qualities of play-able characters (PCs), with particular emphasis on the ways in which players can take on virtual roles. Although we were focused on the PC, we did touch on the contribution of nonplayable characters (NPCs) to the player's experience of a game. In this chapter, we turn our attention to the wider cast of playable and nonplayable characters and consider the aesthetic qualities of the virtual ensemble. Even some of the earliest video games (such as those identified in the Introduction) included virtual character casts that were pivotal to the atmosphere and narrative of the product. The threat and sense of panic in *Space Invaders* {Taito 1978} is in large part due to the fact that the player is under attack from a relentless swarm of extraterrestrials rather than a singular enemy. *Pac-Man* {Namco 1980} may feature a memorable PC, but the arcade game that he is famous for would be incomplete without the distinctive cast of NPCs that he sought to evade. Over time, video game developers have added increasingly complex protagonists, antagonists, henchmen, sidekicks, and companions to their products. Today the games with the biggest budgets can contain casts of hundreds of unique virtual characters. But even games with relatively small budgets demonstrate expert use of carefully designed character ensembles.

In the following sections, we examine a selection of video games that contain notable virtual character casts. We discuss how NPCs can create emotional links with the player through their interactions with the PC, and how multiple PCs can establish a form of coprotagonism that offers a distinctive gaming experience. But first, we consider how casts of characters can have a significant and long-lasting impact on an audience.

CHARACTER APPEAL

When we look to the history of video game casts, one name that instantly springs to mind is Nintendo. While the company is more than 125 years old, consumers are likely to be most familiar with their video game products from 1980 onwards. Early products included the *Donkey Kong* {Nintendo 1981} arcade game, but it was the launch of the Family Computer (or Famicom) in 1983 that cemented Nintendo's place in video game history and that kicked off a succession of TV and handheld Nintendo consoles. Later released in the West as the Nintendo Entertainment System (or NES), this was the console that popularized some of the most memorable casts of virtual characters: casts that continue to appear in video game franchises to this day.

In this first section examining the character ensemble, we examine one of Nintendo's most important franchises: *Super Mario Bros.* {Nintendo 1985}. We look to identify why the characters in this storyworld have been so successful over the last 30 years by considering some of the theories of character presentation and performance that we discussed earlier in the book. Fundamentally, we try to establish an understanding of the appeal of these characters.

We can define *appeal* using the principle of appeal that we first identified in Chapter 6 as part of our discussion of the principles of animation. As you may recall, appeal in animation is considered to be the personality or charisma of a character. It is often difficult to define precisely what will make for an appealing character. More often than not, characters simply have a quality that could be best described as *je ne sais quoi*. Appeal tends to arise from a range of contributing factors, and what makes a particular cast appealing to one audience won't necessarily transpose to another audience or another storyworld. As such, the factors that we identify in this section can be best described as the factors that make the characters of *Super Mario Bros.* appealing. Any analysis of character ensembles from other video game worlds will likely have to take into account other design variables.

First, we should consider the visual design of the key characters in this franchise. Graphical quality has clearly increased over time, and the Mario of *New Super Mario Bros. U* {Nintendo 2012} is a more graphically advanced character than the Mario of *Super Mario Bros.* {Nintendo 1985}. However, what we observe over the history of the series is effectively a graphical evolution of characters linked to underlying technological developments. The visual intentions of the *Super Mario Bros.* character designers have been fairly consistent, despite the emergence of new computer graphics technologies. There are some slight stylistic variations to the core character designs in the franchise: notably in games such as *Super Paper Mario* {Intelligent Systems 2007}. In these instances, we might consider how the chosen visual style is shifted more toward a symbolic form (using the types of visual representations discussed in Chapter 2), and how this relates to the design goals, world aesthetics, and target audiences of the video games. However, even when the visual style is redefined in a *Super Mario Bros.* game, the fundamental visual design characteristics remain fairly consistent. So, what are these characteristics?

Sticking with the theories that we discussed in Chapter 2, we can quickly establish some potential reasons for the continued appeal of characters such as Mario, Princess Peach, and Donkey Kong. Comparing the characters within the storyworld, it is immediately evident that Nintendo makes excellent use of basic design principles such as shape selection, color choice, and silhouette. Mario is a character built primarily from circles: a shape that audiences tend to associate with playfulness and innocence. Younger audiences in particular are drawn to the oval form of Mario. The circular shape is used repeatedly in character design within the *Super Mario Bros.* storyworld, principally in characters that are most strongly associated with either goodness or cuteness (characters such as Luigi and Peach, and especially characters such as Yoshi and Toad). In contrast, while the circular shape is maintained across most characters for consistency in the visual design, we see integration of other shapes into adversarial characters: Wario is rounded but more squarelike in appearance, emphasizing his strength, while Bowser makes repeated use of triangular shapes to exaggerate his role as the chief antagonist.

Color design choices also reflect character relationships. Mario's signature red and blue sets the baseline for the color design of many other characters in the storyworld. He is partially contrasted with his brother and sidekick Luigi through the swapping of red for green, but this contrast is combined with unity in the use of blue. Bowser, on the other hand, is a complete color contrast for Mario: Mario's red and blue conflict with Bowser's green and orange, respectively.

Extending the comparison across characters into more careful examination of silhouette, we can establish that Nintendo has produced recognizable characters with a strong design hierarchy. Any of the main characters in the series could be instantly identified through silhouette alone due to their distinctive (yet simple) features and variations. Key character relationships are communicated visually through similarities, repetition, or contrasts. Luigi is essentially a taller, slimmer version of Mario. The core silhouette is otherwise the same, demonstrating a unity between the two characters. We see this silhouette design approach echoed with other duos in the series. For example, Princesses Peach and Daisy share largely the same silhouette, barring slight variation in hair and dress shape. Meanwhile, size and proportions are frequently used as a means of contrasting characters via their silhouettes. Wario shares similarities with Mario's shape, demonstrating some potential common ground, but he is a much larger, exaggerated silhouette of Mario. Likewise, Waluigi is an exaggeration of the silhouette of Luigi taken to an extreme for maximum contrast.

From here, we can identify key visual design choices within the *Super Mario Bros.* cast that we can relate to our discussion of anatomy in Chapter 1. In other words, there is a biological logic underlying many of the characters' proportions and body shapes. Wario and Waluigi are not just contrasting exaggerations of the basic silhouette of Mario and Luigi. They are also visualizations of somatotypes. Wario is essentially a character defined by the endomorph body shape, while Waluigi has the body of an ectomorph. As we covered in Chapter 1, these body shapes are best considered as extreme categories rather than true descriptions of naturalistic human forms. Most characters (and most people) are not neatly defined by one of the three types. Nevertheless, Wario and Waluigi do, to an extent, embody the endomorph and ectomorph categories. And as a result, connotations of body shape can be more clearly communicated: Wario's shape can support his fun-loving side and physical strength, while Waluigi's lean and lanky appearance can enhance the idea that he is a shifty or sneaky character.

Body proportions and facial features are used to communicate core aspects of the characters in the storyworld, including cuteness, femininity, and temperament. Many characters have extreme head-to-body ratios, particularly those that are intended to appear the cutest (such as

Toad, Yoshi, and Baby Mario). Even Mario and Luigi are designed around a head-to-body ratio of between 2:1 and 3:1. Notably, Peach and Daisy are two of the characters that have a higher head-to-body ratio, drawing more attention to their longer legs and shorter torsos: an exaggeration that serves to communicate their femininity. It is a blunt exaggeration, but one that works well: audiences quickly understand that Mario is cute, that other characters are cuter, and that Peach is feminine. Facial features also mirror a physical exaggeration of youth, through the use of larger eyes and childlike face shapes. Even facial expressions (discussed in Chapter 4) are well used by Nintendo to instantly communicate the basic nature of a character. Contrasting the friendly Toad and the adversarial Goomba characters, for instance, we can clearly see that Toad is a character built around a symbolic smiley face, while Goomba is essentially an expression of anger on short legs.

It isn't just the visual design that serves to establish the appeal of *Super Mario Bros.* characters, however. For example, sound motifs are integral to Mario's appeal, with memorable musical tracks used repeatedly throughout the series and instantly recognizable SFX used to connote specific actions, such as jumping and powering up. And gameplay actions are clearly essential to the appeal of the characters. The joy of playing any *Super Mario Bros.* game tends to boil down to the quality of the jump mechanic, which is arguably one of the most well-executed examples of a jump in any video game. Simple to grasp and difficult to master, running and jumping with accuracy in *Super Mario Bros.* mirrors the overall appeal of youth and freedom that is encapsulated by the visual design. Some games in the series have explored more elaborate use of narrative and dialogue, but it is the gameplay that is fundamental to the appeal of the characters in a *Super Mario Bros.* game. The typical *Super Mario Bros.* game essentially follows a simplified hero's journey, and most of the characters are fairly standard archetypes (or even stereotypes). But complexity or depth of narrative would be counteractive here. Simplicity is key to the appeal of the *Super Mario Bros.* ensemble: a large cast of characters whose roles, qualities, and relationships audiences can instantly recognize.

Consideration of appeal can help us to understand the strengths and successes of a large character ensemble, including fundamental relationships between characters. The appeal of some games—like those in the *Super Mario Bros.* series—might be most dependent on visual design supported by gameplay and sound design. The appeal of other virtual character ensembles might have more to do with the richness of the narrative design, the quality of the acting, or complexity of the gameplay. In designing for or analyzing character appeal, we should therefore be open to considering any of the core theories of presentation and performance that we examined in the first two parts of this book.

DEPENDENCY

While the factors that contribute to the general appeal of a virtual cast can help us to understand character relationships, understanding how those relationships are designed and how they impact upon the player requires further consideration.

In virtual character design, arguably one of the most important roles (other than the PC) is the main supporting character. We've already identified a range of video games that rely upon strong supporting roles. Alyx Vance in *Half-Life 2* is a notable example, for instance. But we could easily reel off many more key supporting characters in video games, from Tails in *Sonic the Hedgehog 2* {Sonic Team 1992} and Daxter in *Jak and Daxter: The Precursor Legacy* {Naughty Dog 2001} to Elena Fisher in the *Uncharted* series {Naughty Dog 2007} and even Leonardo Da Vinci in *Assassin's Creed II* {Ubisoft Montreal 2009}. Some of these characters occasionally become playable within the franchises, but their role is primarily to support the main PC. We could categorize these characters as sidekicks, which we touched on in Chapter 5. As we discussed, sidekicks are often used in narratives to reflect the qualities of the lead character. This could mean something as simplistic as emphasizing the courage of the hero through displays of comparative cowardice, or something more complex such as the scientific rationality of a sidekick being used to frame a lead character's spirituality.

We could use psychological and narrative theories such as those covered in Chapters 4 and 5 to inform the design of excellent supporting NPCs. There are many great examples of sidekicks who enhance a game's narrative due to the fact that they are well constructed, written, and acted. In the context of games, however, we could look to extend the notion of a sidekick further in order to clarify what it is about the relationship between a PC and supporting NPC that makes it so meaningful to the player.

When we examine some of the most notable gaming partnerships, what we tend to find is a degree of either one-way or two-way dependency. With one-way dependency, we see NPCs that rely upon player actions in order to survive or achieve their objectives. With two-way dependency, we see PCs that also depend upon the contributions of an NPC to progress. It is true that we can identify dependency within fundamental archetypes, within great character writing, and with great stories. We generally expect characters to have some form of interdependency that ties them together and enables them to change each other over the course of the narrative. But in games we can look to define character dependency in both narrative *and* gameplay terms. In other words, we can create characters whose personalities, traits, and backstories facilitate a strong interdependency within the narrative, but we can also seek to develop interdependent mechanics that support the nature of the characters and the theme of the narrative. For example, we can look to balance characters so that the PC is confident and strong, while the supporting NPC is cautious and intelligent. We can then take this further by granting the PC access to fighting and climbing mechanics and the NPC access to stealth and lock-picking mechanics. Through the design of appropriate gameplay and narrative scenarios, we can then seek to present gameplay that requires the PC to depend upon the NPC to pass an obstacle that only it can beat (and vice versa), and present narrative sequences that facilitate the development and growth of the characters as a result of their interactions and experiences.

This example is fairly basic, but if we look at video games that make use of character dependency, it becomes clear that it can be a powerful approach to virtual character design. The use of dependency between a supporting and a player character is one tactic that video game developers can use to enhance the quality of character relationships, to promote player engagement with an NPC, and, ultimately, to ensure that a player empathizes with the character that she is controlling. Dependency can provide an instant connection between a virtual character and a player, encouraging the player to feel emotionally invested in its well-being and safety. On the most basic level, we can see this in virtual pets such as Tamagotchis. By exhibiting a need for interaction from the player in order to survive, the player feels compelled to perform the repetitive interactions needed to care for and nurture the pet. Of course, there is a need for a degree of character appeal for this to work: an unappealing character or a character that is poorly written is unlikely to receive positive or sustained attention from a player, but the addition of dependency ensures that players are more attentive and mindful of their supporting characters.

Some video games focus on PC-NPC dependency to the point that we could consider this to be the fundamental aesthetic quality of the game. The games that we look at are *Ico* {Team Ico 2001} and *BioShock Infinite* {Irrational Games 2013}. In the first of these games, the player takes control of Ico, a boy condemned to be sacrificed after being ostracized by his community. After escaping, Ico finds a princess named Yorda who is being held prisoner by her mother, the Queen. With limited use of dialogue and an overall minimalist design, gameplay revolves around environmental puzzles that Ico must overcome if he is to lead Yorda to safety. *BioShock Infinite*, the third game in the *BioShock* first-person shooter series, is set in a floating city called Columbia in an alternative 1912. A totalitarian city-state that seceded from the USA, Columbia at first appears to be an American utopia but is soon revealed to be under the control of ultranationalists and white supremacists. The player takes on the role of Booker DeWitt, a troubled detective with mounting debts. Under pressure, he takes on a dangerous job to locate a young woman called Elizabeth who has been imprisoned in Columbia. Elizabeth has the ability to open up tears between dimensions in the space–time continuum, a power that features heavily in both gameplay and the narrative.

Looking at *Ico* first, we find a basic but nevertheless powerful example of dependency. The player has complete responsibility for the well-being of Yorda, who has very limited abilities. Yorda can jump (but not very far) and is ultimately dependent on the more powerful Ico to successfully traverse each environment. As Ico, the player can not only jump farther than Yorda, but also can move objects, climb, solve problems, and fight off creatures. Yorda can be instructed to follow or to wait. And that, essentially, is the extent of the gameplay actions that can be performed. The relatively simple goals—get Yorda from A to B while protecting her from threats—makes the nature of the relationship between the player and Yorda easy to understand and easy to relate to. The minimalist visual and narrative design become strengths rather than supposed shortcomings. Had *Ico* been encumbered with narrative exposition or with detailed dialogue, then the nature of the relationship between Ico and Yorda could have become muddied. Indeed, the two characters cannot engage in conversation anyway, as Yorda appears to speak a different language than Ico. This is a relationship about action, care, and responsibility in the absence of language. Although the dependency is one-way, *Ico* demonstrates excellent use of gameplay actions and level design as a means of not only communicating a relationship to the player, but also emotionally investing them in the relationship. Yorda is an NPC that the player, as Ico, feels compelled to protect—in much the same way as the Tamagotchi pet—but in a more thought-provoking context.

In *BioShock Infinite*, the narrative is much more explicit than in *Ico*. Both the PC Booker DeWitt and the main NPC Elizabeth speak throughout the game and share many conversations, including during gameplay. As discussed in Chapter 7, this means that Booker does not perform as an empty-vessel character type, as is often the case in first-person perspective games. Booker has a complex personality and backstory that is revealed through his thoughts and speech, creating some distance between the player and the player-character. As a result, controlling Booker DeWitt feels much more like going on a roller-coaster ride, in that the player is given a first-person perspective view of an action-packed experience but with limited agency to act. The metaphor of a roller coaster is given added weight by one of the core gameplay mechanics: the player can make use of overhead rails to race between the islands of Columbia. The speed of gameplay does well to distract players from the fact that they are not playing as Booker (in the same sense that one plays as Gordon Freeman in *Half-Life 2*), but are instead along for the ride. When the pace slows down and Booker's personality is given center stage, his performance can be quite jarring. Booker is certainly not an easy character to empathize with at times, which can make the first-person camera perspective a little unsettling. But creating a PC that would directly appeal to the player was not the intention of *BioShock Infinite*'s designers. Instead, it is through Booker's relationship with Elizabeth (in both narrative and gameplay terms) that empathy with both characters can be established.

As we identified earlier, Elizabeth has the ability to open tears between dimensions. This allows her to find exits, to solve puzzles, and to facilitate escapes through alternative realities. On the other hand, Booker's gameplay actions are fundamentally action-oriented through standard use of weapons, the use of "vigors" (which can be equated to potions or magic in fantasy-themed games), and the use of his Sky-Hook (which allows him to move along Columbia's rails). Although a single-player game, the complementing gameplay actions of Booker and Elizabeth create a form of two-way gameplay dependency. The player becomes dependent on Elizabeth for navigation and escape, while Elizabeth is dependent on the PC for progression through the game (predominantly using Booker's firepower to overcome enemies). In one sense, then, dependency is established in a purely formal manner: the balance of character actions means that the player needs to work with both Booker and Elizabeth to progress. But *BioShock Infinite* aims to extend this gameplay dependency into a more complex narrative involving interrelated character arcs. On a most basic level, we can see balanced archetypes in Booker (the antihero seeking redemption) and Elizabeth (a presumed damsel who is in fact the aspirational heroine with the power to save Booker). A bond is created between Booker and Elizabeth through gameplay and narrative exposition that leads to the characters changing each other over the course of the game. In many respects, Elizabeth is the more human character: more expressive, more emotional, and more realistic. Much like Alyx Vance in *Half-Life 2*, she is designed to reflect the personality and story of the PC. But in *BioShock Infinite*—a game that explores narrative themes such as alternative realities, alternative personal histories, nostalgia, parenthood, and sacrifice—Elizabeth's relationship with Booker becomes poignant. By the time of the game's dramatic conclusion, the player is implored to reflect not only on the true nature of the relationship and dependency between Booker and Elizabeth (across time and dimensions), but also to reflect on their own relationships and life experiences.

In both *Ico* and *BioShock Infinite*, we could argue that the use of a dependency aesthetic helps to make the case for video games as an emotional art form. While much of the gameplay might be formulaic and violent, the quality of the emotional relationship between Booker and Elizabeth in *BioShock Infinite* leaves the player thoughtful and contemplative. Meanwhile, the minimalist design of *Ico* helps to demonstrate that, when one character exhibits a clear dependency on the PC, this alone can generate an emotionally engaging and moving experience. One character's dependency on another character in film and television can be expertly written and acted, leading to a powerful performance that audiences can empathize with. But only video games and interactive media can require the player to address this dependency by taking action, pulling the player directly into the relationship.

CO-PROTAGONISM

In discussing dependency, we focused on a basic two-character relationship, with one character being the PC and the other being the lead NPC in the role of a sidekick. As we have seen, this approach can help to establish empathy not only for the NPC, but also for the PC. However, dependency can be taken to another level of intricacy when one considers that games can offer the player the chance to take control of multiple characters. Indeed, some games may even allow the player to take control of most of the cast. When this occurs, it is likely that we will continue to see evidence of dependencies between the multiple PCs and NPCs. But this approach offers a distinctive player experience: the ability to not only encounter dependencies between characters, but also to see and act from multiple points of view. Dependency might still be an appropriate term to describe the aesthethics of virtual characters in these games, but perhaps a better way of categorizing this type of design is to label it as *co-protagonism*.

Recall that the protagonist archetype is typically linked to that of the hero: the main character whose quest we follow, the character we root for, and the character who undergoes a significant change. Other characters within the narrative might be protagonists of a sort, in that we see them going on their own journeys and also hope to see them succeed. But when one character is most clearly affiliated with the lead role—Booker DeWitt, for example—then the other protagonists are often best described in terms of their relationship to the lead. Elizabeth is a protagonist but also the companion and sidekick of Booker. We witness Elizabeth's journey, but as players we don't have control over her actions. We are more strongly connected to Booker because it is Booker who provides us with agency. When a game gives us the opportunity to directly control multiple protagonists, we become more involved in all of their journeys. These characters might still be sidekicks, skeptics, mentors, or even antagonists, but as players we get to see the world from their point of view. In other words, these characters are co-protagonists.

The two games that we examine in this section make use of both strong appeal and dependency to create memorable characters. However, they offer appeal and embed dependency while also providing the player with opportunities for co-protagonism. The first, *Thomas Was Alone* {Bithell 2012}, is a platform game in which the player initially takes control of the titular character, Thomas. Over the course of the game, the player unlocks a series of other characters and is tasked with making them work together in order to progress through the levels. We compare co-protagonism in *Thomas Was Alone*, a relatively small and simple video game with a low budget, with the big-budget blockbuster *The Last of Us* (2013). Set after an outbreak has turned much of the population into monsters and led to the fall of world governments, *The Last of Us* follows the quest of Joel and Ellie. Not long after the start of the game, it emerges that Ellie possesses an immunity to the infection that might lead to the development of a cure. The game's narrative and gameplay subsequently centers on the journey of Joel and Ellie as they attempt to cross the country through areas populated by monsters and hostile gangs.

Thomas Was Alone, like *Ico*, makes use of a minimalist design. Made entirely by one developer with external support only in music composition and voice-over, *Thomas Was Alone* uses simple graphics and gameplay, with the latter focused on the concept of the jump mechanic. Like the *Super Mario Bros.* series, the simplicity of the jump mechanic is one of the main foundations for the appeal of the game. But the blocky and flat shapes of the world also help to establish a distinctive visual appeal. Most of the game world is presented entirely in black, so that the characters of the game—a series of quadrilaterals of various shapes and sizes—are the primary source of color. Our first impression could be that the game's appeal stems from its simplicity: that the simple mechanics will lead to complex and challenging dynamics in terms of increasingly difficult levels. This is not the case. Indeed, *Thomas Was Alone* is a relatively easy platforming game, when compared to titles such as *Super Meat Boy* {Team Meat 2010} or *Braid* {Number None 2008}. Instead, *Thomas Was Alone* is a platforming game all about characters and their relationships.

The cast of the original game consists of seven characters: Thomas, Chris, John, Claire, Laura, James, and Sarah. Each character has its own rectangular shape and associated color, creating a sense of unity. The characters also have their own distinctive gameplay properties. But most importantly, both their shape and their gameplay properties map across onto the personality of the characters. This mapping might seem quite simple, but again it is the simplicity that makes the experience of co-protagonism in *Thomas Was Alone* all the more powerful. For instance, Chris is presented as a pessimistic and grumpy character with a chip on his shoulder. He is visually represented by a small orange square, making him one of the smallest and most static-looking characters. In terms of gameplay actions, Chris has a very weak jump. Through the narration, it emerges that Chris feels he was doing just fine on his own before the other characters showed up. But in order to progress through the game's levels, it becomes clear to Chris that he needs to work with the others. In contrast, John is a tall, thin rectangle who towers over the others, who has a powerful jump, and who comes across as arrogant, sporty, and in love with the limelight. But John quickly learns to work with others in order to achieve his goals. This pattern is repeated through characters such as Claire (the large square who lacks in self esteem and confidence, but whose ability to float in toxic water makes her a valuable and much-loved team member), James (a character who strives to be different, and accomplishes this by being the only character to walk on ceilings rather than floors), and Laura (who often feels used by others, a sentiment reflected in the fact that her core mechanic is to act as a trampoline).

In gameplay, the player has the ability to swap between characters in order to solve the puzzles. Most levels involve getting all of the characters to their own end points. In effect, no character can be left behind. The player has to make them all work together, utilizing their individual strengths in order to achieve the collective goal. The narration by Danny Wallace exposes the characters' thinking and emotions. Feelings of pride, guilt, pessimism, joy, shame, and irritation are described in the humorous exposition of character thought processes, and are subtly mirrored in the gameplay actions that can be performed. Ultimately, the characters of *Thomas Was Alone* all appear familiar to us: these are people we know in our daily lives, or who may even reflect our own personalities, desires, and anxieties. And through co-protagonism—allowing the player to directly control each character and perform its simple actions in pursuit of collective success—these characters are made all the more immediate.

The Last of Us takes a similar approach, where the experience of controlling either Joel or Ellie mirrors the development of their roles and of their relationship. For much of the game, it appears as though Joel is the only PC and that Ellie is instead locked into the role of an NPC companion. As Joel, the player's core responsibility is to protect Ellie. In a similar fashion to Booker and Elizabeth, we see mutual dependency in the gameplay design: Ellie relies upon Joel's strength, stealth, and ability with weapons, while Joel relies upon Ellie to navigate the environment, climb platforms, and unlock doors. At the same time, a narrative dependency grows between the two characters. It is clear from the outset that Joel—whose teenage daughter was killed during the initial outbreak of disease some 20 years earlier—has a psychological problem with being responsible for Ellie. Unwilling to take risks or place Ellie in danger, Joel eventually finds it necessary to let go of the past and appreciate the development of new relationships and bonds. Similarly, Ellie has issues with trusting others (particularly adults) and has a troubled relationship with Joel after it becomes apparent that he might leave her behind.

Much of the praise for *The Last of Us* has been placed on the quality of the performances, both in terms of the award-winning voice acting and the fidelity of the animation. Indeed, we can examine the animation of Joel and Ellie and find model examples of emotive character performance both in and out of gameplay. For instance, when interacting with Ellie, we often see Joel move in a manner that is consistent with Laban movement analysis (LMA), as discussed in Chapter 6. One of the most obvious uses of LMA is in Joel's performance of body-half movement, where one side of the body moves to attack while the other serves to offer protection or guidance to Ellie. We also see expert use of nonverbal communication (Chapter 4) that reflects the personalities and fluctuating relationship of the two characters.

Perhaps one of the most touching sections of the game occurs after Joel is gravely injured. Ellie (as an NPC) helps Joel to safety before the game skips forward to winter. At this point, the player is thrust into the role of Ellie. The tables have turned, and now Ellie as a PC must do what she can to help Joel, who is incapacitated and critically ill in the basement of an abandoned house. Ellie the player must now hunt for food, fight off infected and hostile humans, and eventually secure drugs to help Joel get better. We are no longer as strong or as skilled as we were when we controlled Joel, but we get to use abilities that we witnessed Joel teach Ellie earlier in the game. This is Ellie coming of age and finding her own feet. The game could have skipped over this section or encapsulated it in narrative exposition. Instead, it was deemed essential for the player to get to experience the narrative from Ellie's perspective and to carry out the actions necessary to save Joel.

Parenthood has become an increasingly prevalent narrative theme in video games, no doubt a result of the number of young video game developers of the 1980s and 1990s who now have families of their own. But not all games offer as broad a representation of family as they could do. As we saw in Chapter 3, the emphasis of representation in games is usually focused on the adult male: the father, the husband, and the brother. This could have easily been the case with *The Last of Us*, a game largely about Joel's coming to terms with the loss of his child and the need for him to fulfill a father role. But by adopting a form of co-protagonism and allowing the player to experience rather than just witness Ellie's role in the narrative, the game more fully acknowledges parenthood as a two-way relationship.

SUMMARY

In this chapter, we sought to identify practices in virtual cast design through a few brief case studies. First of all, we considered the broad appeal of any given ensemble of characters, taking the *Super Mario Bros.* series as our example. We discussed the notion that appeal is not something that we can neatly organize into core variables or factors. Indeed, we described it as a *je ne sais quoi* and discussed how any of the theories that we covered earlier in the book could form the basis of character appeal within a video game. In our *Super Mario Bros.* case study, the factors we identified as being key to character appeal related to the visual design, the use of anatomical knowledge, and the role of gameplay design. Characters throughout the series—whether they were protagonists, sidekicks, contagonists, or antagonists—were shown to share a visual language that reflected their roles, archetypes, and relationships. Had we chosen another game series, we would likely have found that other factors were key to the appeal of the cast. If we were to take the other game casts we examined in this chapter, we could argue that the cast of *Thomas Was Alone* builds appeal through visual design and gameplay, but also more explicitly through narrative design. The casts of games such as *BioShock Infinite* and *The Last of Us* lean much more heavily on narrative design than *Thomas Was Alone* for their appeal, but they also rely on more detailed consideration of character psychology and politics, representation of family, and the authenticity of the animated performance. Ultimately, to conduct an analysis of character appeal, it is necessary to identify the aspects of the character design that are most important to the design and success of the video game.

In the sections that followed, we looked specifically at two approaches to designing character relationships: dependency and co-protagonism. We saw that these were not exclusive categories and that a mix of both methods could be achieved. First, dependency was discussed as a method for designing character interactions so that one or more NPCs could be directly dependent upon the PC through both gameplay dependency and narrative dependency. We also saw that dependency can be two-way, in that an NPC and PC can be mutually dependent on each other. Co-protagonism was introduced as a design that allows the player to switch roles within a game in order to experience the point of view of multiple characters, either at will (as in *Thomas Was Alone*) or as a carefully crafted part of the game narrative (as in *The Last of Us*). Beyond the overall appeal of the character cast, dependency and co-protagonism were shown to be two approaches that could be used to strengthen the bonds between virtual characters and to enhance the player's understanding of their personalities, aspirations, and experiences.

Taking the ideas discussed in this chapter forward into your own practice, it would be a good idea to seek to develop your own original character concepts with these factors in mind. After first identifying what the core appeal of your cast of characters should be, consideration of dependencies within the cast and opportunities for co-protagonism could help you to shape a virtual character ensemble that not only engages players emotionally, but also challenges them to see human relationships in new and perhaps unexpected ways.

CHAPTER 9

Complexity

The Aesthetics of Hyperreal Characters

IN THIS FINAL CHAPTER OF THE BOOK, we aim to explore some of the most complex issues facing the design of virtual characters. Having examined issues of player control and the design of interactive casts in the previous two chapters, we end by considering how virtual characters exist with increasingly intricate simulations, and how this in turn impacts upon our perception and interpretation of character performances.

Before we begin, it is important that we briefly establish a theoretical context for the study of characters within advanced simulations. Specifically, we are interested in the concept of the *hyperreal*. Hyperreality is a term used by postmodern theorists to describe the blurring of perceptible boundaries between the real world and the virtual world. Hyperreality was originally defined by the French theorist Jean Baudrillard (1994), who made the argument that reality has come to be replaced by a system of signs, which ultimately makes it more difficult for consumers to discriminate between physical reality and simulated reality. Although some critics have considered his work to be radical or controversial, Baudrillard's writing has greatly informed game studies (as have the contributions of other postmodern theorists and sociologists), and hyperreality is one of the most important concepts for understanding the evolution of the medium.

In the context of this book, we are specifically concerned with how the advancement of game technologies has led to the development of hyperreal characters. We look at how virtual characters can be imbued with simulated intelligence, and how they might be designed to retain knowledge of our actions. First, though, we consider one of the most well-known issues in virtual character design: the problem of the *uncanny valley*.

THE UNCANNY VALLEY

We first identified the uncanny valley problem back in Chapter 2 when discussing photographic visual styles. The uncanny valley theory predicts that when a character approaches a high degree of visual realism, it is more likely that we will find unsettling flaws in its appearance or performance. This can cause problems for designers who aim to produce virtual characters within a photorealistic visual style. In the early decades of commercial game development, game designers were not able to attempt photorealism, which led to a prevalence of cartoon, stylized, or abstract visual styles. However, as technology has progressed, we have seen increasing use of photorealism in games. CD-based games allowed designers to make use of full-motion video (FMV), but the lack of interactivity meant that this approach was only really applicable in cutscenes. Use of FMV in games declined as three-dimensional (3D) graphics technology advanced, and today it is commonplace to see high-resolution 3D characters capable of complex animation rendered inside game engines. Although a variety of visual styles is used in games, those developers who aim for photorealism in their virtual characters are now achieving visual standards comparable to those of film and animation.

To understand the problems that photorealistic characters raise, we must first consider the work of Sigmund Freud (2003). In 1919, Freud published the seminal essay *Das Unheimlich*—literally "the unhomely" when translated into English, but the term *the uncanny* has been used more widely. In his essay, Freud sought to define the uncanny within the field of aesthetics, which had more often favored studies of the beautiful or the sublime. In contrast, the uncanny is defined as something fearful. More specifically, Freud discussed how the uncanny can be comprehended as a fear of the unfamiliar, that is, in recognizing something that appears familiar to our senses, but which, on some level, appears incorrect, unseemly, or eerie. Through psychoanalysis and literary criticism, Freud went on to discuss the psychological underpinnings of this aesthetic emotion and its deployment within the creative arts. The uncanny can be considered a desired response within works of art that aim to intrigue and terrify: in gothic or horror fiction, for example.

In 1970, a Japanese researcher named Masahiro Mori published an article that made a connection between the uncanny and our perception of humanlike robots (Mori 2012). Mori proposed that the more lifelike a robot appeared, the more we would find the robot familiar. But as the robot more closely resembled a human in appearance, subtle differences between the humanlike robot and a real human being would become noticeable. The response from an observer would therefore be one of disgust, revulsion, or fear: The robot would be uncanny. Mori named the problem of humanlike appearance the *uncanny valley*. Since Mori's publication, computer graphics have advanced exponentially. Computer graphics were rudimentary in 1970. Indeed, as we covered in the Introduction, video games were yet to become established as a commercial medium when Mori first proposed his theory. But by the late 1990s, video games and animated films were capable of representing fairly realistic humanlike virtual characters. And it was clear that the problem that Mori had originally applied to humanlike robots could also be applied to computer graphics.

Many animators and game developers have argued that the uncanny valley problem can be solved with the development of more advanced computer graphics technologies, motion-capture tools, and rendering engines. But the problem of perceived uncanniness in humanlike virtual characters is that, no matter how close to reality we get, there are always likely to be subtle imperfections in appearance that audiences can detect. Virtual characters need to be not only highly accurate in visual presentation, but also have to be capable of performing in a manner that looks realistic. The latter is often the main challenge to video game developers. Subtle humanlike appearance is one thing; subtle performance is quite another. Factor into this, then, that these characters also need to be able to respond to our actions in an authentic manner and it becomes clear that the uncanny valley will remain a key consideration in virtual character design for the foreseeable future.

We could look at early prerendered characters in games as our examples, but it would be more logical for us to examine virtual character performances that are rendered within game engines. As such, we discuss games that were released in the seventh generation of game consoles, when highly realistic in-game characters were first starting to emerge. All of the games were noted for the realism of the character appearances and performances, but were also discussed in terms of the potential uncanny responses experienced by players.

First, we should consider the 2010 game *Heavy Rain* {Quantic Dream 2010}. Presented as an interactive drama, the game tasks the player with taking control of several characters. These characters subsequently become involved in the events surrounding a serial killer known as the Origami Killer. Gameplay encompasses context-sensitive actions rather than specific repeatable actions, and there is an emphasis on gameplay that is similar to quick-time events, or QTEs (pushing labeled buttons to perform bespoke actions). At first, the characters of *Heavy Rain* were noted for the quality of their presentation and performance when compared to previous games set within a photorealistic style. In particular, an early demonstration for *Heavy Rain*—known as *The Casting*—was widely discussed as a sign of things to come on seventh-generation consoles. However, closer inspection revealed subtle inadequacies in the rendering and movement. This ended up becoming a major distraction for some commentators and gamers. While the developer's focus was on introducing a new approach to mature, interactive storytelling in video games, there was clear difficulty in capturing authentic acted movement, especially facial movement around the eyes and mouth. Far from flattening or crossing the uncanny valley, the characters in the final game came across as eerie.

It would be a fair argument to make that, in 2010, the characters of *Heavy Rain* were among the most humanlike virtual characters in any commercial video game. Not only was the rendering and motion-captured animation of an exceptionally high standard, but also the adult nature of the narrative themes and the atypical gameplay design meant that these characters were required to perform in a manner that more closely imitated cinema than traditional action-adventure game design. And yet, with hindsight, it is clear that the characters actually stand out as one of the more problematic aspects of the game's presentation. Despite winning plaudits for the gameplay, narrative, and the wider production design, time has only drawn further attention to the gap between the characters in *Heavy Rain* and our expectations of authentic human presentation and performance.

After the launch of *Heavy Rain*, a range of titles were released that sought to address the identified issues of character rendering and movement. The development of more advanced technologies and more accurate motion-capture tools was discussed as the solution to the uncanny valley problem. This was particularly true of Rockstar Games's *L.A. Noire* {Team Bondi 2011}. Inspired by the film noir genre, *L.A. Noire* places the player in the role of Detective Cole Phelps, with gameplay focused on interrogation of witnesses and suspects. As in *Heavy Rain*, much was made of the fidelity of the virtual character performances in the game, which featured detailed facial movements. Indeed, detecting subtle facial movements formed part of the gameplay, as the player was tasked with deducing whether or not NPCs were lying to them.

While the novel approach to interactive narrative design was arguably the main selling point behind *Heavy Rain*, the motion-capture technologies were the star of *L.A. Noire*'s promotional videos and press articles. By using 360-degree motion capture that was able to detect and record even subtle facial movements, the virtual characters of *L.A. Noire* are about as close to virtual actors as you are liable to find in a video game. Indeed, the precision of the capture technology leads us to conclude that, in many ways, this is actually a form of translated film sequence rather than computer animation. And yet the response from many players was that something was still not right. Certainly the performances and presentation had improved, but the inadequacies had become even subtler: the failure of fingers to make realistic contact with faces, the lack of color change in the skin, or simply an unexplainably alien facial expression. The characters are impressive but uncanny, and once again we find that time only widens the gap.

The audience's rising expectations are arguably the main challenge to character designers preoccupied with crossing the uncanny valley. Newer games always put older virtual characters into context. Quantic Dream's next release after *Heavy Rain* was *Beyond: Two Souls* {Quantic Dream 2013}, which demonstrated a marked improvement in virtual character presentation and performance, supported by impressive motion-captured animation of actors Ellen Page and Willem Dafoe. It was an improvement, but mainly in the sense that the original imperfections became less noticeable. Even the games that have bridged the console generation through eighth-generation remakes—games such as *The Last of Us* {Naughty Dog 2013} or *Tomb Raider* {Crystal Dynamics 2013}—still suffer from visual imperfections.

Given that this section specifically concerns technology in relation to virtual character presentation and performance, it is highly likely that cutting-edge virtual characters will emerge in the months (not even the years) after the publication of this book. Many of the major game studios, publishers, and technology companies have already started to demonstrate virtual characters inside game engines that are astonishingly realistic. Nevertheless, the uncanny valley problem is one that will persist within virtual character design. Fundamentally, gamers will always be aware that the virtual characters are precisely that: graphical representations of humans within a simulation. When we talk about flattening or crossing the uncanny valley in virtual character design, what we are actually talking about is an extended suspension of disbelief. We want players to believe in the virtual characters for as long as possible: to become lost in the narrative and in gameplay and to be moved by the quality of the virtual performance. It is inevitable that something about the presentation or performance of a virtual character will cause the player to blink in disbelief. This is virtual acting, after all, and acting is all about deception. Some of the best actors in the world are still susceptible to giving performances that cause an audience to stop believing in the authenticity of the character. We don't critique an acted performance by commenting on the realism of the character's eyes, skin, hair, or facial movements. Instead, we question whether the character on screen is an authentic representation of a human thought process. When examined in isolation, the characters of games such as *The Last of Us* easily appear uncanny. These clearly aren't real humans; they are simulants. But we don't notice this when playing the game: the quality of the acting, the quality of the writing, and the authenticity of the human personalities suspend our disbelief. From realism in visual presentation and performance, our next consideration should therefore be authenticity in thought process.

THE TURING TEST

Can virtual characters be engineered in such a way that they are capable of exhibiting a thought process that we perceive to be intelligent? As we saw in Chapter 6 when we discussed the importance of thinking to character performance, the imitation of intelligence is central to animation theory. In animation, all entities that we regard as characters—regardless of whether they are photorealistic or abstract—are designed and animated in such a way that they induce a suspension of disbelief in the audience. The emphasis on making animated characters appear alive and sentient is crucial. If we see in an animated character a representation of human intelligence, personality, and thought process, then we can suspend our disbelief and accept the character as credible, even if the character is visually presented as nonhuman.

In video games, the representation of humanlike thinking is much more complex. In linear animation for film and television, there is obviously no requirement for characters to respond to the audience and react in real time. The representation of thought process can be achieved through the iterative creation of frames of animation, guided by the principles of animation and consideration of acting theory. Virtual characters in games and interactive media, however, cater for player interaction. We can create virtual characters that exist entirely within narrative sequences, and whose behaviors are fixed regardless of how the game is played. Depending on the intentions and aspirations of the developer, this can be a valid design choice. However, as interaction is the cornerstone of the video game medium, we could argue that virtual characters should progressively become more reactive to player action, demonstrating a capacity to react in real time to interactions in a manner that maintains our suspension of disbelief.

In the twentieth century, the British computing pioneer Alan Turing posed the question, "Can machines think?" (Turing 1950). What followed was the proposal of a hypothetical test that could be applied to a computer program. The idea behind the test was that a sufficiently advanced computer program could respond to questions posed by human participants in a manner that would fool them into thinking the computer was actually another human being. It was this premise that led to the development of ELIZA (Weizenbaum 1966), the character program that we first discussed in the Introduction. The Turing test has since become a key concept in the field of artificial intelligence. The test has been criticized: for example, there is a discrepancy between intelligence and real human behavior (which can be unintelligent), and the performance of seemingly intelligent behaviors does not mean that a true intelligence exists beneath the surface. However, the broad concept of the Turing test is very useful as a means of framing analysis of simulated humanlike behavior in virtual characters. We might not be deploying an explicit test when we interact with a character in a video game, and we are certainly aware that these characters are not real. (We loaded them when we started the video game; we can see them represented within a virtual world.) But we test these characters implicitly whenever we interact with them. We expect them to respond to our actions, which can include not only dialogue interaction, but also physical and emotional interactions. When our suspension of disbelief is broken by an unusual action, an odd behavior, or a strange piece of dialogue, we could say that the Turing test has failed.

One of the best examples of the Turing test in application is *Façade* {Mateas and Stern 2005}, an experimental interactive drama game that was initially developed as a test of natural language processing and character artificial intelligence. In the final game, players are invited to fulfill the role of a guest visiting the home of NPCs Grace and Trip. The player can move around their small apartment in first-person view and interact with objects. Most importantly, the player can "speak" with the characters by typing in text. The game analyzes these statements and interprets what the text is likely to mean in the context of the game. In consequence, the virtual characters Grace and Trip are able to respond to the player's verbal input by exhibiting emotional responses. This can range from happiness at an implied compliment through to irritation or even fury at insults. But the characters can also react to your text in different ways: One character may perceive a compliment in a positive and enthusiastic manner, while the other might regard the compliment as an intrusion and a threat to the stability of their relationship. The direction that the interactive story unfolds can also be determined by the player's actions. Through the conversation with Grace and Trip, the player might encourage the couple to stay together or, alternatively, cause their relationship to implode. They might even find themselves thrown out of the apartment. Throughout the game, both Grace and Trip give fairly credible performances (given the limited art style) that match their implied emotions and thought processes. On the one hand, *Façade* demonstrates how virtual characters can be engineered so that they respond to a range of both predictable and unpredictable player actions, and how this in turn can progress an interactive story. But at the same time, *Façade* has also been shown to fail the Turing test when the player behaves unusually or shows disinterest, with Grace and Trip unable to interact with the player meaningfully.

The Sims is one of the most accomplished video game series to have an explicit focus on character behaviors and personalities. Over its four main games and numerous expansions and spin-offs, *The Sims* has received broad critical acclaim and commercial success. Essentially a life-simulation game—a subgenre of the simulation genre—*The Sims* is an evolution of digital pets like the Tamagotchi, which we touched on briefly when discussing dependency in Chapter 8. Players create and interact with a series of characters (known as Sims) satisfying their basic needs (shelter, food, careers) as well as addressing their mood states and desires. The characters in *The Sims* establish a dependency on the player but, unlike the games that we looked at in Chapter 7, the player does not take on a specific character role. Instead, the player is omnipresent: a player perspective often used in strategy games and world-based simulation games like *SimCity* {EA Maxis 2013}. So while characters in *The Sims* exhibit a degree of dependency on the player in terms of their need for attention and interaction, this presentation of dependency is more of a driver for continued play rather than a key aesthetic quality of the virtual characters.

Instead, the simulation of human personalities is arguably the most interesting quality of the characters in *The Sims*. Sims are essentially virtual dolls that demonstrate their own thought processes and needs, both of which can be developed through a mixture of simulation and RPG-style gameplay mechanics. Players can engage with creative gameplay by building houses, designing interiors, and developing garden spaces, all of which can impact on a Sim's satisfaction. These spaces can be progressively enhanced and expanded by generating money, known as Simoleons, which in turn can be earned by directing Sims to pursue careers. Sims can also level up a series of skills under the direction of players, who have the ability to intervene and guide Sims to perform certain tasks. Ultimately, the core of *The Sims* series is an artificial intelligence system (that is both autonomous and subject to player interactions), while the shell is a satirical representation of modern domestic life.

Although all of the games in the main series contain Sims that have moods and desires, *The Sims 4* {EA Maxis 2014} introduced the most advanced set of behavioral variables to date. By selecting aspirations (such as family, fortune, and knowledge) and traits (from broad traits such as cheerful, outgoing, or loner through to much more specific traits such as bookworm, materialistic, or romantic), players have the ability to define a complex personality for their characters. We can recognize the personality theories that we discussed earlier in the book in the aspirations and traits of *The Sims 4*. Essentially, players set up their characters with personality traits, views, and attitudes, and these in turn have a significant impact on how Sims will think, behave, and act. Sims will take autonomous actions in order to address their moods or emotional states, and these decisions will be driven by their personality design. At the same time, players can seek to change the emotional state of a Sim by guiding it to perform tasks or interact with objects in the world that match its personality type. The end result is a fairly complex simulation of personality within interactive virtual characters, coupled with animated performances that help to communicate their emotions. The performances in *The Sims 4* (and, indeed, earlier simulations such as *Façade*) may be fairly simplistic and cartoony in comparison to the much more nuanced and authentic performances that can be observed in games such as *L.A. Noire*, but this is because the focus is on runtime dynamics rather than visual realism. Where *L.A. Noire* emphasizes nuanced movement, *The Sims 4* emphasizes nuanced behavior.

By referring to the Turing test as a means of understanding virtual character design, we are highlighting the potential for a virtual character to fool us into thinking that it has a human intelligence. Ultimately, it is not the uncanny valley or Turing test alone that represents an ideal simulation of a character, but a combination of both. In other words, a truly authentic and humanlike virtual character should not only look and move as we would expect a human to, but also think and perform in a manner consistent with an authentic human intelligence.

VIRTUAL KNOWLEDGE

However, we could argue that the combination of authentic appearance and authentic intelligence is still insufficient for the ideal simulation. As the power of computer technologies advances, we are increasingly looking for virtual characters to give performances that demonstrate broad contextual awareness. In other words, we expect virtual characters to act, behave, and make choices in ways that are consistent with the virtual world that they inhabit. Even if character rendering and animation are perfected to the point that the uncanny valley ceases to be a consideration, and even if immensely complex personality simulations can be engineered so that virtual characters pass the Turing test with ease, there is still the potential for a virtual character to act out of sync with the game world.

From this perspective, we could define an authentic character performance as being dependent on the character's development and retention of knowledge. Virtual characters need to have not only a preloaded knowledge of the storyworld, but also an ability to learn from what the player does. This knowledge base should inform how a character performs when interacting with the player, and it should theoretically apply to all characters in a game from background NPCs all the way up to pivotal characters. In *Grand Theft Auto V* {Rockstar North 2013}, for instance, background characters "know" to show disdain toward a player who is acting aggressively or obnoxiously. As the player ups the ante, these characters will know to hurl insults or to fight back. Eventually, crowds will flee as the player shows extreme violence and disregard for pedestrians. But there is limited long-term memory in these background characters, and the world will eventually return to normal. This has much to do with the sandbox nature of the game: if background characters truly remembered the actions of the player, then the game would no longer be playable in the manner that is intended. The background characters have to demonstrate a limited capacity to retain and use complex knowledge of the world and of the PCs, or else it would not be a *Grand Theft Auto* game. Nevertheless, background virtual characters that have the ability to learn are a key consideration for future virtual character design.

Pivotal NPCs have a more immediate need to demonstrate and retain knowledge of the virtual world. In particular, NPC knowledge is most relevant to games that provide interactive narratives: games that allow the player to make choices that impact on the plot. Two of the most prominent video game series of recent years that have focused on narrative interaction are *The Walking Dead* {Telltale Games 2012} and *Mass Effect* {BioWare 2007, 2010, 2012}. *The Walking Dead* is based on the comic book series of the same name, but presents an original narrative based within the shared storyworld. In the game, the player fulfills the role of Lee Everett, a convict who is being transported to a Georgia prison when a zombie outbreak hits. After escaping from an initial attack, Lee finds and subsequently takes into his care a young girl called Clementine. The narrative over the five episodes centers on Lee's care for Clementine. Gameplay is similar to traditional graphical adventure games, with emphasis on player interaction with the environment and dialogue decisions. The *Mass Effect* series follows the story of Commander Shephard, a veteran soldier with a customizable appearance (including selection of gender). Over the three games in the main series, the narrative centers on Shephard's investigation into and final showdown with an alien race known as the Reapers. Again, gameplay involves making decisions (including within dialogue) in addition to action and RPG gameplay elements.

Both games place a strong emphasis on player choice and the subsequent impact on NPC memory of the virtual world. First, it should be noted that player choices don't have a major impact on the storyline, in that the overall narrative remains fairly fixed in both series. This aligns with the modulated plot structure that we discussed in Chapter 5, which can cater for alternative paths through a game's narrative with a potential for subtle variations in a game's ending. The role of player choice in *The Walking Dead* and *Mass Effect* has more to do with the journey (the character interactions and relationships) rather than the plot or conclusion. In *The Walking Dead*, for example, there are many decisions that the player can make that seemingly impact on the narrative. A few of these do open up alternative routes through the game, or alternative experiences. But for the most part, the plot remains fixed. What the player is actually manipulating is the beat-by-beat emotional connection between the PC and the NPCs she encounters. While the dependency aesthetic is used to

212 Virtual Character Design for Games and Interactive Media

reinforce the relationship between Lee and Clementine, it is Clementine's capacity to develop some knowledge of the player's actions that makes her a distinctive virtual character. Her knowledge base might be limited, and ultimately her impression of the PC does not affect the overall narrative of the game, but her subtle responses and memories of the player's ethical and moral choices help to create a touching relationship with Lee.

Like *The Walking Dead* series, *Mass Effect* also incorporates a degree of memory into the character design. One of the most notable features of *Mass Effect* is the player's ability to ensure that decisions made in earlier games impact on their gameplay experience in later games, through the use of a save-file transfer. This essentially means that key decisions made in *Mass Effect* can be transferred into *Mass Effect 2*, and likewise from *Mass Effect 2* into *Mass Effect 3*. Given that it is a challenge to provide an authentic modulated plot structure with multiple decision branches in just one game, the fact that decisions are carried across the series is an accomplishment that goes some way toward establishing continuity of character knowledge. With such a strong emphasis on decisions and character reactions to decisions, the lack of this feature would greatly undermine the authenticity of virtual character knowledge in *Mass Effect 2* and *Mass Effect 3*. Much of what is retained ultimately relates to character survival (characters that die as a result of a player decision do not return, while those who are spared or otherwise survive as a result of player action might return in later games). But subtler decisions also impact on character memory and subsequently on the events that unfold (such as aiding a character in an earlier game or initiating romantic relations with particular characters).

CONCLUSION

In this final chapter on the aesthetics of virtual characters, we have reached a point where we are looking to hypothesize what the future of virtual character design might look like. By considering hyperreality—in other words, the point at which virtual characters become a complete simulation and alter our perception of what is and is not real—we have started to predict what might be possible using the technologies of both today and tomorrow. We broke this hyperreal vision of virtual characters down into three categories: their capacity to cross the uncanny valley, their capacity to pass the Turing test, and their ability to possess and develop virtual knowledge. If we were to combine these qualities, we could define what might be considered the ideal for a complex virtual character as, respectively, a character that gives an authentic humanlike performance, that exhibits humanlike intelligence, and that shows comprehensive contextual awareness.

The emphasis of this book has been on the design of virtual characters within the specific context of video games. Our examples and case studies have been drawn from critically and commercially successful video games and video game franchises. We have sought to understand character design by applying relevant knowledge from biology, visual design, sociology, psychology, narrative theory, game design, acting theory, and animation. We then looked to define key aesthetic qualities of characters in games, culminating in our discussion of the hyperreal. The hyperreality of virtual characters is likely to extend well beyond our traditional understanding of video games and interactive media. Characters already appear as virtual agents within digital devices, offering consumers assistance while they shop, pay for their parking, or navigate an airport. Characters can leap across devices, allowing players to engage with them on their television screen at home and on their mobile devices when they leave for the daily commute. We even see a transportation of characters between the virtual and physical worlds. Video games such as *Disney Infinity* {Avalanche Software 2013} allow players to engage with both collectible figurines and virtual play sets. Essentially, virtual characters are becoming ubiquitous. And the game designers of today—equipped with a solid understanding of the theories of character presentation and performance—will be well placed to lead the way in the production of virtual characters for use not only in video games, but in all manner of interactive media.

REFERENCES

Baudrillard, J. 1994. *Simulacra and simulation*. Trans. S. F. Glaser. Ann Arbor: University of Michigan Press. (Orig. pub. 1981.)

Freud, S. 2003. *The uncanny*. Trans. D. McLintock. London: Penguin. (Orig. pub. 1919.)

Mori, M. 2012. The uncanny valley. Trans. K. F. MacDorman and N. Kageki. *IEEE Robotics & Automation Magazine* 19 (2): 98–100. (Orig. pub. 1970.)

Turing, A. M. 1950. Computing machinery and intelligence. *Mind* 49: 433–60.

Weizenbaum, J. 1966. ELIZA: A computer program for the study of natural language communication between man and machine. *Communications of the ACM* 9 (1): 36–45.

Glossary

AI: artificial intelligence
FMV: full-motion video
FPS: first-person shooter
HCI: human–computer interaction
MMO: massively multiplayer online
MMORPG: massively multiplayer online role-playing game
NPC: nonplayer character
PC: player character
QTE: quick-time event
RPG: role-playing game
SFX: sound effects

Ludography

2K Games Boston. 2007. *BioShock*. PlayStation 3/Xbox 360/Windows/Mac OS X. 2K Games.

Activision. 1982. *Pitfall!* Atari 2600. Activision.

Advanced Microcomputer Systems. 1983. *Dragon's Lair*. Arcade. Cinematronics.

Anthropy, A. 2012. *Dys4ia*. Adobe Flash. Newgrounds.

Atari, Inc. 1972. *Pong*. Arcade. Atari, Inc.

Avalanche Software. 2013. *Disney Infinity*. PlayStation 3/Xbox 360/Wii/Wii U/ Nintendo 3DS/Windows/iOS. Disney Interactive Studios.

Bethesda Game Studios. 2002. *The Elder Scrolls III: Morrowind*. Xbox/Windows. Bethesda Softworks.

Bethesda Game Studios. 2006. *The Elder Scrolls IV: Oblivion*. PlayStation 3/Xbox 360/Windows. 2K Games/Bethesda Softworks.

Bethesda Game Studios. 2011. *The Elder Scrolls V: Skyrim*. PlayStation 3/Xbox 360/Windows. Bethesda Softworks.

BioWare. 2007. *Mass Effect*. PlayStation 3/Xbox 360/Windows. Microsoft Game Studios.

BioWare. 2009. *Dragon Age: Origins*. PlayStation 3/Xbox 360/Windows/Mac OS X. Electronic Arts.

BioWare. 2010. *Mass Effect 2*. PlayStation 3/Xbox 360/Windows. Electronic Arts.

BioWare. 2012. *Mass Effect 3*. PlayStation 3/Xbox 360/Wii U/Windows. Electronic Arts.

Bithell, M. 2012. *Thomas Was Alone*. PS3/PlayStation Vita/Windows PC/Mac OS X/ Linux/iOS/Android.

Blizzard Entertainment. 2004. *World of Warcraft*. Windows/Mac OS X. Blizzard Entertainment.

Bohemia Interactive. 2006. *ARMA: Armed Assault*. Windows. 505 Games/Atari.

Bungie. 2001. *Halo: Combat Evolved*. Xbox/Windows. Microsoft Game Studios.

Bungie. 2014. *Destiny*. PlayStation 3/PlayStation 4/Xbox 360/Xbox One. Activision.

Capcom. 1996. *Resident Evil*. PlayStation/Sega Saturn/Windows. Capcom.

Capcom. 2009. *Resident Evil 5*. PlayStation 3/Xbox 360/Windows. Capcom.

Capybara Games. 2012. *Superbrothers: Sword & Sworcery EP*. Windows/Mac OS X/Linux/iOS/Android. Capybara Games.

Core Design. 1996. *Tomb Raider*. PlayStation/Sega Saturn/DOS. Eidos Interactive.

Crystal Dynamics. 2013. *Tomb Raider*. PlayStation 3/PlayStation 4/Xbox 360/ Xbox One/Windows/Mac OS X. Square Enix.

DMA Design. 2001. *Grand Theft Auto III*. PlayStation 2/Xbox/Windows. Rockstar Games.

EA Canada. 2014. *FIFA 15*. PlayStation 3/PlayStation 4/PlayStation Vita/Xbox 360/Xbox One/Wii/Nintendo 3DS/Windows. EA Sports.

EA Maxis. 2013. *SimCity*. Windows/Mac OS X. Electronic Arts.

EA Maxis. 2014. *The Sims 4*. Windows. Electronic Arts.

Firaxis Games. 2012. *X-COM: Enemy Unknown*. PlayStation 3/Xbox 360/Windows/Mac OS X/Linux/iOS/Android. 2K Games.

Fullbright Company, The. 2013. *Gone Home*. Windows/Mac OS X/Linux/Wii U.

Higinbotham, W. 1958. *Tennis for Two*. Analog computer.

Hofmeier, R. 2011. *Cart Life*. Windows.

HyperBole Studios. 1998. *The X-Files Game*. PlayStation/Windows. Fox Interactive.

Id Software. 1993. *Doom*. DOS. GT Interactive.

Infinity Ward. 2003. *Call of Duty*. Windows. Activision.

Intelligent Systems. 2007. *Super Paper Mario*. Wii. Nintendo.

Irrational Games. 2013. *Bioshock Infinite*. PlayStation 3/Xbox 360/Windows/Mac OS X. 2K Games.

Key, E. 2013. *Proteus*. PlayStation 3/PlayStation Vita/Windows/Mac OS X/Linux.

Konami. 1981. *Frogger*. Arcade. Konami.

Konami Computer Entertainment Tokyo. 2001. *Silent Hill 2*. PlayStation 2/PlayStation 3/Xbox/Xbox 360/Windows. Konami.

Linden Research, Inc. 2003. *Second Life*. Windows/Max OS X.

Lionhead Studios. 2008. *Fable II*. Xbox 360. Microsoft Games.

LucasFilm Games. 1987. *Maniac Mansion*. Commodore 64/Apple II/IBM PC/Amiga/Atari ST/NES. LucasFilm Games.

LucasFilm Games. 1990. *The Secret of Monkey Island*. Amiga/Atari ST/DOS/Mac OS/Mega CD. LucasArts.

MachineGames. 2014. *Wolfenstein: The New Order*. PlayStation 3/PlayStation 4/Xbox 360/Xbox One/Windows. Bethesda Softworks.

Mateas, M., and A. Stern. 2005. *Façade*. Windows/Mac OS X.

Media Molecule. 2008. *LittleBigPlanet*. PlayStation 3. Sony Computer Entertainment.

Midway Games. 1992. *Mortal Kombat*. Arcade/SNES/Mega Drive/Master System/Game Gear/Amiga/DOS. Acclaim Entertainment.

MIT. 1959. *Mouse in the Maze*. TX-0.

Namco. 1980. *Pac-Man*. Arcade. Midway.

Naughty Dog. 1996. *Crash Bandicoot*. PlayStation. Sony Computer Entertainment.

Naughty Dog. 2001. *Jak and Daxter: The Precursor Legacy*. PlayStation 2. Sony Computer Entertainment.

Naughty Dog. 2007. *Uncharted: Drake's Fortune*. PlayStation 3. Sony Computer Entertainment.

Naughty Dog. 2013. *The Last of Us*. PlayStation 3/PlayStation 4. Sony Computer Entertainment.

Nintendo. 1981. *Donkey Kong*. Arcade. Nintendo.

Nintendo. 1985. *Super Mario Bros*. NES. Nintendo.

Nintendo. 1986. *The Legend of Zelda*. NES. Nintendo.

Nintendo. 1987. *Metroid*. NES. Nintendo.

Nintendo. 1996. *Super Mario 64*. N64. Nintendo.

Nintendo. 1998. *The Legend of Zelda: The Ocarina of Time*. N64. Nintendo.

Nintendo. 2004. *The Legend of Zelda: The Wind Waker*. Gamecube. Nintendo.

Nintendo. 2012. *New Super Mario Bros. U*. Wii U. Nintendo.

Number None, Inc. 2008. *Braid*. PS3/Xbox 360/Windows/Mac OS X/Linux.

Nutting Associates. 1971. *Computer Space*. Arcade.

Oliver Twins. 1987. *Dizzy—The Ultimate Cartoon Adventure*. Amstrad CPC/
Commodore 64/ZX Spectrum. Codemasters.

Origin Systems. 1997. *Ultima Online*. Windows. Electronic Arts.

Platinum Games. 2009. *Bayonetta*. PlayStation 3/Xbox 360. Sega.

Polytron Corporation. 2012. *Fez*. PS3/PS4/PlayStation Vita/Xbox 360/Windows/
Mac OS X/Linux. Polytron Corporation.

Project Soul. 2005. *Soulcalibur III*. PlayStation 2. Namco.

Project Soul. 2008. *Soulcalibur IV*. PlayStation 3/Xbox 360. Namco Bandai.

Project Soul. 2012. *Soulcalibur V*. PlayStation 3/Xbox 360. Namco Bandai Games.

Quantic Dream. 2010. *Heavy Rain*. PlayStation 3. Sony Computer Entertainment.

Quantic Dream. 2013. *Beyond: Two Souls*. PlayStation 3. Sony Computer
Entertainment.

Rare. 1997. *GoldenEye 007*. N64. Nintendo.

Remedy Entertainment. 2001. *Max Payne*. PlayStation 2/Xbox/Windows/Mac
OS. Rockstar Games.

Rockstar North. 2008. *Grand Theft Auto IV*. PlayStation 3/Xbox 360/Windows.
Rockstar Games.

Rockstar North. 2013. *Grand Theft Auto V*. PlayStation 3 and 4/Xbox 360 and
One/Windows. Rockstar Games.

Rockstar San Diego. 2010. *Red Dead Redemption*. PlayStation 3/Xbox 360.
Rockstar Games.

Rocksteady Studios. 2009. *Batman: Arkham Asylum*. PlayStation 3/Xbox 360/
Windows/Mac OS X. Warner Bros. Interactive Entertainment.

Rocksteady Studios. 2011. *Batman: Arkham City*. PlayStation 3/Xbox 360/Wii U/
Windows/Mac OS X. Warner Bros. Interactive Entertainment.

Russell, S. 1962. *Spacewar!* DEC PDP-1.

Sega. 1976. *Fonz*. Arcade. Sega-Gremlin.

Sonic Team. 1991. *Sonic the Hedgehog*. Sega Mega Drive. Sega.

Sonic Team. 1992. *Sonic the Hedgehog 2*. Sega Mega Drive. Sega.

Sony Online Entertainment. 1999. *EverQuest*. Windows/Mac OS X. Sony Online
Entertainment.

Sony Online Entertainment. 2003. *Star Wars Galaxies*. Windows. Sony Online
Entertainment.

Sony Online Entertainment. 2004. *EverQuest 2*. Windows. Sony Online
Entertainment.

Square. 1990. *Final Fantasy*. NES.

Square. 1997. *Final Fantasy VII*. PlayStation/Windows. Sony Computer
Entertainment.

Taito. 1975. *Gun Fight*. Arcade.

Taito. 1978. *Space Invaders*. Arcade.

Tale of Tales. 2008. *The Graveyard*. Windows/Mac OS X/iOS/Android.

Team Bondi. 2011. *L.A. Noire*. PlayStation 3/Xbox 360/Windows. Rockstar Games.

Team Ico. 2001. *Ico*. PlayStation 2/PlayStation 3. SCE.

Team Meat. 2010. *Super Meat Boy*. Xbox 360/Mac OS X/Windows.

Team Ninja. 2003. *Dead or Alive Xtreme Beach Volleyball*. Xbox. Tecmo.

Telltale Games. 2012. *The Walking Dead*. PlayStation 3/PlayStation 4/Playstation Vita/Xbox 360/Xbox One/Ouya/Windows/Mac OS X/iOS/Android. Telltale Games.

thatgamecompany. 2012. *Journey*. PlayStation 3/PlayStation 4. Sony Computer Entertainment.

Treyarch. 2010. *Call of Duty: Black Ops*. PlayStation 3/Xbox 360/Wii/Windows/ Mac OS X. Activision.

Turbine Entertainment Software. 1999. *Asheron's Call*. Windows. Microsoft.

Ubisoft Montreal. 2009. *Assassin's Creed II*. PlayStation 3/Xbox 360/Windows/ Mac OS X. Ubisoft.

Ubisoft Montreal. 2012a. *Assassin's Creed III*. PlayStation 3/Xbox 360/Wii U/ Windows. Ubisoft.

Ubisoft Montreal. 2012b. *Far Cry 3*. PlayStation 3/Xbox 360/Windows. Ubisoft.

Ubisoft Montreal. 2013. *Assassin's Creed IV: Black Flag*. PlayStation 3/PlayStation 4/Xbox 360/Xbox One/Wii U/Windows. Ubisoft.

University of Washington. 2008. *Foldit!* Windows/Mac OS X/Linux.

Up Multimedia. 2014. *My Ex-Boyfriend the Space Tyrant*. Windows/Mac OS X/ Linux. Up Multimedia.

Valve Corporation. 1998. *Half-Life*. Windows. Sierra Entertainment.

Valve Corporation. 2004. *Half-Life 2*. Windows. Sierra Entertainment.

Valve Corporation. 2007. *Portal*. PlayStation 3/Xbox 360/Windows/Mac OS X. Valve Corporation.

Valve Corporation. 2011. *Portal 2*. PlayStation 3/Xbox 360/Windows/Mac OS X. Valve Corporation.

Volition. 2013. *Saints Row IV*. PlayStation 3/PlayStation 4/ Xbox 360/Xbox One/ Windows. Deep Silver.

Warner Bros. Games Montreal. 2013. *Batman: Arkham Origins*. PlayStation 3/ Xbox 360/Wii U/Windows. Warner Bros. Interactive Entertainment.

Index